The Political and Social Thought of John Richard Spencer

A nonviolent anarchist

Political and social essays of John Spencer
Politics, Society and Life

TABLE OF CONTENTS

Addendum promoting novel, "Brownout-666; the Inside Story of a Misguided life in the drug and sex trade and the Real Meaning of the Swastika p. 195

Foreword

(July 2020)

The following essays and blog posts have been written over several years. I have tried to place them in such a way as to make a consistent thread. Therefore, to that end, they are not simply placed in date order but are grouped to a large extent by subject. I have placed the approximate date next to each post so that the reader can understand if the post refers to world leaders and events that have been overtaken by subsequent history.

All photographs and artwork, unless otherwise attributed, have been taken from the public domain or belong to the author.

ɞ ♦ ♦ ♦ ♦ ♦ 03

"1984" is coming sooner than you thought

Privacy, Security and Freedom

(Feb 2015)

(from Google images)

Since the recent whistle-blowing of Edward Snowden there has been a huge interest in the USA and elsewhere on the questions of Privacy, Freedom and Security and the price for each. The fact that these questions are even being asked reflects poorly on the intelligence and education of the common man. Privacy, Freedom and Security are all very relative concepts. In absolute terms there is no real freedom in the world and never has been. The freedom of every one of us has always been constrained by natural limitations and the freedoms of others. No-one and nothing is ever really free! Similarly, there is no real security. We are all subject to the vagaries of Fate!

As to privacy, that may once have existed to a considerable extent but anyone in the modern world who believes that we still have any serious degree of it is a fool. It is possible to find out almost anything about anyone. Many politicians and famous people have learned this to their detriment. It was different in the times of Abraham Lincoln and John F. Kennedy. In the contemporary world the technological sophistication of spying techniques is such that none of us have any real privacy anyway. At present, at least our thoughts are our own but how long that will last is anyone's guess.

(from Google images)

If people believe that their details remain at all private in this electronic age they are totally deluded. Some police forces have number plate detection cameras atop their cars that record every vehicle they pass such that everywhere that vehicle has been for years, (and presumably that vehicle's owner in most cases,) can be extracted from a database.

Our smart phones enable enough data about our movements, history, life preferences and politics to be grabbed by governments and companies to fill volumes. Scores of shopping centres around the world are extracting data from such phones and sending it who knows where? Much of the data ends up in the USA, which possibly has some constitutional protections for its own citizens but none for the rest of us.

"WHO CONTROLS THE PAST
CONTROLS THE FUTURE
WHO CONTROLS THE PRESENT
CONTROLS THE PAST"

(from Google images)

If that isn't enough our use of Facebook (and other social media) give governments even more information about ourselves to fill in any gaps in their knowledge. Doubtless, my views expressed in this blog have been collected somewhere by various government authorities. However, I am probably too insignificant for those bodies to be concerned by them.

Edward Snowden's revelations caused considerable protest against US spying by governments in Europe and elsewhere. Unsurprisingly, the Australian government along with both major political parties said nothing. It just hoped that the public would forget about it quickly.

Unfortunately, democracy is only as good as its Lowest Common Denominator. That translates as "democratic governments reflect the values and attitudes of the lowest level of their citizens where that lowest level boasts the largest numbers."

(from Google images)

It would seem certain that the power brokers of our planet will destroy the environment and any semblance of a decent society at the same time as politically destroying the last vestiges of human freedom. In his vision of the future the only thing that George Orwell got wrong was the date!

The coming world will much more resemble *"1984"* than Aldous Huxley's one portrayed in *"Brave New World,"* as in the latter vision the populace at least were given drugs to keep them content. Our world wants to tax or remove any chemical help and leave control by war and terror.

American gun massacres and the 2nd Amendment

(Mar 2018)

George Washington
(from Google images)

Andrew Jackson
(from Google images)

When the founding fathers of the U.S. constitution framed the Second Amendment, they certainly couldn't possibly have even imagined the massacres of innocent people and children by lunatics with high powered, rapid fire weapons. Obviously, they didn't foresee heavily armed people massacring innocents, including children in their schools. So, what could they have been thinking in instituting the second amendment; the right to bear arms?

In an age of flintlock muskets and pistols and with the Revolutionary war against the British fresh in their minds, the founding fathers wanted to be easily able to establish militia groups. That was most likely their immediate objective. Perhaps a longer-term objective was to enable an armed citizenry to resist any attempts at the establishment of a dictatorship.

We currently see quite a few dictatorships (e.g. the People's Republic of China) in the world, and many quasi dictatorships such as those of the Russian Federation, and Turkey. However, given the overarching power of most modern nations and their highly armed military forces the chances of an armed citizenry successfully resisting rotten governments are virtually zero. Military coups are quite a different matter.

It is more than obvious that the U.S.A. needs to either abolish the second amendment or drastically modify it. No amount of AR-15s and other assault rifles in the hands of civilians will be able to resist the US military. As we have seen, their only function is to enable ghastly massacre after ghastly massacre. Perhaps the National Rifle Association romantically envisages armed citizens defending the freedoms of the U.S.A. The grubby reality however is the needless and tragic number of deaths attributed to gun violence.

Be afraid of the Future

(Aug 2018)

There are too many leaders and those waiting in the wings who only care about their own egos, power and wealth and are not concerned with the good of their countries or the planet as a whole. Sensible policies and positive action are mostly ignored.

Donald Trump (from Google images)

Ego and power grabbing are all consuming. This will spell disaster for humanity and many other species.

The only real solution to the Refugee Crisis

(Aug 2019)

With every increasing human floods of refugees seeking safe havens, the world is facing a logistical nightmare in addition to increased political, social and economic problems. It is simply impracticable to have multi-millions of people traversing the world in search of a safer or better life.

The solution to the refugee crisis that is rocking the world is perhaps, glaringly simple. If people can have a safe and reasonable life in their homelands, they are not going to risk the lives of their families in leaking boats in search of a future. They are not going to line up in thousands at the Mexico/USA border either.

It would be wise for the EU to ensure that Libya has a proper government, with or without any permission. Military force would be an option. Syria is a much more difficult problem because of the involvement of Putin and the Russians. Military action there is simply not a realistic possibility.

The thousands of refugees at the Mexican/USA border are predominantly from small Central American countries where drug gangs simply run amok. It would be cheaper in the long run and more reasonable for the US to use force to clean up these small countries, with or without their cooperation, than to pursue the Trump Administration's crazy anti-immigrant policies. The only long-term solution to the refugee crisis is to clean up and rebuild the countries from where the refugees are fleeing!

Why the world's economic system destroys people

(Mar 2018)

(from Google images)

Every day we are bombarded with assertions from many of the world's governments that taxes for multinational corporations and *very rich people should be lowered.* *"It's good for the economy,"* they say, "and everybody will benefit." When the costs of lowering such taxes are pointed out, the argument runs that since other countries are doing it, we must also do it to remain competitive. Donald Trump grants huge tax concessions to the wealthy and so the other countries must follow suit.

Working poor
(from Google images)

In the somewhat optimistic decades of the 1960's and 1970's, the vast majority of people wanted to raise the wages and living standards of those in third world and other poor countries. Mind you, they also believed that technology would allow shorter working hours and higher wages! Neither of those things happened. In both the third world and in the OECD countries, working hours either stayed the same or increased and wages gradually declined against the relevant cost of living. The top 2% or so of the world, in terms of wealth, massively increased their standing while everybody else went backwards.

Without a voluntary surrendering of excess wealth nothing would ever improve. The exception proves the rule. Philanthropists like Bill

Gates and Warren Buffet make a very small proportion of the mega wealthy. It is likely that the rich getting richer and the poor becoming poorer will continue until the world's entire financial system collapses.

(from Google images)

Such economic collapse would surely be accompanied by social collapse. We haven't yet even mentioned global warming, overpopulation and the aging of the population. Scary isn't it?

Beyond Good and Evil

(Jun 2014)

The essential problem of humanity is that basically we only care about ourselves and ours. What appears to be good for us, our families and our tribes we call "good." What appears to be bad for the same we label as "bad." Greed, stupidity and most of the ills that befall our world that are caused by our species come down to the simple fact that most of us are trapped in our own egos and identities. We fail to see the big picture; our individual selves are just little tiny cogs in a much bigger environment. We must think outside of this little selfish square.

14

Artificial Intelligence – the way forward or precursor to the doom of humanity?

(Mar 2015)

[dreamtime.com]

Don't think of the brilliant Steven Spielberg movie with all of its predictions and pathos. Scientists and engineers in the field are widely claiming that already the learning capacity of machines is equivalent to that of an insect brain. Furthermore, they are claiming that in accordance with Moore's law, (technological advance roughly doubles every 18 months or so) by 2030 the intelligence and learning capacity of A.I. will exceed that of humans. While the use of algorithms is already quite advanced within narrow ranges, it is the capacity of artificial "brains" to learn by themselves and acquire values and opinions that is both tremendously exciting and frightening.

A super intelligent machine would be useful for its ability to find plans that its programmers never imagined, to identify shortcuts that they never noticed or considered. That capability is a double-edged sword: a machine that is extraordinarily effective at achieving its goals might have unexpected negative side effects, as in the case of robotic laboratories damaging the biosphere.

15

There is no simple fix: a super intelligent system would need to learn detailed information about what is and isn't considered valuable, and be motivated by this knowledge, in order to safely solve even simple tasks.

[The Value Learning Problem Nate Soares

Machine Intelligence Research Institute

nate@intelligence.org]

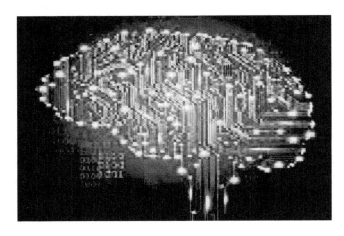

[dailysciencejournal.com]

Soares' concern doesn't even mention the possibility that such machines may acquire the value of satisfying their own issues of well-being before considering those of humanity or anything else. After all that is precisely what our species has done and why the planet's ecosystem is on the verge of collapse. Would such super intelligent examples of artificial intelligence be likely to challenge the human race as in the *Terminator* movies?

Given the advantages and risks to ourselves of continued development in this sphere should we continue with it? That is somewhat of a hypothetical question since, throughout history, humanity has never erred on the side of caution. If something can be done, it surely will. The development of artificial intelligence will continue regardless of cost or risk. This habit of our species is unstoppable regardless of whether new discoveries will prove positive or catastrophically negative.

Adam Conner-Simons describes how results of tests that were run showed that assembly line workers actually preferred a robot boss to a human one. In all likelihood this preference is a result of the machine boss not possessing the emotions, (including favouritism and prejudice,) so often exhibited by the human variety.

[Adam Conner-Simons | CSAIL

August 21, 2014]

[bipb.com]

Yet the unstoppable increase in machine intelligence presumably will result in A.I. that experiences something akin to human emotions and value judgements. Will workers be happy to take orders from these more advanced bosses? In short, when the rise of machines reaches a certain but unknown point will they possess the same weaknesses and shortcomings, (in terms of emotions – including selfishness and greed) as humans but with a huge technical superiority?

To illustrate this point further think of how the human race has advanced throughout history. In prehistoric times, for example, you had two tribes warring. Each had roughly an equal number of men armed with spears. The result was probably a Mexican standoff at a very limited cost, (a few thousand dollars in terms of today's money). Now we have numbers of adversaries, (nations and groups) armed to the teeth with nuclear weapons, cyber knowledge and heaven knows what. The result is still more or less a standoff but at the cost of billions, if not trillions of dollars. Add to that the knowledge that today's weapons could spell the end of us all and we can see exactly how humanity has progressed. Technically our species has made huge strides. From a spiritual and ethical standpoint, however, we are still in the Stone Age!

When artificial intelligence takes its place in the sun will it do any better?

Adolf Hitler
(from Google images)

Hitler and Jesus were both right

(May 2013)

Jesus (and Buddha) were right in saying that you should love all things, including your enemies. On a spiritual level that is the most sensible way to approach life. Stop to sniff the flowers and love them! On a personal and individual level, that is all there is.

Yet on a biological and species level it is more than likely that Hitler was right. If one desires that humanity goes on and prospers, such ruthless policies as elimination of the disabled and weak make a great deal of sense. Post WWII the world we have inherited is worse than ever. Aging populations, ever increasing numbers of humans and finite resources are all spelling doom.

At present we have multitudes of people in nursing homes, many with dementia. In the near future; (unless humanity entirely becomes enlightened) I can't see the rich and the greedy sacrificing anything for these unproductive individuals. I suspect it will be a case of "Arbeit macht frei" (Work sets you free). You guessed correctly, that is a slogan of Nazi Germany.

I don't have to dream very hard to imagine a coming world where people who no longer work are disposed of. No, this is not a world created by Hitler. This is the world that prospered after his defeat. It is more than just for amusement, economic advancement and the occupation of time that the elderly continue to work. It probably makes them feel safer.

After all, if humanity doesn't quickly get its act together, both from an individual and species perspective, nature almost certainly will remove us, one way or the other.

Are the ever-increasing financial complexities of the contemporary world destroying your peace of mind?

Time and money are becoming increasingly intertwined and more difficult to manage.

(from Google images)

If you are over 40 you may well remember the days when most goods and services had a roughly standard price. Technology was comparatively in its infancy and life could be lived within relatively simple human equations. Work may have been arduous enough but retirement was a realistic goal with a comfortable pension or super-annuation to see you through your old age.

(from Google images)

The world has changed in a blink of an eye. People are forced to gamble with their retirement incomes by choosing safe, moderate or aggressive portfolio investments. The ordinary man is forced to make extraordinary and difficult choices. The wrong choice will condemn him or her to miserable twilight years or early extinction.

(from Google images)

Even the simplest of tasks such as shopping now involve considerable intellectual endeavour. Prices for items or services vary wildly from one outlet to the next and sensible purchasing involves extra research and time. As well as traditional stores there are now thousands of online ones. Except for the wealthy few, choices for all purchases from food to big-ticket items are matters of vital importance. The weekly grocery shop involves looking constantly for specials and only buying those. In all probability, the price of a special is what the price of the item should be in any case.

Simple financial survival in the day-to-day world is becoming an increasing headache. The countless advertisements bombarding us further damage our equilibrium. We are continually told that brand X sports drink will save us from dehydration and damage, while in truth simple tap water will do just as well for all but the most extreme of athletes and even then it is a toss-up. The very vitamins that we used to intake with a healthy balanced diet are now being marketed to us at a high price as a "must have" if we are to avoid ill-health.

Rupert Murdoch caricature
(from Google images)

The web of lies, disinformation and complexity doesn't end there. Politicians bend the truth with increasing alacrity and the mass media are ready to support their chosen ones with all sorts of distortions. The unfettered support of the Murdoch Empire for its pet causes and politicians beggars belief. To see past all this spin, which threatens our own and our children's existence, requires a considerable effort and time on our part in doing our own research. It is now no longer sufficient to read a newspaper and believe that we are basically receiving facts and truth. Now it is necessary to search countless sources, including social media, to arrive at reasonable conclusions.

(from Google images)

Life appears to be becoming more complex by the minute. Let's just hope we are all close to being geniuses and can accomplish all the tasks required of us in record time. If that is not the case something big will have to give. It will either be the excesses of capitalism or our own wellbeing if not actual survival. On every front, from intellectual to economic, the world is becoming one categorically divided into winners and losers. Mind you, if the environment goes, everyone and everything will be a bigtime loser.

Environment, Society and Economy

(Aug 2013)

As political players around the world have tried to recover from the GFC one wonders what the ultimate objectives are. Austerity seems to create as many problems as it solves; spending other people's money to spur the economy does likewise and in the meantime, we can see our environment crapping out at a rate of knots. Most politicians have valued economy, society and the environment in that exact order: the wrong order.

Using common sense, we can see that there has to be an intelligent balance between environment, social justice and economy. Protecting the environment has to come first; both for ourselves and the other creatures on the planet. If we have any pretence at all of a reasonable social order; then social justice and a sustainable, as fair as possible, society must be a priority. That leaves economy. If we mean by economy that you can't spend wealth that has not been created that is a correct assumption, (although many governments love to spend money that they hope to raise in the future from taxes on a probably impoverished generation). On the other hand, if economy means a robust capitalistic system that enables the rich to get richer, then we should simply forget about that particular parameter.

BREXIT – LIKE A BITTER, EXPENSIVE AND UNNECESSARY DIVORCE WHERE EVERYBODY LOSES

Marriage counselling would have been better for the UK and EU. A hasty divorce will hurt the children (Scotland, Northern Ireland and London). Who knows which parent (the UK or the EU) each child will live with?

(Jul 2016)

The decision to continue with the likely disastrous Brexit process on the result of the flimsiest and most careless of referendums is strange to say the least. The pound continues its slide and the future looks extremely uncertain. The current situation with the incoming PM, Theresa May, preparing to press ahead willy-nilly is analogous to a lengthy, acrimonious, expensive and unnecessary divorce.

Theresa May
(from Google images)

Sure, there are problems with quite a few of the EU arrangements. However, to refuse to deal with these within the existing structure is like a refusal to accept marriage counselling. It seems that the British government is determined to press ahead with a hasty divorce that will hurt the children, Scotland, Northern Ireland and London. The expense will be massive and both the UK and the EU will be seriously damaged as a result for little actual, positive gain.

David Cameron
(from Google images)

Outgoing PM, David Cameron, appears like a shell-shocked husband and father who has suddenly been served divorce papers from out of the blue. The shock seems to have caused him to meekly accept the catastrophe and impending disaster rather than fight against it.

It is interesting to note that the architects of this divorce, Nigel Farage, Boris Johnson and his double-crossing sidekick (analogous to greedy, self-seeking divorce lawyers), have removed themselves in one way or another from dealing with the mess.

The British parliament is the only body that can introduce Article 50 and begin the process of leaving the EU. There is no legal compulsion for them to do this. Nigel Farage (in an interview with Australian 60 Minutes) claimed that there is however, a moral one.

In view of the entire situation, just about any reasonable person would surely claim that, in light of the facts that have appeared since the Brexit vote, there is a moral imperative that they do not introduce Article 50 to a vote and pass it. Whether they decide to hold a second referendum or not, Article 50 should be left alone and considered as a virtual atomic bomb. There will be no turning back once this missile is launched and the button should NOT be pushed.

The missile was launched. However, it is still just possible that it can be recalled.

Julian Assange – champion of Freedom and Transparency

The Assange case exposes the common trumping of justice by power and politics

(Feb 2016)

In the contemporary world very few things make me at all proud of being Australian. However, the fact that Julian Assange is a country man of mine and from the state where I live, is one of those few. For years he and Wikileaks, the organisation he founded, have strived to expose gross wrongdoing and corruption on the part of governments, worldwide. Unfortunately, such wrongdoing and corruption is the norm rather than the exception. Unsurprisingly, the targets of these attacks use any and all methods to strike back.

Julian Assange
(from Google images)

The very recent UN judgement that Assange's predicament is a form of detention, unfair, unreasonable and a violation of human rights cannot but be seen as a substantive vindication of the justice of his cause. His fear of being extradited to the USA and receiving a massive judicial punishment for his whistle blowing activities, can hardly be viewed as unreasonable or unfounded. One of the Wikileaks informants, Bradley Manning, is currently serving a massively lengthy jail sentence in that country.

The fact that the United Kingdom and Sweden are currently ignoring this UN judgement is also less than surprising. Both countries (as is Australia for that matter) are heavily leveraged by the USA's power base and situation. They simply dare not challenge the government of the USA on this question as they would have too much to lose.

Additionally, I can't imagine any governments that would enjoy their secrets being exposed by Wikileaks. Corruption and abuse of power is so much the norm that it is probably the major reason that humanity is rather quickly descending into a gloomy and miserable future. The USA may be bad enough but the governments of Russia and China are probably much worse. Undoubtedly, they would be hot on Assange's trail if he had managed to expose their darkest malfeasances. If that had been the case, he may not have even been alive now.

It is becoming obvious that, around the world, ordinary honest people are becoming increasingly marginalised and finding it more difficult to simply survive. Fewer and fewer champions of any semblance of decency are to be found.

The symbol of Anonymous
(from Google images)

Organisations such as Anonymous, appear to be largely noble-minded rather than self-serving. All over the world, most politicians are commonly viewed as feeding at the trough at our expense. The few admirable ones seem to support the adage that the exception proves the rule. Of course, part of the human condition involves imperfection and inconsistency.

Politicians may sometimes act for the common good and then return to the old habits. Also, the better world leaders are often constrained by the undesirable powers behind them. It may well be the case that personally, Barrack Obama, would like to publicly abandon any pursuit of Assange. However, this is simply not possible. Obama hasn't thus far safeguarded his improvements to the US health system and has made almost no headway in gun control. Mind you, fear of governments and politicians has probably contributed to the resistance about changes to the Second Amendment.

Donald Trump
(from Google images)

Despite his outrageous and populist statements Donald Trump has done very well so far in the presidential race. In all likelihood this success comes down to two facts. Firstly, he is NOT a politician (so far). Secondly, he is using his own money to fund his campaign.

In a non-politically correct world Julian Assange might be accused of having attractive females representing him as legal counsel.

Jennifer Robinson, Julian Assange's lawyer
(from Google images)

Since this is a politically correct word, except in so far as justice and honesty are concerned, Jennifer Robinson's looks are entirely irrelevant to the whole Assange question. Likewise, any other female spokespersons who act on his behalf cannot be considered on any other grounds than their integrity and ability.

In all probability the old allegations of sexual misconduct originating from the Swedish Prosecutor's office are anything but fair and reasonable. Increasingly, the entire Assange case looks like a case of a corrupt and powerful Goliath attempting to squash a little 'David'.

The whole Assange case and its ramifications for World powers exposes the most alarming of situations. Although terrorist organisations, such as ISIS, ISIL, Daish, Islamic State or whatever they call themselves, are quite apparently grossly barbaric and driven by a lunatic ideology, they have one thing going for them.

The blindingly obvious corruption of the majority of governments around the world, and particularly over the Middle East, fuels support for any entity that is standing and fighting these governments. Under current circumstances, any organisation challenging the world status quo would receive wide support amongst the impressionable young particularly. Given ISIS's skilful use of social media as a way of sidestepping the world's power base their hitherto success in attracting foreign fighters is hardly surprising.

Islamic State fighters
(from Google images)

Bombs and warfare alone will not put Syria, Libya, Iraq and much of the world back in order. To regain public support and belief; the world powers must reform their own houses first. Chasing Julian Assange and other whistle blowers to the ends of the earth is hardly the way to do this!

Populism, short-sightedness and the height of Folly

As the challenges facing humanity grow more and more complex and difficult to overcome it is natural that people look with critical eyes on the ruling establishments and desire a quick fix. However, quick "fixes" generally only exacerbate underlying problems rather than providing a real solution. With the proliferation of possible news sources, it is becoming increasingly difficult to know what to believe.

(Feb 2017)

Theresa May
(from Google images)

Taking advantage of democracy's essential weakness (the lowest common denominator factor) populist movements and leaders have sprung into action around the globe. Fear of immigrants had much to do with the foolish Brexit vote. Despite the fact that most of the UK's voters now have a much clearer idea of what the real costs of Brexit will be, Theresa May and her government seem determined to carry on with this folly rather than offering the people a second referendum. The likely outcome will be the breakup of the UK itself in addition to a very large economic burden.

There is no denying that the EU needs a significant amount of re-form. It expanded too fast admitting several countries whose econ-omies were too low compared with the UK, France, Germany and Italy. This, coupled with the fact that many Europeans can speak English while relatively few British people can speak a European language, means that the UK receives a net immigration from the EU. Despite this only genuine complaint that the Brexiteers might have, the cost to the UK and to Europe as a whole of Brexit and a weakened EU is just far too high.

Donald Trump
(from Google images)

The election of Donald Trump to the presidency of the USA is another example of voters being so desperate for change that they forget that a disastrous change is much worse than no change at all. With an unpredictable loose cannon in the White House, the USA and the world must surely experience increasing levels of anxiety.

Marine Le Pen
(france24.com)

The third apex of the triangle hasn't happened yet. If far right leaders, such as Marine Le Pen succeed in their presidential bids in upcoming European elections the collapse of the European Union would seem all but a certainty. The loss of Britain is a huge blow for the EU but the additional loss of France would be fatal. The collapse of the EU would be disastrous for Europe and the world. The outbreak of more armed conflict in the region would be all but certain.

With Putin's Russia prepared to assert itself at all costs and China's determination to steal sovereignty of much of the South China Sea the world is becoming an increasingly dangerous place. It is no wonder the Doomsday clock was reset at two and a half minutes to midnight after the inauguration of Donald Trump.

We haven't even considered yet that global warming and climate change is increasing all the time and has probably already reached tipping point and that the looney dictator of North Korea, Kim Jong Un is getting ever closer to having nuclear ICBMs. As the main suspect in the recent murder of his estranged half-brother, Kim Jong Un apparently will stop at nothing to maintain his grip on power. While the war in Syria drags on and millions of innocents suffer, the power brokers in the world seem much more concerned with their own well-being than with any ethics, altruism or even common sense.

Kim Jong Un leader of North Korea
(from Google images)

We are facing desperate times. Any more short-sighted populist quick fixes are likely to throw us all over the edge.

The Evil Triangle of World Power

(Apr 2018)

Donald Trump

Vladimir Putin

Xi Jinping

(all above photographs from Google images)

Donald Trump, to put it nicely, appears to be erratic, unable to formulate any reasonable and consistent policy and seems to lack the moral compass and integrity required for a U.S. president. His election campaign was centred round the phrase, "Make America great again." It is more than unlikely that he will even vaguely succeed in this quest. Most of the good news about the U.S. economy is a result of the efforts of his predecessor, Barack Obama.

Vladimir Putin, the president of Russia, has the aim of basically restoring the Soviet Union to its former powerful position and is prepared to invade countries (the Ukraine and Crimea) and overlook or contribute to the murder of innocents, including children (his support of Assad's regime in Syria) in pursuit of this goal. He is pursuing any means available, including cyber warfare, in pursuit of his aim. He even had the temerity to tell Russians to prepare for possible nuclear attack. His mojo might as well be called, "Make Russia great again" and he is effectively conducting a semi-clandestine war against the West.

Xi Jinping, China's president for life, wants to make the "reunification" of China his legacy. (One must remember that the original inhabitants of Taiwan were not Chinese, and that it is only in the last three centuries that large numbers of Chinese people inhabited that island. Taiwan is not, and was not, an integral part of China.) He has said that China is prepared to use force to take Taiwan.

He also desires to extend Chinese power as far into the Pacific as he possibly can. You might as well say that he wishes to make China great, or greater again and probably aims to make it the world's number one super power. Again, questions of morality or legality are not even considered. Here we have another dangerous maniac in full flight.

These three presidents, Trump, Putin and Xi, are much more likely to cause a catastrophic nuclear war than achieve their aims. None of them knows how to be sensible, reasonable and back down when necessary. We have every reason to be scared, and much more so than in 1962.

China's uncompromising plan to take over much of the world

(Dec 2018)

Xi Jinping President (or more correctly, Chairman) of China (slate.com)

China, under President for life, Xi Jinping, has set a course to "conquer" as much of the world as possible; covertly (with bribery and bullying "loans" to small and vulnerable nations), and overtly such as the takeover of much of the South China Sea and the simple denial of historical fact as is the case concerning Taiwan.

The really terrifying aspect of China's march is an apparent total lack of a moral compass. The current trial of China's social credit system is "1984" stuff. Everyone is photographed and a file kept on the entire population. Those who are good Party members etc. can travel wherever they like and can afford to. Others who might buy too much liquor or criticize the government, suddenly find themselves unable to even travel to the next town. They are stopped from boarding trains or buses etc.

The recent admission of genetic alteration of human embryos by a Chinese scientist could be even scarier. It is not a huge stretch to see a future where human embryos are altered to create model citizens and die-hard supporters of the Chinese government.

We should be afraid, very afraid.

Theresa May's Brexit obsession is a recipe for disaster

(Dec 2018)

Theresa May
(from Google images)

Despite a number of prominent leaders in the UK, including two former PMs stating that a second Brexit referendum is the only sensible thing to do, Mrs. May erroneously thinks that another referendum would further divide the nation. Perhaps her aim is simply to go down in history in a big way. The nation is already bitterly divided and headed downhill fast. A second referendum with all the options on the table is the only way to move forward.

Carrying on with her chosen course is only likely to divide the nation further. Scotland and Northern Ireland will demand independence referendums, (the second for Scotland and the first for Northern Ireland) and the breakup of the UK is a likely result. If this is not further dividing the UK then what is?

The UK and Europe at the Crossroads

(Mar 2017)

Recent weeks have been momentous in the unfolding of the fate of Western Europe and the Western world generally. Scotland is now clamouring for a second independence referendum. As far as Scotland is concerned the Brexit folly was the last straw. Nicola Sturgeon, Scotland's First Minister, is leading a determined push for another independence referendum and soon.

Nicola Sturgeon
(from Google images)

Theresa May's insistence that such a referendum can only be granted by Westminster is hardly likely to placate the Scots.

British PM Theresa May
(from Google images)

A very real possibility of the breakup of the UK is now presenting itself. It would be much simpler and more sensible to have a second

Brexit referendum. Such a referendum could simply be the conduct of another vote, without any campaigning since most of the British public now have a fair idea of what Brexit would entail, including many undesirable consequences that they hadn't even considered at the time of the referendum last June. If Theresa May's government needs an excuse to hold a second referendum it needn't look very far.

Further evidence that Putin's Russia may have not only interfered in the US's presidential election but may have been involved in the financing of Donald Trump's business interests, (when Wall Street wouldn't touch him) has presented itself.

Donald Trump
(whitehouse.gov)

Vladimir Putin
(businessinsider.com)

Some British MPs have claimed that Putin's Russia may have interfered in the Brexit campaign. Even the possibility of this would be a perfectly reasonable excuse for holding a second Brexit referendum vote.

It is quite clear that Putin has been conducting a clandestine campaign to destabilise Western Europe and the EU as part of his aim to make Russia a great power again. "Make Russia great again" has a familiar ring doesn't it? His bloody and bloody-minded support of Assad has cost the lives of countless innocents and created the greatest refugee crisis since WW II. To be accurate the Soviet Union (and Russia) had a lot to do with that refugee crisis too.

Assad President of Syria
(from Google images)

Putin obviously knew that his support of Assad's regime would prolong that hideous civil war and send millions of refugees in the direction of Western Europe and the EU.

The Netherlands' very recent election has resulted in the return of the current Dutch PM. In resisting populist and far right politics, have the Dutch people shown themselves to be fundamentally more intelligent and thoughtful than the British and the Americans, or is it a case of the Dutch having seen the unfortunate results of the Brexit debacle and the election of Donald Trump?

Although under the American political system it would be very difficult to dislodge Donald Trump now, (impeachment seems a very unlikely possibility) and you can just forget about the removal of Putin in Russia, it is very simple for Britain to conduct a second Brexit referendum vote. It would seem that Theresa May wants to rush through the Brexit folly and trigger article 50 as a sign of her power. Perhaps she would also like to go down in history as the person who did the most to destroy the UK and hugely damage Western Europe.

Marine Le Pen (leader of France's National Front)
(from Google images)

If the French, in their coming presidential election, can resist the fallacious populist appeal of the far right, then perhaps Europe has a chance. However, if they elect Marie Le Pen and France leaves the EU, the European Union will be finished and Western Europe will be massively damaged and in a worse situation than it was prior to the Second World War.

The person with the greatest opportunity to stop this disastrous slide is Theresa May. If the British government decides to hold a second vote on Brexit before the French elections are held, a clear signal will have been sent that the West will resist the attempts of Putin to bring it to its knees. Hope in a reasonable future could then return.

Vladimir Putin's War on the West

Vladimir Putin
(from en.wikipedia.com)

(Dec 2018)

A person may wonder why the Russian Federation, under Putin's leadership, would not only support but actively assist Assad's murderous Syrian regime in its disgustingly vile and brutal attacks on children and other civilians under the guise of attacking rebels/terrorists. It is becoming increasingly obvious to anyone with a modicum of intelligence that Mr. Putin will stop at nothing in his cherished attempt to recreate a Russian (Soviet style) empire in Europe. Evidence for this includes the annexation of the Crimea and support for rebels attacking the forces of the Ukraine.

His, all but absolutely proven, interference in the US presidential election and the Brexit referendum are additional evidence that he desires nothing short of a massive weakening of Europe, starting with the EU, and of the United States. Who can tell what his ambitions will result in after a sufficient weakening of the West?

It is almost certain that he will position Russia as close as possible to China, (remember, the Chinese president has more dictatorial power than any of his predecessors) and do all he can to promote subtle forms of conflict between the USA and Chinese. This would be largely economic, (both Russia and China are hoarding gold and trying to reduce any dependence on the US dollar) but may well include promoting some degree of military confrontation. I am not suggesting, however, that Putin wants to start any kind of nuclear war.

Returning to the horrors occurring in Syria and the myriad images of severely injured children on our TVs, we again ask ourselves why does Putin support this horror? Only a day or so ago the Russian ambassador to the UN vetoed a proposal to establish a ceasefire in that heavily bombarded rebel enclave near Damascus. The answer, although horrifying, is relatively simple. The lives of all those children and others mean nothing to Putin compared with his aim of massively weakening the West.

Without Russia's intervention in Syria it is probable that the civil war in Syria would be largely over by now. Putin wants to keep it going so that the flow of refugees to the West is ever increasing. This flood of refugees certainly weakens the strength and economies of Western Europe, (regardless of cultural questions such as the possible Islamisation of those countries). When you think about it, without the flood of refugees into Europe the British Brexit referendum is likely to have gone the other way.

The "Leave" campaign dishonestly distributed leaflets showing unnamed maps of Syria and Iraq. This fear of a refugee horde undoubtedly influenced many British voters to support the Brexit idea. It is becoming increasingly clear how much of a disaster, both for the UK and the EU, Brexit will be. Only today the President of the EU made a public statement that Theresa May is living in a fantasy land as regards her wish list for Brexit.

One thing is certain: Vladimir Putin will be smiling. Many historians argue that both Stalin and Mao were even worse than Hitler was, as regards crimes against humanity and the number of deaths of innocents that they caused. Perhaps in the future Vladimir Putin will be added to that vile list.

What the rise of China, Putin's Russia, America's Donald Trump and Brexit mean for Freedom

Xi Jinping
(news.yahoo.com)

As if the looming disasters of climate change and overpopulation aren't enough, we now face a huge challenge to our very notion of freedom. Although Xi Jinping's China could hardly be called a socialist or communist society, it has a massive ideological agenda built around authoritarian power. This China could best be described as a state-run capitalist oligarchy with loads of attendant corruption.

Recent history is likely to provoke ample alarm. From building military fortifications on an artificial island in the South China Sea to unilaterally claiming the Spratleys, China has ignored the other claimants to those regions and forged ahead in its quest to become the world's greatest military and economic power, leaving any notions of freedom and human rights dead in its wake.

Any vague notion of liberty for the billion odd inhabitants in that country was quickly dispelled with the advent of the new social credit system, whereby the smallest transgressions against the state ideal can result in a person being unable to leave his or her home town.

The "One Belt One Road" program has amounted to China making loans to poor countries in the Pacific and Africa and, when those nations are unable to repay, they become vassals of China. It doesn't take a genius to see where all this is going. If you didn't like the USA's behaviour when it dominated the planet you "ain't seen nothin' yet" as China's ascendancy rises. Xi Jinping's installation as leader for life (read absolute dictator) is the icing on the cake.

Bob Hawke
(from Google images)

Kevin Rudd
(from Google images)

Australia is caught in an ungodly position. Its defence strategy depends heavily on the USA but its main trading partner is China. The chair of parliament's powerful Security and Intelligence Committee, Andrew Hastie warned Australia against underestimating China and compared its rise to that of Nazi Germany and Stalin's Soviet Union. Unsurprisingly, this didn't go down well with China.

How did this unfortunate position happen to Australia? It is fair to blame the Australian Labor Party. Bob Hawke began Australia's dependence on China and Kevin Rudd increased it. Under their policies Australia has experienced a huge increase in immigration from mainland China. The big problem here lies in the fact that many of these people consider that their first loyalty is to China. Xi Jinping has also stated that such Australian citizens owe such first loyalty to China.

Putin and Xi
(chinadaily.com)

China's strategic alliance with Putin's Russia, (another authoritarian state, although it denies it) presents major challenges to the Western countries which value freedom. Putin's Russia is another nation hell bent on increasing its power at all costs. Its track record includes the annexation of Crimea, starting a war in the Ukraine, and direct complicity in countless civilian deaths, including children, in Syria. It is safe to say that without Putin's intervention the war in Syria would have finished years ago. Strangely enough Putin is popular with the majority of Russians. Of course, like the Chinese, they probably don't have all that much access to unfiltered or uncensored information.

The China-Russia duo is a massive assault on the West and its notion of freedom. This brings us to the Brexit debacle. Only by remaining united under the EU can Western Europe withstand the political and possibly military assault from the East. It has been established that Russia interfered in both the Brexit referendum and the U.S. presidential election, which resulted in the installation of Donald Trump.

The Cambridge Analytica saga demonstrated how cunning use of personal information can achieve political ends. It is true that Trump is challenging China's unfair trade practices. However, he is doing it in the most foolish of ways. Instead of joining forces with the EU he insisted on America going it alone. He even imposed tariffs on steel from the EU along with goods from China. Trump seems to love the idea of Brexit. Along with fellow narcissist and ego maniac Boris Johnson, the new British PM, Trump projects an enormous optimism in the face of an ever-increasing danger.

Donald Trump narcissist
(from Google images)

Boris Johnson fellow narcissist
(from Google images)

Both of these men downplayed the seriousness of the Covid-19 pandemic but Johnson changed his mind after nearly dying from the disease. (July 2020)

Once Britain leaves the EU, Trump has planned a new trade deal between Britain and the USA. This trade deal would very likely involve a massive weakening of Britain's National Health system and make health care as unaffordable for many as it is in the U.S. Donald Trump is obviously intending to challenge both Britain and the EU economically.

Divide and conquer. Xi Jinping and Putin must be laughing themselves sick. It is small wonder that the USA hates Julian Assange and Wikileaks. The only reason that China and Russia aren't after him as well lies in the fact that he wasn't able to get his hands on any of their dirty secrets. Whistle-blowers are a rarity in those two authoritarian states as the penalties are so extreme that fear prevails.

The almost total loss of privacy doesn't just exist in China and Russia. Social media invasions, along with almost universal camera and detection systems, are on the rise in the West. Under the guise of security, states around the world are increasing their control over their citizens. The use of algorithms doesn't just mean targeted ads. It is also likely to mean extremely accurate predictors of human behaviour.

It would appear that the only thing George Orwell got wrong was the date!

(from Google images)

Islamist Jihad, Freedom, Refugees and Human Rights

(Mar 2015)

Capitalism, delusional masses and endless war

Isis fighters
(cfr.org)

(Mar 2015)

Terrorism and Islamic jihad are on the increase almost every-where, from the nightly news to neighbourhoods perhaps only a few miles away. The burning and oft discussed question is, "How do we end this delusional violence while protecting the freedoms and human rights of all?" Western folk often used to condemn teenage rebellion and the fondness of the young for sex, drugs and rock n' roll. This social phenomenon seems somewhat mild compared with its Islamic equivalent. In order to have a realistic chance of ending this sickening and savage violence, humanity needs to understand the causes in all their complexity and have the courage to act.

Wars fought in the name of religion are the height of stupidity and ignorance. However, such wars often have much deeper causes and issues beneath the surface.

Beliefs in themselves

It is absurd to try to coerce others as to their beliefs. People can believe what they like and nobody can stop them from this in any case. Muslims, and others, have a perfect right to believe whatever they will. Such beliefs may be illogical, self-delimiting and crazy but the person holding them can continue to do so regardless, until such time as Orwell's thought police become a reality. In fact, faced with a jihadi sword, many a potential victim must have pretended to convert to the particular enforced version of Islam. Certainly, overt actions such as religious observances and rituals can be monitored but a person's actual set of beliefs remains im-mune. Legislation or force cannot change a person's beliefs. Only education and knowledge can effectively impact on humanity's be-lief systems.

Actions and the Rights of Others

(from Google images)

It would seem inherently reasonable that people can pray and perform rituals however they wish, as long as their practices do not harm or interfere with the rights and freedoms of others. Likewise, they should be able to keep elements of their native cultures, as long as that culture does not interfere with the rights of others or with the cultural traditions of the lands in which they live.

In the case of Islamic folk who reside in the West, this should and must mean that the **practice** of their religion does not interfere with the right of free speech; including the right to criticise or satirise anything, or with long established traditions such as Christmas. Most people in Western countries are able to not only tolerate but also have a laugh at religious jokes that appear amusing. It is sad that so many followers of Islam seem to have lost their sense of humour.

(from Google images)

The Rights of Refugees

(from Google images)

In the wake of anti-Islamic sentiment that has followed terrorist attacks and the pursuit of jihad, western nations have experienced public demonstrations of opposition, and often downright hostility, to the arrival of refugees from Muslim lands. Surely, we don't want to harden our hearts against those, particularly children, who through no fault of their own are in desperate need. Genuine refugees, who appreciate the kindness of their host nations and are prepared to co-operate with the cultures and laws of their new homes, should be welcomed and assisted.

Unsurprisingly, a problem is always at the ready to spring up! In this case it appears in the guise of significant numbers of refugees who are unwilling to co-operate with the cultures, practices and laws of their host nations. These individuals cannot simply be dismissed as a few jihadis who pretended to be refugees and arrived in western countries as sleepers, ready to strike at any time. The numbers of "home grown" terrorists in western nations and jihadis who travel to the Middle East to join ISIS are too great to be explained in such a way.

Islamic demonstrator
(from Google images)

A more rational explanation is that there are large enough numbers of refugees who flee countries where war, Islamic jihad and terrorism are rife, find homes in the west, and then seek to introduce, if not impose, the very elements of their original culture and interpretation of Islam that were the major causes of the destruction of their original countries in the first place. In many cases it is the children of these particular immigrants who, despite being born and raised in the west, are now active proponents of radical Islam and jihad.

I take pains to emphasise that these particular immigrants, although a sizeable enough number, are still a small minority of refugees. These uncompromising jihadi types who bite the very hand that feeds them can be compared to a spreading cancer. It is these individuals and their practice of Islam that need to be stamped out and quickly. The grateful refugees should still be welcome. It is beyond obvious that refugee screening procedures should be more thorough than they have been in the past. Nevertheless, we have still to examine the underlying causes of all this wanton violence and terror!

Capitalism, War and the Arab Spring

WE BUY THINGS WE DON'T NEED WITH MONEY WE DON'T HAVE TO IMPRESS PEOPLE WE DON'T LIKE.

(from Google images)

It is no accident that the Arab Spring occurred before the rise of ISIS and the rapid increase in jihadi terrorism. For decades the despots in many of the Arab nations have stolen their populaces blind. Likewise, western nations have profited from the poverty of those populations while propping up corrupt and despotic regimes for the west's own perceived geo-political interests. The failure of the Arab Spring to improve the ordinary people's lives fuelled just about every kind of extremist violence imaginable. With nowhere to turn it is unsurprising that unemployed and dispossessed youths flocked to extremist calls.

History tells us that it is economics more than actual notions of freedom that spur underclasses into action. Modern day China is a case in point. Despite a lack of freedom there the rulers have managed to keep a lid on discontent by substantially increasing living standards (economically at any rate) for large numbers of the population.

The young people of the Middle East have seen any vestiges of an opportunity for a decent life slip away or stolen from them. Despite the almost unimaginable horror and brutality of ISIS and their jihadi cohorts, they appear relatively free from the stain of corruption that hangs over the traditional rulers and the western powers. Hence it is small wonder that thousands flock to what they see (probably unconsciously) as their last hope. Add to that the recipe of excitement and "idealism" and the mix is a very potent one. Many youngsters have joined ISIS to the horror of their own parents.

War and Capitalism

(from Google images)

Those of us who have read George Orwell's novel, "1984," can probably see the ghastly parallel between his three super nations, constantly at war with each other, along with the occasional change in alliance structure, and our modern world. The mega rich and their greed have their interests served by perpetual conflict and war as these assist the capitalist model nicely.

After all, those who decide on having wars don't actually fight in them. It is ordinary folk who fight and die for the wealth and power of others. Freedom and human rights are never served by wars, (in the long run at least) as nothing ever really changes for the better. Different groups of powerful mega rich keep the game running as our world society and environment deteriorate in a spiral that is rapidly running out of control.

Without fundamental reform of human society and capitalism any military victory over Islamic jihadism or any other form of ultra violence will be shortlived. There will always be more greedy and powerful individuals and more expressions of radical terror!

Self empowerment of the People

Anonymous hacker group
(from Google images)

If there is any solution at all to the woes that are bringing the human species down at an exponential rate it probably lies in the anarchist dictum; "People, do not replace overthrown rulers with others that will do the same, but rule yourselves from the ground up!" [my own statement]

Recep Tayyip Erdoğan

(Mar 2019)

The murder of 50 innocent people, and the injuring of many more by a nameless Australian man at two mosques in Christchurch has brought out the best and worst in humanity. The New Zealand Prime Minister, Jacinda Ardern, and the emergency services in Christchurch all performed magnificently showing their empathy and genuine humanity. This is quite apart from their efficiency in minimising the effects of this horrible tragedy as much as possible. .

Recep Tayyip Erdoğan (abc.net.au)

Alas. the same cannot be said for the President of Turkey. Erdog˘an couldn't resist making stupid inflammatory comments to bolster up support from his radical Islamist base before upcoming elections. His remarks about sending home people with anti-islamist attitudes in coffins, particularly Australians, if they visited Turkey are of the same ilk as the views of the nameless assassin of those innocent people in the mosques. What does this turkey (the president not the country) want? More violence and more terrorism?

To add ignorance and absurdity to his statements he said that the Gallipoli campaign of 1915 was an attack by the Anzacs against Islam. How ludicrous! The attack on Turkey was an attempted backdoor strike against Germany, a Christian country that was allied with Turkey in the Great War. Religion had nothing whatsoever to do with it.

The great Ataturk, the founder of modern Turkey, took great care to make Turkey a secular state and quickly forgave the Anzacs for their attack. After that Australia, New Zealand and Turkey became great friends. The lunatic current president of Turkey, by his extremist promotion of Islam has not only prevented his country from joining the EU but is also endangering its membership of NATO.

This is not to even mention his strident steps towards creating a dictatorship; jailing his critics at the slightest pretext. No wonder the Turkish military attempted a coup. How else could they protect the legacy of Ataturk? It is a shame that the coup didn't succeed! Let's just hope that the people of Turkey will quickly wake up and see this man for what he is and how he is attempting to destroy a previously happy and successful nation!

Were Nazi Economics the Real Cause of WW II?

(Mar 2015)

Alred Rosenberg
(from Google images)

In his "Myth of the Twentieth Century", Alfred Rosenberg stated the essence of Nazi economics. He declared that capital was nothing more than the value of stored labor. In short, the Nazis saw capital as the savings, put away for the future, of the fruits of labour, honestly earned.

They did not approve of the capitalistic system of the present world, where the rich get richer (without work) and the poor get poorer (with more and more work). Despite the various crimes of the Third Reich their economic policy was second to none. They achieved a balance between capital and labor that not only made sense but was also fair. Some elements of the Nazi party, including the Strasser brothers, wanted to outright ban any unearned income, whatsoever, apart from pensions.

Despite being reduced to an economic ruin after WW I, the Treaty of Versailles and the Great Depression, Hitler's Germany performed an economic miracle in less than five years. It was the first country in the world to fully emerge from the depression. Economically, it was the envy of most of the world. The world's bankers (both Jewish and non-Jewish) were not as pleased by Germany's brilliant progress as it threatened their world of usury and huge, easy profits. If other countries followed in the steps of Germany the banking behemoth would lose much of its ill-gotten wealth and power.

The halls of gross capitalism may well have been felled forever. Apart from Hitler's words in Mein Kampf and those of Rosenberg, there are a number of sources that suggest that a formidable banking and economic group did their best not only to keep WW I going and assist the demise of the Kaiser's Germany but also to bring about WW II. This group of virtual illuminati wanted at all costs to keep the world's dollar and borrowing systems going and were behind a worldwide Jewish boycott of Germany's trade goods early on in the Third Reich.

[Adolph Hitler, The Greatest Story Never Told - https://www. youtube.com/results?search_query=adolf+hitler+the+greatest+story+never+told+part+1] Although some sections of this 27-part documentary are not very convincing, others make a profound statement and refer to facts that are quite verifiable. This is particularly the case with its assertion that Nazi Germany's economic miracle may well have been a prime cause of WW II.

In terms of economic fairness and consideration for the environment, the defeat of the Nazis has seen no improvement for mankind and the other creatures who inhabit this planet. The GFC of 2008 was a product of the same global economic powers that the National Socialists railed against all those years ago. The greed and shortsightedness of the mega wealthy and powerful has not only caused misery for billions but is also now threatening the very fabric and survival of our world.

The Brexit Debacle

(Aug 2019)

The ludicrous situation of Brexit threating to destroy the very existence of the UK begs one very significant question: how was it that the 2016 referendum was run in such a careless way? For such a major constitutional change, surely it should have been a minimum requirement that, apart from a simple majority, there should have also been the requirement that a majority of all four countries (England, Scotland, Northern Ireland and Wales that make up the UK) agreed to leave. Generally, for such constitutional changes a 66% majority is required.

Former PM
(from Google images)

Boris Johnson, new PM
(from Google images)

Yet the diehard Brexiteers ignorant of the consequences, are taking to the streets demanding that their votes, be enshrined as the cornerstone of democracy. Common-sense demands that a second referendum be held, now that the UK populace has some idea of what is involved and the costs.

Now that Boris Johnson is the Prime Minister of the UK, the situation resulting from that flawed referendum has become even worse, as Johnson is advocating an exit from the European Union by the end of October 2019 at any price, including a no-deal Brexit which is likely to see chaos and renewed violence in Northern Ireland.

Leaders the World would be better off without

There are a considerable number of world leaders whose influence and action are predominantly negative in the struggle to achieve a happy, just and cohesive world. Here, we look at just some of the more remarkable and prominent ones amongst them. Some are downright criminals of the worst order with innocent blood on their hands. Others are corrupt and/or incompetent and yet others have short-sighted attitudes and huge egos which cause them to damage their countries and the wider world around them.

They are not listed in any particular order. While some are indeed horrendous, they lead not-so-powerful countries and their negative effects are limited largely to their own populations. Others, while not being in the same moral league, head much more powerful nations and therefore have a greater effect at large.

1. *Kim Jong Un of North Korea*

Kim Jong Un
(guardian.com)

Kim Jong Un stands accused of many crimes and executions and has zealously developed North Korea's nuclear weapons and missile technology; undermining the stability of the region and making countries further afield nervous. Despite having the benefit of an education in Europe, he seems to be somewhat paranoid and boasts a love of absolute power, unhindered by ethical qualms.

2. *Bashir Al Assad of Syria*

Al Assad
(from Google images)

Assad has led a murderous war against his own people that has killed hundreds of thousands of civilians, including many children, apparently without giving it any more thought than if he was just squashing flies. Right at the beginning of the demonstrations against his rule during the Arab spring, he could have simply resigned with all of his wealth intact. It was once reported that his own mother suggested he do this. Yet he was determined to remain President of Syria no matter what the cost in innocent lives.

3. *Vladimir Putin of the Russian Federation*

Vladimir Putin
(en.wikipedia.com)

Putin has ruled Russia for two decades and has managed to stifle what democracy it had when he came to power. It is obvious that he wants Russia to be the power that it once was in the glory days of the Soviet Union and is none too fussy about what means he uses to achieve that end. He apparently is doing all he can to weaken Western Europe and the United States. It seems that he did indeed attempt to influence the outcome of the U.S. presidential election last year. Surprisingly perhaps, Putin is popular with the majority of Russians and also with the Russian Orthodox Church.

The church likes his conservative stand against gay rights and the population perhaps fall for the nationalist drivel that so many of the world's people do. Apart from standing accused of having masterminded several state-sponsored murders, Putin's support of Assad's murderous regime is undoubtedly a crime against humanity. Without Putin's support the war in Syria may well have ended a couple of years ago and the dreaded ISIS may never have come into existence.

4. Donald Trump of the United States

Donald Trump
(forbes.com)

Regardless of whether Trump colluded with the Russians during the election campaign or not, it is becoming increasingly apparent that he simply does not have the ability to effectively govern the world's most powerful nation. A man with a huge ego and a belief in simple solutions to complex problems is simply not up to the task. Nearly six months into his presidency he seems to be still in campaign mode. His simple "solutions" often appeal to the most selfish and unreasonable side of human nature, marginalising minorities in the process. A person who is addicted to Twitter, especially one in his position, could be fairly described as a twit.

5. *Nicolas Maduro of Venezuela*

Nicolas Maduro
(from Google images)

Nicolas Maduro has done little if anything to fight corruption in his country and has so mismanaged it that it is facing economic ruin, social collapse and civil strife. Certainly, the falling oil price has exacerbated the economy's position but there has been no plan to develop other sources of foreign revenue and no effective measures to deal with the situation. He is clinging to power regardless of popular dissent. The recent helicopter attack on a government building has been widely reported as being possibly staged so he can further clamp down on the country's freedoms and ensure a virtual dictatorship.

6. *Xi Jinping President (for Life) of China*

Xi Jinping
(cnbc.com)

Apart from the fact that he apparently can't speak much English, which is disgraceful for the leader of a world power, Xi Jinping, the president of China appears not to care a fig about human rights and is set on flexing China's muscle. Like most of the other members of China's oligarchy he is more likely corrupt than not. Power seems to motivate him much more than any sense of justice or compassion. If the eyes are the window to the soul, he looks in bad shape.

He must be held largely responsible for the disgraceful treatment of dissidents in China. He also lacks a sense of humour, banning Winnie the Pooh in the nation after associations were made between himself and that famous cartoon character. If Winnie the Pooh, on any level, were to be compared with Xi Jinping, Winnie the Pooh should feel insulted.

7. Recep Tayyip Erdogan President of Turkey

Recep Tayyip Erdogan
(en.wikipedia.org)

Another destroyer of any semblance of democracy is the president of Turkey. He is a populist who makes Donald Trump look mild and harmless in comparison. His mission appears to be the destruction of the secular state established long ago by the great Ataturk and the creation of an Islamic state.

Ataturk's wisdom saved Turkey from the excesses and dramas of radical Islam and now Erdogan wants to destroy this. He has used the excuse of the failed coup to jail many thousands of people, and dismiss from their jobs hundreds of thousands more and markedly increase his own power through a narrow referendum result. At the end of the day many people are probably sorry that the coup wasn't successful.

8. *Rodrigo Duterte President of the Philippines*

Rodrigo Duterte
(from Google images)

Duterte came to power as his tough stance on the war on drugs appealed to many voters. There is no denying that the Philippines has had a serious drug problem for many years. Amongst the worst of those drugs is Meth Amphetamine or Crystal Meth, known in the West as "Ice" but in the Philippines as "Shabu." This drug reached prominence in the Philippines more than 20 years before it grabbed headlines in Western countries.

Many of these addicts in the Philippines have been responsible for countless murders, in addition to robberies and other crimes. "Addis-addis," as they are called in the local language, have provoked fear and loathing across the nation. The police already knew how to deal with the worst of them. Multiple murderers, who terrified potential witnesses so much that none would testify against them, would often be found dead in a ditch somewhere. This extra-judicial removal of the most terrifying of criminals is known in the Philippines as "Salvage." Although this "Salvage" may offend Westerners' sense of legal niceties, in this country it has been actually necessary quite often.

Yet Duterte has actively promoted the extra judicial killing of many thousands of people, including those who were simply selling a little marijuana. Along with such relatively harmless folk it would seem that his war on drugs has included the elimination of political rivals without any convincing proof at all. He has even expelled foreign missionaries who dared to criticise him.

9. *Hun Sen President of Cambodia*

Hun Sen
(from Google images)

The president of Cambodia is another leader who boasts a love affair with power. Despite having the benefit of an education in Australia he hasn't adopted any principles of democracy or social justice. He rules his country with an iron fist and it is most unlikely he will ever be removed by popular will.

10. Boris Johnson new Prime Minister of the UK

Boris Johnson
(from Google images)

Boris Johnson is notoriously known for his insistence on any form of Brexit, including a no-deal one, by the end of October 2019.

This man, who was once a colourful and unconventional major of London, has quite obviously pursued personal power at any cost. After, then PM, David Cameron, announced a Brexit referendum in 2016 Boris prepared two very different speeches. One was a "Remain" speech if he chose to stay in the Cameron Remain camp. The other was a "Leave" speech. He chose the latter as he realised his best chance of becoming Prime Minister lay in siding with Nigel Farage and the "Leave" camp.

During the referendum campaign Boris told some real "whoppers" or plain lies. One of them was how much money the UK would save by leaving the EU. He suggested that this money could be ploughed into the National Health system. Not only were his claims untrue, it has now become apparent that leaving the EU is going to cost the UK a truly colossal amount of money, enough to seriously weaken its economy for years to come. This is quite apart from the very real risk of Scotland and Northern Ireland splitting away from the UK.

Despite all of this the Conservative Party still elected Boris as its leader and therefore PM.

11. *Jair Bolsonaro President of Brazil*

Jair Bolsonaro
(www.nationalpost.com)

Jair Bolsonaro, the new president of Brazil, is a homophobic denizen of the far right who wishes to clear more of the Amazon's rain forest to make way for more farming and presumably logging. He is not worried that *a football field amount of rainforest is being cleared every minute!*

The Amazon rainforest provides 20% of the earth's oxygen, is home to a million indigenous people and countless species of flora and fauna. Many new medicines are likely to be sourced from this rainforest. In August 2019 a record of more than 500 major separate fires, (along with hundreds of thousands of smaller ones) have been lit in the forest, an 85% increase on the previous year. Instead of employing the military to guard the forest against people lighting fires on virtual pain of death, this idiot seems to encourage the fires. He is also opposed to Brazilian workers receiving a liveable minimum wage. How did this guy get elected in the first place? What were the voters thinking?

Further evidence of Bolsonaro's total unsuitability is provided by his utterly inept and foolish response to the Corona crisis in his country. This has resulted in many thousands of deaths and millions of infections. (July 2020)

12. *Benjamin Netanyahu, longstanding Prime Minister of Israel*

Benjamin Netanyahu
(from Google images)

The last in our rogue's gallery is the present Prime Minister of Israel. Over the years he has been implicated in a number of corruption scandals but has escaped unscathed. His hard line and almost Zionist approach to the occupation of Palestinian lands and encouragement of more and more Israeli settlements on those lands, has made the prospect of a meaningful peace deal between the Palestinians and Israel all but impossible.

A realistic charter of human rights

(Jul 2013)

Preamble

Given the precarious state of life on our planet it would seem reasonable that the long-term survival of the human race is subject to some considerable doubt. Globalisation has more rapidly brought negative consequences more so than positive ones. Although circumstances would seem to be rapidly spinning out of control there is no going back. We are on a one-way journey wherever that is leading.

If we are to have any hope of overcoming these horrendous obstacles it will be necessary, in the fairly near future, to arrive at some sort of world government. That could be a UN with real teeth and power, although given its charter and the various rights of veto belonging to super powers who seldom agree, this is probably a pipe dream. A significant number of powerful nations would have to be willing to surrender most of their sovereignty. Millions die while nations and their governments follow their own agendas.

A democratic world government could only work if the bulk of humanity had sufficient education and intelligence to think both long term and fairly rather than chasing after immediate self-interest or ludicrous agendas and promises of extremist groups. The West's promotion of democracy in the Middle East is an obvious example. The moment a genuine democratic election is arranged it is often the case that a majority elect an Islamic government tending toward the extreme and the West is mortified by the results.

A world government dictatorship is undesirable as the likelihood of an enlightened leader (in the mold of the Dalai Llama) is remote. Even more so than leaders of democracies, dictators seem only interested in their own well-being and that of their immediate circle of support. Syria and North Korea are obvious cases in point.

The Dalai Lama
(from Google images)

How we are to begin in saving our species and many others is a bothersome open question. Unless we can reign in the greed and philosophical stupidity of the mega rich and the very powerful, we have little chance. The capitalist ethos of congregating more and more wealth in the hands of individuals or small groups is certainly doomed. The question is; will the survival of the human race go down with it?

A new charter of human rights will have to start from a non-capitalist standpoint. The very idea of human rights also necessarily includes the concomitant notion of human responsibilities. The idea, of rights without responsibilities, tends toward the absurd and is totally useless.

Charter of human rights

1. *All humans should respect all forms of life and live and let live wherever reasonably possible.*

2. *Every human being has the right to basic shelter, food, water and the necessary means to sustain their lives.*

3. *All people have the right to produce and raise children, (although not too many given the overpopulation of the world) in as much safety as possible. All children have the right to at least a basic education and preferably one beyond that.*

4. *People have the right to accumulate modest amounts of property and have that property protected. Such property should be subject to reasonable limits so as not to condemn others to poverty.*

5. *All humans have the right to defend themselves up to a reasonable use of force. This specifically does not include the right to bear arms. We have all seen how this amendment to the US constitution has played out. The right to bear arms actually diminishes personal safety rather than increases it.*

6. *Everybody has a right to work and an obligation to do so, health permitting, until a reasonable retirement age has been reached. Such retirees have a right to modest support for the rest of their lives. People likewise have the right to reasonable amounts of non-work time and to be compensated fairly for their work.*

7. *All humans have the right not to be exploited, economically and generally, by others. This in turn translates into the obligation not to exploit others.*

8. *All governments, from world down to local, should be secular. Human beings follow many different, and quite often competing religions. No-one, and no religion has the right to assume a monopoly on truth and hope. People can believe what they want to believe and it is impossible to stop this in any case.*

9. *All governments and large private companies should be required to be completely transparent in all their deliberations and practices. The obvious exception to this requirement is weapons-technologies and military matters. This exception is necessary to prevent such technologies falling into the hands of terrorists or criminals.*

General transparency in governance is about the only effective way to fight corruption and corruption is one of the greatest blights on humanity, blocking our way forward.

Conclusion

Unless our outdated means of coordination between nations is quickly superseded it is all but certain that our species is going to follow the dinosaurs. There is little time left to act. Violence destroys much more than it gains. The various wars are testament to this. We must find non-violent ways of disempowering those who presently run this world, and are either possessed by greed and stupidity or else hamstrung by that of others. It could be argued that Barrack Obama is one of the most enlightened presidents in US history but is hamstrung by the realities of the power and wealth cliques that lie behind him. He may possibly even believe personally that Julian Assange, Bradley Manning and Edward Snowden are right deep down. However, there is no way he could say that or exonerate them without risking a very likely assassination of himself. His position prohibits him from making many decisions and choices that he may otherwise like to make.

The only way forward is for each individual to do what he or she can to follow a path of enlightenment and fight greed and stupidity at every turn, on every level!

The Global Corona virus pandemic and its aftermath – What will follow?

The most frightening aspects of this pandemic are the myriad unknowns. The virus is spreading more rapidly than expected and it appears to be gaining more virulence. More people are dying, including those in their prime.

I can see two possibilities.

1. *We are faced with a 1930's-style Great Depression, coupled with more deaths than from the 1918 Spanish flu. This is the better scenario.*

2. *The second one is indeed terrifying. A total breakdown of the world's economic and social system, coupled with a death rate exceeding that of the great plagues or black death. This scenario would lead to complete anarchy and all the Doomsday preppers would feel completely vindicated.*

Certainly, the wealthy and powerful elites (often referred to as Illuminati) would do their level best to preserve their wealth and power and try to reset the world economic order in such a way that it would be the ordinary people who would lose their savings and suffer massive pain. This would be a type of Debt Jubilee where the slate is wiped clean and everybody starts again, (the poor and the middle class of course being the losers). These elites with their foolish debt-fuelled economic model created the mess that we now find ourselves in but they don't want to pay for it. The ordinary folk will!

However, if everything sufficiently crashes and dissolves into dust the elites may simply not be able to push the reset button. Chaos and anarchy everywhere would create an uncontrollable world. Every cloud has a semblance of a silver lining though. A massive cull of the human race, say the removal of 5 or 6 billion people, would allow the planet to have a reset. Abnormal climate change would become a thing of the past and millions of other species would have a brighter future. Assuming the surviving portion of humanity learned from their past mistakes and dramatically cut down on greed, stupidity and fear, the human race could then prosper in a sustainable way. This is a huge "IF" and in all probability the same mistakes would lead to the disastrous cycle beginning again.

The possible causes of the Corona virus and their implication for geopolitics

Amongst the disinformation spread on the Internet are claims, fostered by the Chinese government, that the virus was deliberately started and spread by the USA. Such claims are simply ludicrous. Then there is the official line from China that the virus began in a food market in Wuhan. This is possible but somewhat unlikely. The Chinese government has a biological warfare unit in Wuhan! It also has one in Beijing where the SARS virus began.

What is more likely is that the Wuhan virus was an experimental one being worked on and accidently released. Some Indian scientists claimed that this virus appears to be a standard Corona one spliced with elements of HIV and Ebola. This may be just speculative but who knows? The Chinese government arrested the doctor who first raised the alarm and he later died from the virus. Not only that, but they deliberately delayed reporting the outbreak to the World Health Organisation, although it was just before Chinese New Year when most of China's population was on the move. WHO appears to be scared of China and commended its efforts when it should have condemned them. China's government is opaque at best and truth telling is not its strong point.

At this time hundreds of thousands of Chinese headed into Italy, which signed up to the One Belt One Road project. The results are plain for all to see. Xi Jinping has long held a fascination with, and desire for power, both for himself and for China. He is determined that China should be the one and only global power, at all costs. Only a few weeks ago he was beginning to lose face in Hong Kong as the protests there showed no sign of abating.

The outbreak of the virus was a godsend for him as the demonstrations had to suddenly stop. This was suspiciously convenient. Then as the pandemic began to grip China a vague possibility emerged that the Communist Party might lose its hold on power. Two months after the outbreak, Xi turned up in Wuhan, wearing a face mask and standing behind glass. In the streets below there were a few stooges clapping him and numbers of angry people shouting defiance.

Now, if their government is to be believed, they have contained the outbreak via draconian measures and everything will soon return to normal. Then there is the added bonus that they will have broken most of the power of the West. Xi is smiling from his face to his arse.

There is also the possibility that the COVID19 virus was a deliberate biological warfare attack. I doubt that China's government cares that, in the process, it killed several thousand, or however many, of its own people. This outbreak has put China in the box seat to rule the world. That thought in itself is terrifying.

If, however, proof of a deliberate biological attack by China appears then, to coin a phrase, "It will be on for young and old!"

Retaliation from the West, particularly the USA, would be a certainty; tit for tat biological strikes or nukes, who knows? I could easily imagine Donald Trump itching to push the button. In such a scenario I think the US military would actually carry out his order!

Whichever way you look at it, Xi Jinping's China is a pariah!

Australia and the PRC Chinese Diaspora

Scott Morrison
(from Google images)

The spat between the Australian government and that of China's CCP is well known by now. However, it is only recently that Australia's PM, Scott Morrison, announced that Australia would grant students from Hong Kong a five-year extension to their visas in the wake of China's new national security law. In addition, Australia is considering granting humanitarian visas for those pro-democracy leaders who are now in serious danger.

Xi Jinping
(from Google images)

Unsurprisingly, the government of Xi Jinping is less than happy with this. While commenting on Scott Morrison's announcement, federal Labor senator, Penny Wong stated that this move couldn't compare with the late Bob Hawke's sudden granting of permanent residence visas to Chinese students who were in Australia in 1989 at the time of the Tian'anmen Square massacre.

Penny Wong
(from Google images)

Bob Hawke
(from Google images)

What many people fail to understand is that the Chinese government did not want these students to return as they probably knew about the massacre and would spread the news. Those same students, if they had returned to China and not undertaken any protests, would have had nothing to fear. While not denying his earlier achievements, the tears that the then PM, Bob Hawke, shed would prove to be very expensive ones.

We have no idea how many of the students in Australia at that time were pro-democracy. However, I have a friend whose father was a high ranking official in the CCP and she was sent to Australia to spy on pro-democracy students. She said this herself.

Gerry Hand
(from Google images)

A year or two later, the then-Minister of Immigration, Gerry Hand, appeared on television and was asked by an interviewer if Australia's family reunion policy, coupled with the grant of permanent residence visas to the roughly 20,000 students who were in the country in 1989, would mean that 300,000 additional immigrants would arrive over the next ten years. Mr Hand replied, "Yes," a very forthright answer from a politician. Three days later he was no longer Immigration Minister.

While Bob Hawke had not done anything illegal, in hindsight it would seem that he had accepted some kind of implied quid pro quo from the Chinese government. This became apparent when, not long after he had left politics, Hawke became a highly paid consultant to the Chinese government. This was the very same government that had committed the 1989 massacre. What a reversal of sentiment!

I saw Bob Hawke, in the early 2000s, on television trying to convince the Aboriginal traditional owners of land in the Northern Territory to accept spent uranium waste from China in return for financial incentives. In the years since then a large pro-CCP Chinese diaspora has emerged in Australia. They have often clashed with Hong Kong students during demonstrations.

Let's hope the present Australian government is much more careful about the granting of visas to the current Hong Kong students. We don't want any more pro-Beijing students sneaking in. I think the current government will be much more circumspect than the Hawke government was. Additionally, we can be sure that Xi Jinping's government will not be offering any "quid pro quos."

The Expansion of China and the rise of Covid-19 virus

(July 2020)

While the exact origins of the current pandemic remain a little murky it is clear that the CCP (Chinese Communist Party) of China under Xi Jinping are absolutely committed to increasing that country's expansion and power by any means possible. As the world is preoccupied with the virus and what to do about it, China is ramping up its aggression towards other nations like there is no tomorrow. Common sense, fair play and genuine diplomacy have been tossed out the window.

LEADERSHIP OF THE CENTRAL COMMITTEE OF THE COMMUNIST PARTY OF CHINA

Members of the Standing Committee of the Political Bureau of the CPC Central Committee

Xi Jinping

Li Keqiang Li Zhanshu Wang Yang Wang Huning Zhao Leji Han Zheng

Top leaders of the CCP (china.org.cn)
(from Google images)

Presented with any action, statement or communication it doesn't like, the spokespeople for the CCP respond with classic twisted logic that would make any sophist proud. Almost anything that you might think of is claimed as an internal Chinese matter. Therefore, other countries should simply butt out. According to these officials, the complaints of Britain, and any other country, over the introduction of the new all-encompassing and vague security law in Hong Kong are totally unreasonable and a gross intrusion into China's internal affairs. Never mind the fact that China has trashed the formal agreement with the UK of one country, two systems that was solemnly promised for 50 years, beginning in 1997. The agreement didn't even make it to the half-way point.

Threats of economic punishment and the use of military force often spill from the mouths of the CCP. To date, only economic actions, along with arbitrary quasi legal detentions of foreign citizens, (such as the fate of two Canadians after the arrest of a Huawei executive in Canada) have occurred. Threats of direct military action have so far been reserved for the island state of Taiwan.

The CCP has bullied the rest of the world into accepting its claim that Taiwan is an integral part of China for years, despite the fact that Taiwan has its own government, issues its own passports and has its own military. Its athletes have been forced to compete in Olympics under the name of Chinese Taipei. Airlines around the world have been pressured into listing flight destinations as Taipei, China. Many have acceded to these demands out of fear of losing mainland China flights.

A brief history of Taiwan

Map of Taiwan
(nationsonline.org)

The CCP and its online trolls love to distort history. Although it is true that both PRC China and Taiwan ROC claimed each other's territory, for years Taiwan was not historically part of China. After the civil war in China concluded in 1949, the Nationalists under Chiang Kai-shek fled to Taiwan, angering many of that island's inhabitants. Dreaming of a return to the mainland the Nationalists (or KMT) claimed that they had the right to rule over all China. Taiwan ROC was the rump that was left of the Republic of China. In effect, mainland China was a breakaway region of the ROC having begun as an illegal insurgency.

Returning to the history, the indigenous folk of Taiwan were a native group akin to Malays and other dark-skinned peoples. They were not ethnically Chinese. The first group of foreigners to occupy the island were the Dutch who called it Formosa (beautiful island). They arrived in the early seventeenth century and stayed for almost a hundred years. During the late seventeenth century Chinese traders from Fujian and Guangdong began to arrive and settle.

The Qing dynasty sent an army to Taiwan in 1683 and annexed the island. Taiwan was a part of China until the first Sino-Japanese war, when the Qing dynasty ceded it to Japan in 1895. Japan ruled the island until 1945 when it was returned to the Chinese Nationalists after WWII ended. The Nationalist forces fled to Taiwan in 1949 after losing the civil war. Their forces had borne more of the fighting against the Japanese than the Communists had and were therefore weakened, contributing to their defeat.

It is a fact that the British ruled over Hong Kong for a longer period of time than China ruled Taiwan. The New Territories were leased from China but Victoria Island and Kowloon were ceded to Britain in 1842 following the first Opium war. Yet nobody claims that Hong Kong was not historically part of China. Using the logic of truth and historical fact Taiwan is not an integral part of China. Quite apart from historical facts, why should the majority of people be forced to accept the authoritarianism of the PRC? Likewise, why should Taiwan's 25 million people be compelled to join authoritarian China when it is clear that the overwhelming majority of them do not want to.

Tsai Ing-Wen, the president of Taiwan, has very eloquently and rationally explained Taiwan's position. The criminal and rogue regime of Xi Jing ignores this common sense and continues its quest to dominate as much of the world as it can.

Tsai Ing-Wen
(Wikipedia)

The emergence of the Corona virus

Despite some claims that evidence of Covid-19 has been found in Europe a year or more earlier, (the research is not solid enough to be accepted) it is all but certain that the virus did indeed first emerge in Wuhan, China late last year. Reports within China began in November 2019. Initially, the Chinese government tried to completely suppress any information about it and sanctioned the doctors who reported it in the first place, one of whom later died from the disease.

It seems more than likely that the Beijing government was to some extent aware of the danger the virus posed by December 2019. It began the lockdown of Wuhan on 23 January 2020 and soon extended lockdowns over much of China. Three flights a week from Wuhan, capital of Hubei province, to Milan continued until Italy suspended them on 31 January. The Beijing government banned all flights between Hubei province and the rest of China on 23 January in an apparent effort to reign in the outbreak domestically. Further harsh lockdowns followed in many regions. Yet it happily allowed international flights to continue until the end of March. By that time this new plague had been fully unleashed on the world.

Taiwan health officials informed the World Health Organisation (WHO) of the dangers of this virus back in December, 2019 but senior officials at the WHO refused to even listen. Canadian Dr Bruce Aylward, **a** senior adviser the WHO, when interviewed by Yvonne Tong of Hong Kong's RTHK about why Taiwan's warning was not acknowledged, replied: "Well, we've already talked about China. And when you look across all the different areas of China, they've actually all done quite a good job." and then apparently cut off the video interview link.

Dr Tedros
(guardian.com)

The head of the WHO, Dr Tedros, was praising Beijing's response to the virus and downplaying its seriousness for quite a while. It was only some months later that he was warning the world to take the virus much more seriously. By this time the pandemic was totally obvious. It would certainly appear that the PRC government pressured the WHO to ignore the seriousness of Covid-19 until the contagion had well and truly spread.

Taiwan is probably the country in the world that has had the most successful response to the virus with few cases and hardly any deaths. It achieved this without even imposing lockdowns apart from the isolation and monitoring of returned travellers. Taiwan reacted earlier than anybody else to the virus by ignoring what China and the WHO were saying and implementing sensible measures such as mask wearing and contact tracing.

When Australia's PM, Scott Morrison, announced the banning of arrivals from China and advised Australians not to travel there on 1 February, the Beijing government complained bitterly. It certainly appears that it wished the virus to spread as far as possible globally.

A purely natural virus or not?

Although many experts and China itself claim that the virus originated in a Wuhan wet market, (when it is not claiming that the virus came from the USA) one has to wonder. It is a fact that a number of countries are researching viruses under the guise of looking for medical breakthroughs. It is more than likely that some of them are researching biological weapons although these are outlawed under the Geneva Convention.

As time has gone on the awful effects of this virus are becoming more apparent. Not only does it cause injury to the lungs but can also cause strokes, heart attacks and damage to the brain. Additionally, there are long term effects emerging amongst some survivors, which include chronic pain. I find it difficult to believe that such a complex virus could simply come from nature. More likely, I suspect, this is a virus that has been tweaked in a laboratory. Wuhan has one such lab amongst a number in China. Whether the release of the virus was deliberate or accidental is a matter of pure conjecture.

The People's Republic of China has obviously caused the spread of this Corona virus to other parts of the world such that it has become a global pandemic, with massive loss of life and inestimable economic damage. It is continuing to use the pandemic as an ideal opportunity to increase its power and aggressive expansion.

The outrageous imposition of the security law in Hong Kong is a prime example. Even before the outbreak of the pandemic, China was economically bullying small countries in the Pacific and Africa by seemingly bribing their political leaders to accept dubious loans under the One belt, One Road program and then threatening to take over parts of their infrastructure if they are unable to repay these loans. A few countries have experienced just such a result. Sri Lanka is one of them.

Another example of Chinese expansionism is the illegal annexation of parts of the South China Sea and the construction of military bases on artificial islands created there. Another one is the attack on Indian troops in 2020, while trying to expand over the line of control that separates the two countries.

China continues its march toward world domination and the emergence of the Corona virus is just another battleground. Xi Jinping and the CCP have no interest in ethics or real diplomacy. They are only interested in power and money. Any reasonable actions they have performed are generally the result of having been compelled to take such, again by the exercise of power (economic or other) on the part of others.

Essays about Humanity and Lifestyle

This next section deals with commentary on the human race which, although some of it may have political ramifications, deserves its own place in the sun.

(Jul 2013)

The Singularity.

Prof. Vernor Vinge
(en.wikipedia.org)

Every day millions of people have the task of constantly learning new things merely to be able to perform their employment duties properly.

It is undoubtedly true that the task of keeping up with constant changes is becoming more and more demanding as well as expensive. The rate of change in the modern world is increasing exponentially. Just to be able to cope with our work and our lives in general, we will have to increasingly learn much more.

Given the exponential rate of change the human race is going to reach a point where we are simply unable to learn and remember the amount of information that we will need to in order to survive. Professor Vernor Vinge coined the phrase, "the singularity." The singularity is that point when the rate of change against the time axis goes off the chart. There is simply no way of stopping or slowing down this exponential rate of change. Perhaps the only solution will lie in humans becoming androids, with powerful computer chips embedded in their brains.

A Metaphor for Humanity

(Feb 2018)

(from Google images)

Humanity's progress through the ages could be described as a very powerful automobile with very poor steering. Technologically, humankind has become somewhat advanced. Science and medicine are progressing at a pace. Yet with each technological advance, Man has employed it to produce more sophisticated capacity for killing, albeit at a huge economic cost.

Likewise, although we are grateful for advances in medicine, there has been insufficient consideration given to the problems of ever-increasing overpopulation and an ever-increasing proportion of elderly people in those populations as life expectancy increases.

Following the dollar trail gives a great insight into what our species as a whole considers really important. Financial investment and incentives are thrown at science and technology, while almost no resources are directed towards philosophy and the humanities. Philosophy can be considered as the steering of our metaphorical vehicle, whereas science and technology equate to the power of the engine.

What is the value or point of ever-increasing speed and power without adequate thought being given to the direction of travel? The questions of the environment, society and ultimately even the economy have been subjugated to the pursuit of power. While science and technology certainly increase the scope and depth of our knowledge, without accompanying philosophical considerations they do little to add to our wisdom.

Testosterone and Youth

(Aug 2013)

Have you ever wondered why so many of our youth come to violent ends? Many die in car accidents and others perish in needless social violence, often fuelled by drugs and alcohol.

As part of the growing process it seems certain that risk taking, particularly amongst young males but also to a much lesser extent among females, is here to stay. Why? It would appear that such behaviour, although undesirable, is a part of the human condition. After the Second World War there was much less deliberate risk-taking by youth than is the case today. The reason is simple: the youth then, had totally got this behaviour out of their systems because they were exposed to massive risks during the war. Those that survived had moved past that stage of development.

The question today is: "How do we accommodate this natural but undesirable behaviour in our current world?" I would suggest that teens who feel this primal urge, be encouraged to undertake dangerous but socially beneficial work as charity workers in war zones or places that are simply too dangerous to attract most people. In that way the "danger urge" of youth is spent while improving the world rather than detracting from it.

Healthy attitudes to sex go a long way towards a healthy society

So many human social problems have their origins in sexual matters.

(Oct 2015)

Mental illness is an ever-expanding scourge of human society and much mental illness stems from sexual problems. Quite often, the problems a person has in relating to others originate from sexual issues. Without a secure, non-threatening childhood and a reasonably smooth passage through the teenage years, a person can find him or herself confused and angry, although this state may not be entirely on a conscious level.

The consequences of such a state can manifest themselves as a "bomb waiting to explode." It is small wonder then that viciously violent crazies, such as those who seem to make up the Islamic State gang, have enshrined sexual crimes into their operational program. Female prisoners from conquered areas are, all too often, forced into sexual slavery.

Without appeals to sexual opportunity, despite supporting a religion that has very strict views about relations between the sexes, how would ISIS, ISIL etc. attract so many Jihardis to their cause?

(from Google images)

Regardless of sexual mores promoted by various religions or even by total libertinism, a society must establish clear ideas of appropriate family relationships and a lucid understanding of appropriate sexual and non-sexual relations. While not denying the existence of physical or sexual desire, a healthy society promotes respect for the rights of all individuals and discourages the view that men or women can ONLY be sex objects. This respect and understanding are fundamental to healthy relationships. I am not denying the role of (voluntary) prostitution in handling various and overwhelming physical needs outside of a normal relationship. Yet it is vital for each of the sexes to view their counterparts of the opposite sex as people with thoughts, ideas and feelings.

(from Google images)

What do the predominantly male Jihardis see when they imagine women? Do they see their own women dressed in burkas as the epitome of the fair sex or do they fantasise about scantily clad women as objects of desire? It is easy to see that this dichotomy is not likely to promote healthy human relationships.

(from Google images)

A balanced, fair and reasonable view about sex is vital for healthy human societies. Mass education on these points will reduce instances of paedophilia, incest and child sexual abuse. Sexuality gone wrong is one of the greatest causes of human suffering known. Sometimes it takes years to emerge and bursts forth in the strangest of ways.

97

When considering matters religious and political, it is absolutely vital that whatever creed a person follows promotes healthy attitudes towards sex. Without sex a species quickly dies. With inappropriate or disturbed sex, the seeds of a society's destruction are quickly sown. Globalisation means that the evils of one locale rapidly spread to another.

The World spends more of its Scarce Resources on prolonging the lives of the frail elderly, many of whom are in a terminal condition, than it does in promoting the health of babies and young children.

Why is this absurd situation allowed to happen?

(Feb 2016)

In most of the world's countries more money is spent on prolonging the lives of the elderly than in promoting the health of their greatest resource: children. The situation reaches the height of absurdity in the case of dementia patients. The resources required to provide daily care for these people are considerable. Especially for those in the final stages, there is no quality of life and it is difficult to imagine that they could actually wish to remain alive.

I have personally experienced both ends of this medical-resources scandal in Australia.

Expensive care of the elderly when no quality of life remains.

My father, Peter Spencer, with his granddaughter, Claire.

This was probably not long after his dementia began.

Firstly, my own father died in 2015 after a long battle with vascular dementia, at the age of almost 91. The last three years of his life were spent in a high care nursing home and I would candidly assert that he did not have a good quality of life for several years before that. For the three years before he entered the nursing facility, my sister lived in his house and acted as his carer. By 2012 he had deteriorated to the point where she could no longer cope.

Unfortunately, my father had not made any sort of advanced health care directive so the nursing home was legally obliged to keep him alive for as long as reasonably possible. During the three years he was resident in the home I had occasion to see the detail of medical tests and treatments he had been receiving. The number and estimated costs thereof were truly staggering. My dad was a truly kind and wonderful person. However, by this time, his essence had largely gone.

My father in his nursing home

As a self-funded retiree, it was my father's own money that paid for his care in the facility. In addition, he was required to pay a similar amount in the form of government taxes. However, the situation is completely different for those on the aged pension. Eighty-five percent of their pension is taken for their keep in nursing homes. The rest of the considerable cost is borne by the public purse and hence the tax payer.

Fewer resources are directed at the health and welfare of babies and young children.

Again, my understanding of this side of the equation is from my personal experience. My little daughter, Claire, died on 6 June 2008 from no known cause. She simply went to sleep and didn't wake up. This was ten days before her second birthday. This phenomenon is known as SUDC (Sudden Unexplained Death in Childhood – website is www.sudc.org) and is applied to children, over one year of age, who die this way. It is much rarer than SIDS.

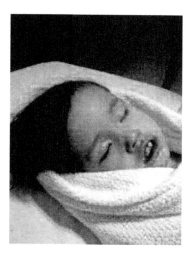

Claire

I don't wish to digress from the topic too much but Claire was a totally gorgeous spirit. Even before she could walk, she would willingly share her toys with other children and her food with the dog. Later, she would walk up to the lonely and dispossessed, and brighten their day. I had never seen such a shining light before in my entire life.

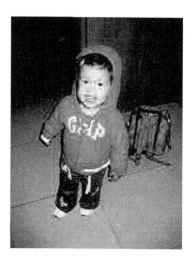

Claire

Two months before she passed away, Claire experienced four febrile convulsions in a 12-hour period. During the first one she stopped breathing for 30 seconds. She was taken by ambulance to a private hospital. They assured us that febrile convulsions were harmless and sent her home with instructions that she be given Panadol to lower her temperature. Late that evening, she had another minor convulsion and then another major one. Again, we called an ambulance. This time we took her to the public hospital on the Gold Coast in Queensland, where we live.

We were placed in a corner and left for several hours. Then, in front of a group of doctors, she suffered a major convulsion. Finally, her situation was taken seriously and she was admitted to the Children's Ward for 24 hours. We asked what tests could be performed to discover the cause of the convulsions and what could then be done. The doctors suggested that because of her age she wouldn't be able to keep still enough for an MRI. To this day I still don't know if their reluctance to perform any tests was due to the question of financial cost. We even offered to pay for any tests but none (apart from simple blood tests) were offered.

Her febrile convulsions were ascribed to a high temperature caused by an unknown virus.

After 24 hours in hospital, Claire was discharged and we were given instructions to monitor her temperature and judiciously administer child doses of Panadol. We followed this advice and all was well for a while. Then on that fateful day, two months later, Claire died in her sleep.

My wife and I can't help wondering if the situation would have been any different had the amount of resources expended on the elderly been applied to the health of babies and young children. Statistics from around the world will bear out the fact that the expenditure on prolonging the lives of the elderly is much greater than that devoted to the health of young children! Although I am somewhat elderly myself, I see this situation as a gross travesty of natural justice.

A more complete account of her life is given in my book, "Waiting for A Miracle – Life in the Dead Zone" available in either eBook or printed form on Amazon.

Early Demise for the Elderly The Ugly side of the Future

(Feb 2015)

(from Google images)

In late 2013 China announced that it was relaxing the one child policy. Despite the fact that this policy was an attempt at preventing critical overpopulation, the Chinese government is relaxing it because they already have too many old people in their society. With not enough young workers, who will pay to keep the elderly? You are probably right when you gasp, "No-one!" This would-be solution is obviously a very short-term fix.

Climate change is a bad enough problem but at least it can be mentioned! The question of how to deal with the elderly is a problem that, around the world, politicians won't touch. The reason is that, if they were honest, it would cause panic amongst the not-so-young.

My prediction is probably as correct as it is chilling: within ten years or so, around the globe, (short of a pandemic that reduces the world's population by at least half and particularly hits the elderly), euthanasia will go from being illegal to compulsory. The rich and powerful are not going to pay to keep the "dead wood" alive. The future for them looks ugly and bleak.

Pile of skulls and bones
(from Google images)

It is simply going to be impossible to keep ever increasing numbers of very elderly people, the majority of whom have dementia, in nursing homes alive. Forgetting for the moment the miserable quality of their lives, there isn't the money, the resources, nor the numbers of young people to act as nurses and carers, to sustain this ridiculous situation much longer. It costs more than twice as much to keep a person with dementia alive as it does to save a critically ill baby.

baby girl
(from Google images)

Within ten years or so I predict that euthanasia will go from being illegal in most countries to compulsory for those who are no longer independent or vaguely productive. Some politicians and community leaders vehemently argue that human life must be preserved as long as possible no matter what the cost.

Nonetheless, more intelligent and logical leaders and forces in the world are most likely already working on this problem. It goes without saying that the world of the near future will make Hitler look like a boy scout. (In a way, albeit a cruel one, that leader did try to prevent some of the disasters that are now swamping the world). I strongly suspect that the global plan for dealing with the problem of the elderly will follow these steps; firstly euthanise all residents of nursing homes with dementia, secondly get rid of the rest of the residents of nursing homes, thirdly remove all retirees (apart from the wealthy and powerful) and lastly the extermination of the long-term unemployed.

It is already possible that certain scientists around the world are attempting to develop and produce viruses that will only target the elderly. Governments in Australia will, in all probability, merely make it too expensive for the elderly to receive any medical attention.

The future for the elderly is scary, ugly and horrible but I fear, short of a natural pandemic that wipes out more than half of mankind, it cannot be avoided.

Buddhism and Christianity

(Mar 2015)

Buddhism has its origins in the teachings of the Buddha who lived several hundred years before Christ. Perhaps the most striking of Buddha's teachings were his desire to overcome suffering and his discovery of the middle way; it is not necessary to deny the needs of the flesh in order to achieve spiritual enlightenment.

To be accurate, it should be mentioned that this religion shares some common background and concepts with Hinduism and both religions were influenced by the ideas of the more ancient tantric practice of Yoga. Today, Buddhism has several branches but all of which promote a common respect for all living creatures. Buddhism does not single out mankind as the only significant and worthy life form. In its great precept of overcoming suffering, Buddhism encourages vegetarianism and has always disavowed violence.

Christianity shares a common historical antecedent with both Islam and Judaism. That common origin flows through the teachings of the Old Testament; the Torah and the Koran. Christianity was essentially a dramatic revision of all Judaic teaching that had occurred before the time of Christ.

Christ's teachings, while maintaining the fundamental framework of the Old Testament scriptures, offered something else, something fundamentally different from Judaism and from the later teachings of Mohammed. Jesus preached a much "softer" view of the world. Animals had a respected place in it and the precepts of love and mercy assumed a much greater importance than those of simple obedience and punishment for transgressors.

Given the inherited background of Christianity, how and where did Jesus come by his completely radical ideas? It is probably fair to say that, in many respects, his ideas were fundamentally different from and more radical than those of Judaism or the later Islam. It is quite possible that Jesus Christ was heavily influenced by Buddhist teachings as the journey from Palestine to India was not a huge one, even in ancient times.

Tobacco taxes, poverty and organised crime

(Jan 2019)

Scott Morrison PM
(from Google images)

Richard Dinatale leader of the Greens
(from Google images)

While nobody would argue that smoking is healthy or that it shouldn't be discouraged, the entire Australian federal parliament is guilty of the unintended and horrendous consequences of the current "tax them till death" policy. Australia's approach to this issue not only makes us the laughing stock of the world but also causes massive harm to our own society. Various political parties and groups have factored in to projected revenues these draconian tax levels.

The hypocrisy is evident to anyone with half a brain. Are "Quit Smoking" aids free? Of course not!

The Negative consequences of this stupid policy

There are many people, who cannot or will not (for various reasons) quit. Quite often these people are amongst the poorest in our community. This reads as "children without shoes or enough to eat."

Tobacco products are so expensive in Oz that smokers drag their fags until the very end, thus consuming more tar and poisons. The mentally ill tend to smoke and it is always much harder for them to quit than for the general population. My own sister suffers from bipolar type 1, is a pensioner and one of her doctors told her not to try to quit as it would increase her stress levels and thus her illness. I, myself suffer from severe depression and OCD. I can't see a way to quitting either.

Organised crime is laughing all the way to the bank. This policy is expanding and enabling the reach of organised-crime networks. Tobacco is now more expensive than marijuana or meth amphetamine ("ice)." Troubled youth, who may have previously resorted to smoking are now taking the drug ice, which is far more dangerous for both the individual and society as a whole.

Alternatives

There are many ways to discourage smoking without targeting the extremely vulnerable. It is possible to set an age for purchase of smoking products (demanding ID) and raising it every year. That should assist in keeping the young from the evil habit. Progressive reductions in public areas where smoking is allowed can also help.

An example of a sensible tobacco policy that I am familiar with, springs to mind. In Taiwan the rate of smoking amongst the young is much lower than that in Oz. Their campaigns against smoking have become a cultural norm. Yet they do not target the vulnerable sections of their society such as the hopelessly addicted elderly, the mentally ill (my brother-in-law in Taiwan is battling schizophrenia fairly successfully, he smokes and is a low-income earner).

The Future.

Will any of our parliamentary leaders have the courage to try to solve this problem and set tobacco taxes at reasonable and sensible levels? I can only hope so but I doubt it! Australia is heading for third world status in a rush in all areas but one: tobacco prices!

Want to be rich for a day or a month?

How to experience the sensation of being wealthy

(Feb 2015)

[pininterest.com]

Most of us complain from time to time that we are having a tough go of it financially in this life. We may occasionally glance at the trappings of wealth displayed by others with a hint of wistful longing. Almost all of us, at some time or other, have remarked that we would like to be rich for a week or so just to see what the experience is like.

The good news is that wealth is relative. If you were a millionaire living in a village entirely populated, apart from yourself, with billionaires you would undoubtedly feel impoverished. The sensation of feeling abundantly wealthy in a material sense derives from comparisons with others. Therefore, it is perfectly possible for an ordinary person to temporarily experience a life of relative wealth.

[engineeredlifestyles.org]

The way to do this is to take a vacation to another country that has a much lower standard of living and a favourable exchange rate for one's home currency. Quite apart from areas of natural, social and cultural interest, such a destination will instantly offer the traveller a personal situation of newfound riches. Goods and services that hitherto were beyond reach are now easily attainable. The visitor can enjoy upmarket accommodation, gourmet restaurants, stunning entertainment and the purchase of luxury goods at bargain rates.

If a little voice in your head cried, "There must be a catch!" you are right. In this land, with a much lower standard of living, you may find that standards of personal security and safety are much lower than what you are used to, but not necessarily so. Perhaps the risk of theft or even personal attack is greater in this destination. In any case this would be a valid portion of the experience of being rich. In most nations the wealthy find it necessary to protect their possessions and even their personal safety with more rigorous security than do the rest of us.

[aljazeera.com]

[thehackernews.com]

Of course, the lucky, or well-researched traveller who finds a low-cost destination with little crime risk is much more likely to have a thoroughly enjoyable holiday. However your vacation pans out you will have had the experience of being rich for a day, a week or a month! No longer will you have to exclaim in conversations at dinner parties, "I'd just like to try being rich!"

Notes about my first novel, "Brownout – 666: The Compelling Inside Story of a Misguided Life in the Sex and Drug Trade and the real meaning of the Swastika."

The third and final section of this book includes a number of posts about the background of my novel. Many of its themes relate to some of the posts in the preceding two sections, which is why I think it may interest you.

The author

(Dec 2018)

Why I wrote this novel

Although I was teaching at Cromer High School as the cold case disappearance of Lynette Dawson and the male teacher and school-girl sex rings were unfolding, and although I had first heard of the allegations of murder in the 1990's, this intriguing case has nothing directly to do with my reasons for penning this tale.

In fact, the only and indirect reference to Cromer High in my story was somewhat a matter of chance. Much of my novel, "Brown-out-666: or the real meaning of the swastika," is based on real events. I could have written part of the story as a nonfiction work but, (aside from the constant danger of being sued for liable or def-amation), I also wanted to include my take on what is happening to human society and its disastrous consequences around the world. Political inaction on climate change, corruption, greed and abject stupidity, (along with short sightedness on many levels) have all long concerned me.

In addition, I wanted to explore exploitative sexuality along with the passion of Eros and romantic love – hence the graphic sex scenes. In Australia of the 1970s and 1980s many young men were sexually frustrated. That, in addition to the prevailing culture of the time, probably caused a sexually exploitative and conquest attitude amongst many males. It is these themes that are common to "The Teacher's Pet" podcast and my novel.
https://www.youtube.com/watch?v=2XzhquLFYGI

Cory Aquino
(from Google images)

The word "Brownout" appears many times and has meaning on numerous levels. When I lived in the Philippines in the late 80s and early 90s, I told people that one day I would write a book called "Brownout." Brownouts (or the sudden cutting of electricity supply) were ubiquitous during my sojourns in that country. On another level the term has metaphorical meaning: cultural clash or an inability to deal with problems in a logical and systematic way is just like the dying of the light. Many of the problems that I experienced in the Philippines, including the massive corruption, exist everywhere but in more subtle forms.
https://www.youtube.com/watch?v=g1CWJjVeJuI

Truth and justice are almost impossible to achieve, but every year our world seems to slip further and further from those ideals. My novel is both a warning and a call to action for humanity.

Rick Daly, the central character in the novel

(Dec 2018)

The central character, Rick Daly, is a composite from many people I have known, along with some fictional elements. Portions of his makeup I have taken from myself but I would certainly disown some of the actions he undertakes during his journey of self-discovery. Some of his attributes are considerably more extreme and apparently somewhat callous, than any that my younger self, possessed.

Some of the apparently heartless actions undertaken by Rick, (such as the way he treats a drunk female passenger who can't pay the fare in his cab,) were taken from real life but not mine. His happy-go-lucky attitude during the beginning of the story and his predatory behaviour relates to many young Australian males of the seventies and eighties and in all likelihood stems from some deep sense of sexual frustration, along with a failure to fully understand women as people on many levels.

Joanne Curtis c. 1980
(expressdigest.com)

This theme is in evidence in "The Teacher's Pet" podcast and its allegations of teacher-schoolgirl sex rings at three high schools on

Sydney's northern beaches. Youngish males who were obsessed with their sexual gratification and used any available means to achieve it, were referred to repeatedly in this podcast, along with the allegations of murder against Chris Dawson who was arrested and is currently on bail.

Cromer High School c. 1979 – 1982
(frasercroastchronicle.com.au)

Cromer High School c. 1979 – 1982
(northernstar.com.au)

Rick, the product of his time, operates his life against a background of constantly wanting to "get his end in" in the most enjoyable way possible. He certainly possesses some hedonistic values at the beginning of the novel.

Fortunately, over time he learns some of the subtleties and more important values, albeit, in many cases, the hard way. He also learns about love and its pitfalls, corruption and the inescapable fact that life is not fair. By the conclusion of the story he realises just how rotten the world and its powers can be. He manages this without surrendering his interest in sex and love but, by putting everything into perspective, achieves a level of inner peace.

The other major characters in Brownout – 666

(Jan 2019)

The character of Marilyn Delgado, Rick's love interest, is largely based on that of a young woman I once employed as a secretary. Many of Marilyn's actions in the story are entirely fictional.

Typical Filipina secretary at work
(from Google images)

Marilyn is a moderately devout Catholic but remains a physical person with the usual hopes and aspirations. She is a proud Filipino but is often the victim of her own culture.

Christopher Daly, Rick's uncle, is a really a composite of people I have known. He is a highly moral man who always tries to do the right thing. His own morals often give him a weakness that makes him an easy victim of unscrupulous people and organisations.

Typical SS soldier
(from Google images)

Hans Werttenburger, is a diehard Nazi and former SS man, whose views on Hitler and WWII have changed little over the decades. I based him on SS men I met in Germany in the 1970s.

Precocious schoolgirl
(from Google images)

The Character of Alma Lopez, the 14-year-old schoolgirl, was based on a number of precocious teenagers I met over the years in the Philippines.

Typical Filipina nurse in uniform
(from Google images)

Cecilia Crisputa, was based on a qualified nurse who once worked for me as a maid.

120

My novel is available on Amazon in both eBook and print formats.

The minor characters in Brownout-666: or the real meaning of the swastika

(Jan 2019)

Quite obviously it would not be practicable to discuss every minor character in the novel, so I shall restrict my comments to the more important ones.

Typical Filipina bargirl
(from Google images)

Lina/Maria – the bargirl who kept her job hidden as much as possible.

Lina was actually based on a number of girls I personally knew in that "fishing" village in Northern Samar, Philippines. These girls plied their trade in Manila, Cebu or other parts of the country but pretended to have innocent jobs when they returned home. Considering the amounts of money they would send to their families, it would beggar belief that their jobs were as maids or shop assistants. Their families obviously knew but would pretend that they didn't. The money came and that was OK.

Ricardo Gordon – the mixed blood fixer

This character was formed from a number of foreigners and mixed blood people who had taken unto themselves the worst aspects of Filipino character and motivations. Hence the quote from the book that you don't trust your own mother once she sets foot in that land.

The Colonel, Major and other military men who often drank with Rick at Alfred's Kitchenette in Cebu City.

Philippine army soldiers in action
(from Google images)

These people are simply described as they actually were and are taken from real life.

The police captain, his sergeant and members of his squad.

Philippine police ready for action
(from Google images)

Apart from name changes most of the actions, including the visits to Rick's house, are simply taken from actual events. These include the Armalites stacked against the wall of his lounge room and Rick's visit to the private hospital and subsequent "arrest." Truth can indeed be stranger than fiction.

Christopher Daly's children

George, his son is a typical child who has had a difficult childhood and then goes off the rails as a teenager.

Likewise, Rebecca is a somewhat rebellious teenager but improves with growing maturity.

Elizabeth, Christopher's youngest child is based on some of the brightest and kindest children I came across during my time as a school teacher. When Elizabeth dies from meningococcal disease I, as the author, felt sorry that we had lost her.

My own young daughter, who mysteriously died from no known cause (Sudden Unexplained Death in Childhood – the website for the support organisation is www.sudc.org) just before her second birthday and is the subject of my book about grief, "Waiting for a Miracle – Life in the Dead Zone," was still alive when I wrote the initial draft of my novel. In a crazy way I wondered if my "killing" of Elizabeth had tempted fate.

The characters of the Organisation

These are mostly fictional but portions of them are from people I knew or heard about. The Organisation is a sophisticated international crime ring.

Hannah Chibber

Blonde Jewish girl
(beauty-around.com)

Hannah is the niece of a very senior Organisation member.

The Delgado family

This family is largely based on a family I personally knew in the Philippines. I hope the above background increases your desire to read this novel.

The Teacher's Pet, Chris Dawson and me

(Dec 2018)

Chris Dawson
(the morningbulletin.com.au)

Chris Dawson, Joanne Curtis & Lynnette Dawson c. 1980
(tremr.com)

Robyn Wheeler (student c. 1980)
(dailymercury.com.au)

John Spencer, author of "Brownout-666: or the real meaning of the swastika" was a teacher at Sydney's Cromer High School between 1979 and 1981 and he personally knew many of the protagonists in this cold case probable murder and story of lust, schoolgirls, betrayal and improper sexuality that is currently grabbing headlines around the world and is the subject of The Teacher's Pet podcast by Hedley Thomas of the "The Australian" newspaper.

John's novel is largely based on true events and, while only making one indirect reference to Cromer High School, explores in depth many of the themes apparent in this podcast; including male predatory sexual behaviour from that era, changes to such attitudes over the decades and the legal ramifications thereof, older men pursuing young girls, and the particular socio/sexual problems of Australian men at that time that may have led to their hunter/conquest at-all-costs attitudes.

John's book is available on Amazon
https://amzn.to/2Mn8bHC
and from his website.
His email address is jspe3506@bigpond.net.au and his website is
www.creativityandpower.com

All photographs and artworks depicted, unless otherwise attributed, are from the public domain or are owned by the author.

ℰ   ✦   ✦   ✦   ✦   ✦   ℭ

Printed in Great Britain
by Amazon

27489764R00071

THE BLOODY ROAD TO CATANIA

A History of XIII Corps in Sicily, 1943

Barrie S. Barnes

Helion & Company Limited

Helion & Company Limited
Unit 8 Amherst Business Centre
Budbrooke Road
Warwick
CV34 5WE
England
Tel. 01926 499 619
Email: info@helion.co.uk
Website: www.helion.co.uk
Twitter: @helionbooks
Visit our blog at blog.helion.co.uk

Published by Helion & Company 2021
Designed and typeset by Mach 3 Solutions (www.mach3solutions.co.uk)
Cover designed by Paul Hewitt, Battlefield Design (www.battlefield-design.co.uk)

Text © Barrie S. Barnes 2021
Images © as individually credited
Maps drawn by George Anderson © Helion & Company Ltd

ISBN 978-1-914059-93-3

British Library Cataloguing-in-Publication Data.
A catalogue record for this book is available from the British Library.

For details of other military history titles published by Helion & Company Limited contact
the above address or visit our website: http://www.helion.co.uk.

We always welcome receipt of book proposals from prospective authors.

For my French girl Brigitte, whose steadfast, loving and supportive nature gives me a solid base from which to work; she keeps my feet firmly on the ground.

And for my very good friend Arthur Bullement, who passed away in July 2021, after suffering so much. Brigitte and I miss him and there is a gap in our lives that can never be filled.

Other Books by Author

This Righteous War: A History of the 92nd (Hull) Brigade in the Great War (Netherwood Ltd, 1990; Sentinel Press, 2008)

The Sign of the Double T: A History of the 50th Northumbrian Division, Sicily 1943 and North-West Europe 1944 (Sentinel Press, 1999/2008)

Known to the Night: A History of Reckitt's Factory of Hull during the Great War (Sentinel Press, 2002)

Operation Scipio: A History of the Eighth Army in the Tunisian Campaign 1943, Culminating in the Battle of the Wadi Akarit, 6th April 1943 (Sentinel Press, 2007)

Known unto God: A History of the East Yorkshire Town of Beverley in the Great War (Sentinel Press, 2014)

The Infinite Debt: A Study of the Lives and Deaths of Beverley's Fallen Sons and Daughters in WW2 (Sentinel Press, 2016)

The 50th at Bay, the Years of Defeat: A History of the 50th Northumbrian Division 1939 to September 1942 (Helion & Co., 2018)

Stars in a Dark Night: A History of the East Coast Town of Hornsea During the Great War (Helion & Co., 2019)

Chaos in the Sand. A History of XIII Corps at Alamein: The Southern Sector (Helion & Co., 2019)

Contents

Glossary

Adj	Adjutant
AP	Armour-piercing solid shell
Bangalore torpedo	Metal tube packed with explosives for blowing gaps in barbed-wire entanglements
Getting a Blighty	To receive a wound that is not life-threatening but is serious enough for the recipient to be sent home
Bomb happy	Shellshock, damage to the mind as a result of being under intense fire for long periods of time
Bought it	To be killed
Breda	Italian light machine gun
Bren-carrier	The Universal Carrier was a light armoured tracked British vehicle, also known as the Bren-carrier
Bren	British magazine-fed light machine gun
Brewing up	A British soldier making tea, or a stricken tank that is burning fiercely with the crew still inside
Bully beef	Tins of Fray Bentos corned beef, issued to troops in the Second World War
Boche	A derogatory name for Germans given to them by the French in the First World War, meaning beast
C-47 Skytrain	Made by the American firm Douglas and known as the Dakota, this versatile aircraft was used to tow gliders, transport weapons and supplies and to drop paratroopers on their landing zones
CLY	County of London Yeomanry, an armoured unit
Compo rations	Short for composite rations; a field or combat ration issued to British soldiers in the Second World War
CO	Commanding officer
Coy	Company
CRA	Commander Royal Artillery
CRE	Commander Royal Engineers
CSM	Company Sergeant Major
D-Day	Day of action

DFC	The Distinguished Flying Cross, awarded for valour in the face of the enemy
DZ	Drop zone
FDL	Forward Defensive Line/location
Flak	Ground-to-air anti-aircraft fire
Flimsie	British petrol cans known for their thin skin that made them very dangerous
FUP	Forming-up point/place
Green Devils	German airborne troops (*Fallschirmjäger*)
HE	High explosive
H-Hour	The hour of attack
HMS	Her Majesty's Ship
Horsa	British troop- or cargo-carrying glider, made by Airspeed Ltd
In the bag	Taken prisoner
Itie	British slang for Italian troops
IO	Intelligence officer
Jerry can	German petrol tins, much preferred by the British troops to their own Flimsies as they were made from heavier-gauge steel
KIA	Killed in action
LAA	Light Anti-aircraft
LCA	Landing craft assault
LCI	Landing craft infantry
LCT	Landing craft tank (capable of carrying six 40-ton tanks)
Lance Bombardier	The rank of Lance Corporal in the Royal Artillery
Lance Corporal	The lowest non-commissioned rank in the British Army
Lt	Lieutenant, lowest commissioned officer rank in the British Army
Luftwaffe	German air force
LZ	Landing zone
Mae West	Slang for life preserver/vest
Matelot	Sailor, from the middle French
ME 109	Messerschmitt Bf 109, single-engine German fighter aircraft designed by Willy Messerschmitt and Robert Lusser in May 1935; saw service throughout the war in all theatres of operations
MO	Medical officer
A Murder	A type of engagement invented by the commander of the 2nd New Zealand Division in 1942, entailing the concentration of a division's artillery (72 guns) onto a single point for two or three minutes, originally called 'Method A'.

NCO	Non-commissioned officer; ranks below lieutenant but not a private
OC	Officer commanding
OP	Observation post
OR	Other ranks (sergeant and below)
Panzerfaust	One-shot recoilless hand-held anti-tank projectile
PBI	Poor bloody infantry
PIAT	British light anti-tank projectile
Pillbox	Reinforced concrete bunker
POW	Prisoner of war
RAF	Royal Air Force
RAP	Regimental aid post
Recce	Reconnaissance
Red Devils	Name given to British parachute troops by their German counterparts; or small red Italian grenades
REME	Royal Electrical and Mechanical Engineers
RN	Royal Navy
RSM	Regimental Sergeant Major; the most senior NCO
RTR	Royal Tank Regiment
Sapper	The rank of private in the Royal Engineers
SP	Self-propelled gun
Spandau	German MG 42, fast firing machine-gun
SRS	Special Raiding Squadron; formed in early 1943 from the 1st Special Air Service and fought with distinction in Sicily
Sten gun	British sub-machine gun
Stonk	Artillery barrage
Strafe	The practice of attacking ground targets with machine-gun fire by a low-flying aircraft
Tedescish	Slang used by British troops for anything German
Tiger	German heavy tank weighing 68 tons and armed with an 88mm gun
Tommy or Thompson Gun	Thompson sub- machine gun, favoured by soldiers for its accuracy and high volume of automatic fire
Tommy cooker	A field stove used by British soldiers, or the German name for a British tank that is burning fiercely with the crew still inside
Vickers	British water-cooled heavy machine gun
Waco CG-4	American troop- or cargo-carrying glider
88	German 88mm anti-aircraft gun, used effectively in an anti-tank role; feared by tankmen as no British tank could stand up to its high-velocity 88mm round

"In war, however much you calculate, in the end it is down to the visceral force of irrational violence and the release in otherwise perfectly normal human beings of murderous fury."

(Leonardo Da Vinci on war)

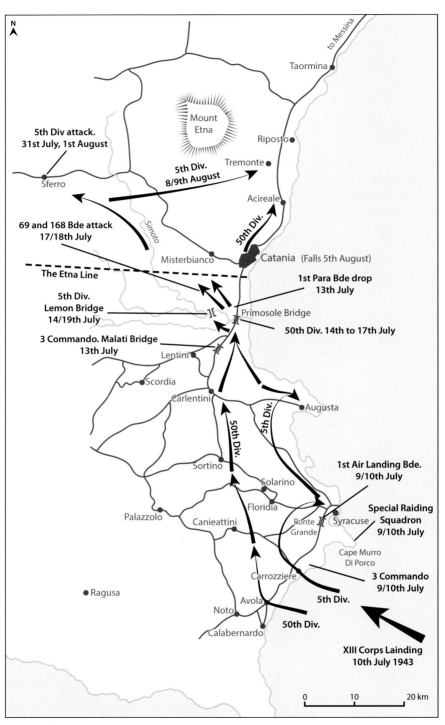

N

5th Div attack.
31st July, 1st August

Mount
Etna

to Messina

Taormina

Riposto

5th Div.
8/9th August

Tremonte

Sferro

Acireale

69 and 168 Bde attack
17/18th July

50th Div.

Simoto

Misterbianco

Catania (Falls 5th August)

The Etna Line

1st Para Bde drop
13th July

5th Div.
Lemon Bridge
14/19th July

Primosole Bridge

50th Div. 14th to 17th July

3 Commando. Malati Bridge
13th July

Lentini

Scordia

Carlentini

5th Div.

Augusta

50th Div.

Sortino

1st Air Landing Bde.
9/10th July

Solarino

Palazzolo

Floridia

Special Raiding
Squadron
9/10th July

Canieattini

Ponte
Grande

Syracuse

Cape Murro
Di Porco

Ragusa

Carrozziere

3 Commando
9/10th July

Avola

5th Div.

Noto

5th Div.

Calabernardo

50th Div.

XIII Corps Lainding
10th July 1943

0   10   20 km

XIII Corps operations in Sicily, July-August 1943.

1

Operation *Husky*
The Invasion of Sicily,
10 July 1943

The Allied re-entry into Europe via Sicily was to be a hazardous leap hedged with uncertainties. The eventual success of the Sicilian landings owed much to factors that were not at once obvious. Firstly, the capitulation of eight Axis divisions in Tunisia had left Italy and its islands almost bereft of defensive cover. With these forces, the Axis powers could have provided a very strong defence for the Italian gateway into Europe, and the chances of an Allied invasion succeeding would have been very slim. Hitler and Mussolini had poured men and resources into the latter part of the Tunisian campaign in an attempt to save face. Neither of the Axis leaders would listen to any argument in favour of evacuating German and Italian forces from North Africa while there was still time and opportunity to get them away. Secondly, Italy had no strong mechanical forces left, and the Italian generals asked the Germans to provide a powerful reinforcement of armoured units. Hitler at once offered five divisions, but Mussolini, fearful of so many German troops on Italian soil, sent a reply requesting only three. Mussolini's pride did not want the world to know he was so dependent upon German aid, and although he was anxious to keep out the Allies, he was equally anxious to keep out the Germans. Mussolini's chief of staff eventually persuaded him that more German troops were necessary if a successful defence of Italy and its islands was to be made, but by the time he accepted the need to have more German help, Hitler was becoming dubious about providing it. The *Führer* suspected that the Italian people might overthrow Mussolini and sue for peace, thus isolating badly needed German forces that could be cut off if the Italians changed sides. Hitler also disagreed with the the view of the Italian command and Field Marshal Albert Kesselring – who as Commander in Chief South commanded all German troops in the Mediterranean theatre – that the Allies' next assault would fall on the shores of Sicily; he predicted they would land in Sardinia or Greece.

Operation *Mincemeat*: Deception, setting the trap and taking the bait

Hitler's beliefs for where the Allies would strike were encouraged further by fake documents found on the body of a Major William Martin, RN, washed up on the shore at Huelva in Spain, on 30 April 1943. The idea of planting a corpse carrying false information was the brainchild of Lieutenant Commander Ewen Montagu, RNVR, and Flight Lieutenant Charles Cholmondeley of the Air Ministry Intelligence. Their plan was eventually sanctioned by the military chiefs and by Churchill himself, who had no misgivings as to its worth. Thus was born Operation *Mincemeat*. Montagu later wrote:

> It was decided that we could not hope to persuade the Germans that we were not going to attack Sicily, but we might persuade them that we would try to surprise them by capturing Sardinia first and then come down to Sicily afterwards from the north. And, if we were successful, we might get even the professional German High Command to believe that we were going to be rash enough both to try that and begin a Balkan invasion almost simultaneously.[1]

Churchill knew that the invasion of Sicily was obviously the next step for the Allies, and that only a fool would think otherwise. It was now the job of Montagu and Cholmondeley to persuade the Germans that the Allies were not going to do the obvious. What started out as a wild idea to plant a corpse and seemingly genuine papers that would hopefully be accepted by the Germans as true, evolved into one of the most brilliant deception operations of the war. After a lengthy search, a suitable body of a deceased young man was found, and permission was gained from his next of kin to use the corpse on condition his identity was never to be revealed. The corpse was given the identity of an officer of the Royal Marines whose plane had crashed into the sea off southern Spain. He was given the name of a serving Marine officer, Major William Martin,[2] and letters from senior officers and official documents were placed in his clothing. One letter considered future tactics and the general situation in the Mediterranean, containing detailed information about the intentions of the Allies and subtly stating the deception of how the British wanted the Germans to believe the next blow would fall in Sicily.

On 19 April 1943, the submarine HMS *Seraph*, commanded by Lieutenant N.A. Jewel, RN, set sail from Holy Loch, Scotland, with its mysterious cargo sealed in a steel container. The crew had no idea of its contents or of their real destination, and because of the container's shape and size it was soon christened 'John Brown's Body'. Eleven days later, in the early hours of 30 April, the *Seraph* moved into shallow waters

---

1   E. Montagu, *The Man Who Never Was* (London: Evans Bros, 1953), p. 143.
2   The government identified the corpse in 1998 as that of Glyndwr Michael, who had taken poison and committed suicide. He was buried with full military honours in *Cementerio de la Soledad* in Huelva, Spain, where he still lies. In 1998, the headstone inscription was changed to 'John Glyndwr Michael, served as Major Michael Martin, RN'.

off the southern coast of Andalucia, a mile from the town of Huelva, which had been chosen as it was known that German spies were active in the area. The submarine surfaced in darkness, the strange cargo was brought on deck and the vacuum-sealed canister opened. The corpse of a young Marine officer was revealed, and chained to his waist was a black dispatch-case with the Royal Seal in place. The body's life jacket was inflated and the young skipper of the *Seraph* said a prayer as they committed the body to the sea, where it began its journey inshore. When the submarine was out to sea, it released an inflated rubber life-raft and one oar, while the canister was thrown overboard and riddled with bullets to sink in 400 fathoms. The corpse was dragged from the sea by Spanish fishermen and handed to the Spanish authorities. Within hours, the body of Major Martin was presented by the Spanish authorities to the British vice-consul, minus the dispatch-case. The following day, Major Martin was buried with full military honours in a local cemetery.

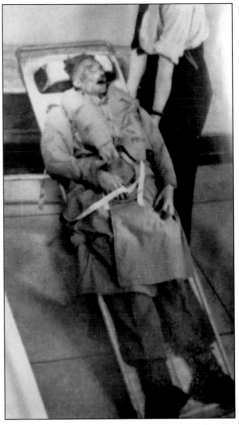

The corpse used in Operation *Mincemeat* being fitted into its metal container and packed with dry ice. (Author's collection)

Urgent signals flowed from London in an attempt to keep up the façade, expressing deep concern that the dispatch-case and its top-secret contents had gone missing. Appeals were made to the Spanish by the British Naval Attaché that the case should be returned without delay, and on 13 May it was handed back with its contents. Tests in London proved that envelopes in the case had been tampered with; there could be no doubt now that Major Martin's secrets had indeed been passed on to the Germans. *The Times* recorded Major Martin's death in its list of casualties; by coincidence, an aircraft had been lost in the area about the same time. By a further piece of luck, the local Spanish medical examiner had failed to notice that Major Martin had not died as a result of drowning.

The Germans took the poisoned bait, and within days copies of the fake correspondence were on their way to Berlin. Hitler met with Grand Admiral Karl Doenitz, commander-in-chief of the *Kriegsmarine*, and is reported to have said that Sardinia should be held by all available forces and that an invasion of Sicily was unlikely. The deception was complete. The Italians, however, were not convinced by this subterfuge, never doubting that the pattern of Allied air operations pointed to an attack in Sicily. The careful deception had no effect on Italian military thinking. In early June, a German signal intercepted by the Allies stated that the entire 1st Panzer Division was to move from its base in Southern France to the Peloponnese in Greece. The presence of this unit in Sicily might have been decisive when the Allies landed, but now it was being sent on a wild goose chase 1,000 miles away. On 21 May, an order was sent to Kesselring stating:

> The measures to be taken in Sardinia and the Peloponnese (Greece) have priority over any others.[3]

The German High Command swallowed the bait hook, line and sinker, but their appreciation of the situation, made long before the end of the Tunisian campaign, contradicted their present stance. At that time, they had correctly predicted that the Allies would direct their operations where the enemy forces were weakest, and that upon the conclusion of fighting in North Africa it would be imperative for them that Italy should be knocked out of the war by means of air attacks, with Sicily offering itself as their first target.

Churchill took a great interest in this act of deception. While the audacious plan was being put into operation, he was in Washington attending the Trident Conference with US President Roosevelt. When it was certain the Germans had taken the bait, a cryptic message was sent to him from London; it read simply:

> Mincemeat Swallowed Whole.[4]

Leading up to the invasion of Sicily, a number of hazardous operations were taking place all along the Sicilian coastline. At night, British submarines surfaced off the coast and launched collapsible canoes manned by Royal Navy officers and ratings and men of the Royal Engineers. Their task was to make reconnaissance trips all along the 105-mile length of coast that would be targeted by the Allied assault divisions. Each landing area had to be forensically investigated for its suitability for a landing and any points of interest recorded, such as gradients of the beaches and the composition of the ground to be passed over. In certain areas of the Sicilian coast, submarines cruised at periscope depth close inshore, an officer making notes on what was observed. One man from each foldable canoe team would remain in the canoe several hundred yards out to sea while his comrade swam ashore to study coastal batteries and build-ings close to the sea, beach defences, searchlight positions and radar facilities. These brave men and made one of the most important, if lesser known, contributions to Operation *Husky*, the codename given to the invasion.

On 19 January 1943, the Allied combined chiefs came to the decision to move against Sicily to relieve the pressure on the Russian Front, secure the Mediterranean

---

3   PRO (CAB 44/285).
4   E. Montagu, *The Man Who Never Was* (London: Evans Bros, 1953), p. 117.

line of communications and increase the pressure on the Italian mainland. The next day, the British put forward an outline plan codenamed Operation *Husky*. US General Dwight Eisenhower became Supreme Commander, with British General Harold Alexander as his deputy in charge of the Allied 15th Army Group, emphasising the role of the USA as the senior partner in the alliance, even though Alexander was senior in rank and experience and the British were to provide the bulk of the invasion forces.

A swift landing in Sicily immediately after the final surrender of Axis forces in Tunisia would have found the island almost defenceless, but the pause that followed enabled the Italians and Germans to reinforce the defences of the island. Churchill had called for the landings to be made in June, but the Allied army commanders were not able to launch the invasion until 10 July. In the plan that was finally agreed, General George Patton's American Seventh Army (Western Task Force) would land in the south-east of the island, alongside General Bernard Montgomery's British and Canadian troops of the Eighth Army (Eastern Task Force), with both armies supported by airborne landings. US troops were originally scheduled to come ashore on the western end of Sicily, but this plan was dropped. The Allied forces would now be more concentrated, with their landing points close together. This tight massing of the invading forces was agreed upon because of the fear of a heavy Axis counter-attack, though with hindsight, such was the initial weakness of the defenders that it was unnecessary. In scale, this simultaneous landing by eight Allied divisions was to be bigger than the invasion of Normandy 11 months later, and would be the first large-scale seaborne assault in the Second World War on a coast held by the enemy.

On the afternoon of 9 July, the convoy of Allied ships began its journey west of Malta. The wind speed increased dramatically, churning up the sea to such an extent that it threatened to dislocate the landings. Later that night, however, conditions improved, leaving just a troublesome swell. The forces of the British 1st Airborne and US 82nd Airborne Divisions were more severely affected by the winds as they launched their assault, the American parachute troops being scattered over an area of 50 miles, while the British glider troops were also widely scattered, with 47 of their 134 gliders coming down in the sea. However, the unintentionally scattered distribution of these troops caused great alarm and confusion over a wide area behind the enemy front, and enabled key bridges and road junctions to be seized. The sudden storm that had plagued the attackers served to lull the defenders into a state of false security, even though the convoy had been spotted during the afternoon while advancing from Malta. Italian troops in Sicily had been on alert for many nights and were very tired, but their weariness was more than just physical; many were tired of the war itself. The troops defending the coast were Sicilian men of the Italian 213th Coastal Division, the reasoning behind this being that they would fight all the harder for their own homes and reputation as fighting men. However, this did not take into account the longstanding dislike of the Germans by the Sicilians, nor the realisation that the harder they resisted the invasion, the less there would be left of their homes.

Pre-emptive Strikes: George Beach, 9 July, 3 Commando

Inland from the main invasion beach, just south of Syracuse, there was stationed a gun battery of 10 Italian artillery pieces manned by 400 men that would create havoc if it directed its fire onto the troops coming ashore. If it was left intact, many casualties would be taken, so 3 Commando was given the unenviable task of landing the night before the main assault and neutralising it. They were to land south of Syracuse and advance through enemy-held territory to eliminate this threat. Lieutenant Colonel John Durnford-Slater, DSO and Bar, OC of 3 Commando, left a description of the ship, the *Prince Albert*, that would take the commandos to their landing point and act as their base during the campaign:

> It was good to get under way, heading back to Europe. The *Prince Albert* was another cross-Channel steamer fitted with eight landing-craft, in the bows of each landing-craft we had mounted a Vickers K Machine-gun and the purpose of these guns was to engage the beach defences as we landed. They were light weapons with a great fire-power and each magazine carried 100 rounds.[5]

Captain Peter Young, 3 Commando, recalled the bustle as the troops made ready to leave their mother ship:

> At 23:00 p.m. our troops began to get dressed and we joined them on the deck where they were grouped ready to make their way to the boat deck and embark. They were in tremendous form, singing at the tops of their voices. The ship was blacked out and there was only a dim light between decks, hardly enough to see people's faces. Because of the weather we stood in closer to the land than originally intended. We were about seven miles from the coast when a little after mid-night we filed along to our boat stations and were lowered into five landing craft, each carrying about 35 soldiers. Conditions were not easy with a strong head wind, a heavy swell and a black night as we slowly crept in towards the shore.[6]

The *Prince Albert* had approached Sicily in the late afternoon of 9 July, with the brooding peak of Mount Etna clearly visible in the distance. The sea was very rough and the chance of a surprise attack did not seem likely. Yet the troops were still in good heart as the ship anchored 10 miles off shore and the men began transferring into the small landing-craft. Other ships were going in all directions, and as the light faded a large transport, the *Sobieski*, appeared on the port side of the *Prince Albert* and a collision was only narrowly avoided. The cover of darkness then descended to conceal the small landing-craft as they slowly headed for the beach.

---

5   J. Durnford-Slater, *Commando, Memoirs of a Fighting Commando in World War Two* (London: Greenhill Books, 2002), p. 132.
6   P. Young, *Storm from the Sea* (Northamptonshire: Wren's Park Publishing, 2002), p. 81.

Lieutenant John C. Erskine was among those who landed with 3 Commando that night:

> Creeping gently in towards George Beach in our own little craft with a warming glass of rum inside me I felt very much at ease. The waning moon was well up in a clear sky so there would still be light until dawn took over. About two miles in we located a tiny red beacon that was flashing Morse-code Gs (for George Beach, the canoe beacon had been placed there by a submarine days before), from which a compass bearing to our own landing was known.[7]

Lieutenant Anthony Daniell, commander of the submarine HMS *Unison*, had prepared the flashing beacon to guide in the attacking force:

> We had to fix our position accurately on the days previous to D-Day and bottom in our allotted position having laid a sonar buoy to seaward. We then surfaced after midnight, still in position of course. One tragic thing I remember clearly was seeing gliders coming down in the sea a mile or two away, and my taking the decision that we mustn't move to look for survivors in case we misled the approaching craft.[8]

Durnford-Slater began to get his bearings as the dark outlines of mountains against the skyline became visible. He had studied these shapes beforehand from maps and photographs, which enabled him to see that the beacon had drifted from its intended position due to the strong winds and tides. The main feature near the landing beach was a prominent rocky escarpment called the Scoglio. Durnford-Slater hailed a destroyer for a compass bearing to take him to the feature, and it was not long before this natural pillar of rock – some 200ft high – came into view.

As the commandos looked towards the headland from their small craft, other features became recognisable through the gloom. They approached slowly, hoping that the Italian troops holding the beach defences would

Lieutenant John C. Erskine, 3 Commando. (Courtesy of M Denney)

7   *Commando Veterans* <www.commandoveterans.org> (accessed 15 December 2019).
8   S.W.C. Pack, *Operation Husky* (London: David and Charles, 1977), pp. 91-92.

open fire too soon and give away their positions. The Italians did indeed open fire, and came under direct and accurate fire themselves from the commando machine-gunners on the open deck of each craft, who plastered the Italian pillbox apertures and forced the defenders to take cover. The landing craft then headed over the final approach at full speed until the beach was hit and the ramps went down. Lieutenant Erskine recalled:

> We paid little attention to the seven enemy machine-gun posts but threw our wire netting rolls over the beach barbed wire and ran inland between two of the enemy posts. Then we formed into a long column two soldiers wide and set off on the first compass bearing heading towards our first check point, which we knew from aerial photographs; we had to turn onto a new compass bearing to avoid an enemy position. We went on for five miles towards our objective which was the German/Italian Battery. We were nearly an hour late as we had wasted a lot of time creeping onto the beach. The colonel had promised the Corps commander [Dempsey] that the guns would be silenced before the divisional landings at first light. We pressed on as fast as we could with the colonel leading, as usual. We were all terribly loaded down with extra mortar bombs and extra Vickers ammunition.[9]

Able Seaman Leslie Harris, who served on HMS *Prince Albert* and was in one of the landing craft that took the commandos to the beach, remembered:

> The first wave of boats landed and then we went back for the second wave. As we approached the beach, we saw objects in the water but could not stop. After the second landing, on the way back, we picked up 15 glider soldiers, these fellows were in the sea but they did not call out for help because they knew we had a job to do, they waited patiently for our return.[10]

Captain Young of 3 Commando immediately moved off the beach with his troop and headed inland:

> We had come under fire a couple of hundred yards from the shore. From a pill-box some Italians were firing at us with a machine-gun when from our seven craft 25 machine-guns returned their fire and it took only a few seconds to convince the Italian garrison that they were doing no good. The commando struggled through a mass of barbed-wire, ran up the beach and struck off inland ignoring the beach defenders. We could hear the moans and cries of the wounded as we passed. It was a bright moonlit night and, led by John Pooley and the Colonel, we set off across country at a good speed with the leading troops marching on a

9   <www.commandoveterans.org> (accessed 20 December 2018).
10   Letter to author from L. Harris, Hampshire, 1989.

Commandos training for a beach landing. (Author's collection)

compass bearing and one man counting the paces. At one point a farmer fired his shotgun at 6 Troop, [but] this act proved fatal to him.[11]

Lieutenant Colonel Durnford-Slater and his batman survived a close shave as he prepared his troops to push further inland:

> We formed up a hundred yards inland, exactly as we had practised. I crouched down to tell my batman, Charlesworth, something and our faces were inches apart when a tracer bullet flashed between our noses. We both reared up like startled horses and neither of us spoke. Then the firing stopped. The countryside was flat and open with a high stone wall dividing the fields every few hundred yards. We started our advance preceded by two scouts 50 yards ahead of us. It was a bright moonlit night and now everything was still.[12]

Durnford-Slater was uneasy about the situation, as he had promised Lieutenant General Miles Dempsey of XIII Corps that the operation would be completed within 90 minutes of landing. He went ahead with Lieutenant Pooley and kept flashing a shaded torch back to his men so they would know the direction they had to move in. This saved valuable time and kept the double-file column moving in the right direction. The heavily laden men did little talking; only essential orders were given by the officers in lowered tones.

11   P. Young, *Storm from the Sea* (Northamptonshire: Wren's Park Publishing, 2002), p. 85.
12   J. Durnford-Slater, *Memoirs of a Fighting Commando in World War Two* (London: Greenhill Books, 2002), p. 133.

As the commandos reached their final check-point, which was a dry water-course 200 metres in front of the enemy defences, the battery guns opened fire at the troops landing on the beach, getting off at least 20 rounds. The commando mortar crews then began to direct fire into the battery positions, forcing them to cease fire and take cover.

Captain Young looked on as an Italian ammunition dump exploded:

> Then the battery began to fire with the commando still not in position. John Durnford-Slater was racing against time. From our dry watercourse in front of the battery he sent a party to harass the Italians with rifle fire and a two-inch mortar. On the flank of the guns and about 400 yards from them he placed a three-inch mortar and four Bren-guns under Roy Westley and they dropped a mortar bomb into an Italian ammunition dump, which went on exploding for some time. Most soldiers carried two three-inch mortar bombs suspended round their necks. As they passed the position of 2 Troop, they dumped their bombs with loud clanks and sighs of relief.[13]

The attack plan was for the Heavy Weapons Platoon to set up their two Vickers machine guns at the base of a large tree identified from aerial photographs, and to fire on fixed lines along a compass bearing in case the poor light prevented them from seeing a target to aim at. However, the sky was perfectly clear and the machine-gunners had plenty of light to see their targets in the gun battery. The double column of commandos filed passed the tree, and as they did so each man dropped off the heavy mortar bombs and boxes of Vickers ammunition he had been carrying since landing. The start line for the attack had been identified from aerial photographs, and the troops moved into their allotted positions and waited. The Vickers machine-gunners opened up a continuous and heavy fire at their tactically important targets in the battery position, while the three attacking troops crept closer to the enemy wire at various targeted weak points in preparation for the assault. The other mortar crews then opened fire on the enemy, firstly with star shells to illuminate the scene, then with high-explosive and finally with smoke to conceal the attackers.

When Durnford-Slater was satisfied that the enemy had been softened up sufficiently, he gave the order for his men to prepare for a bayonet charge which he hoped would take the position with the first shock. Peter Young watched as the first attack went in:

> The Colonel [Durnford-Slater] had formed up three troops, two forward and one back [the latter was Lieutenant Erskine's troop] and the battery was illuminated with flares, by the light [of which] the assaulting troops poured in a heavy fire on the defenders. Charlesworth, the Colonel's batman, sounded the advance on his trumpet and in they went, blasting the wire with Bangalore torpedoes. The Italians had been firing back with a number of automatic weapons.[14]

---

13   P. Young, *Storm from the Sea* (Northamptonshire: Wren's Park Publishing, 2002), p. 83.
14   Ibid.

Lieutenant Erskine watched this first charge go in from the north but founder in confused fighting around the position:

> My section, which was the Colonel's final reserve, had to complete the job with one final charge. My little force of 29 men were crouched out of sight behind a low stone wall just in front of the eastern barbed-wire. As soon as I gave the order to fix bayonets my men were like racehorses straining to get started. It was difficult to hold them back.[15]

Lieutenant Colonel John Durnford-Slater, 3 Commando. (Courtesy of M. Denney)

Erskine twice called out to Durnford-Slater to be allowed to release his men but was told to hold them in check as this was the final throw of the dice and timing was everything if they were to succeed. Durnford-Slater knew that if they failed in their mission, they would become embroiled in a confused fire-fight 5 miles behind enemy lines, with no possibility of help and no reserves of ammunition. The enemy, meanwhile, would be in vastly superior numbers, with reinforcements close to hand. Finally, Durnford-Slater gave the order for Erskine and his eager warriors to go. Erskine recalled:

> We jumped over the wall and then over the barbed-wire, [and] my long line of 29 men, with bayonets fixed, rushed at the enemy. As soon as they saw the bayonets most of them lay down on the ground, put their hands over their faces and allowed themselves to be captured. The battle was quickly over and, except for enemy soldiers lying on the ground, all I could find was one German officer scrambling away at the base of a stone wall. He was just out of range of my Tommy-gun so I let him go.[16]

Durnford-Slater also remembered the attack that captured the position:

> Charlesworth sounded his bugle for the final assault and we went in. We came to concentrations of barbed-wire and blasted paths through it with Bangalore torpedoes, long metal tubes filled with explosive. We dashed through the gaps firing

15   *Commando Veterans* <www.commandoveterans.org> (accessed 9 December 2019).
16   *Ibid.*

from the hip. I was using my Garand [an American infantryman's semi-automatic rifle], I was fond of that weapon. The Italians stuck it fairly well until near the end, replying to our fire with automatic weapons. When we had cleaned up, we proceeded to blow up the guns when some enthusiast decided to blow up the ammunition supply of the battery, about 1,000 shells. It was a very loud bang and there was plenty of stuff flying about. The battery was blown up 85 minutes after landing, redeeming my word to General Dempsey with five minutes to spare.[17]

The commandos had got to their objective, fixed bayonets and launched their attack, leaving the Italian troops so terrified that when the commandos entered the position, the defenders were laying face-down and were all taken prisoner. However, radio communication with the rear had, not for the first time in this campaign, broken down, and the message of the success of the operation was not relayed back to Montgomery. Lieutenant Erskine was given the job of trekking back to the beach and passing on the news:

I was sent post-haste back to the beach carrying the message personally. I got back through the enemy lines easily and ran straight through the beach mine-field, not knowing I was doing so, and delivered my message to the senior officer on the beach, only to be told that their radio had this minute got the message.[18]

After the Italian artillery emplacement had fallen and all was secure, Lieutenant Colonel Durnford-Slater decided it was time for his men to get some food inside them and have a hot drink. Lieutenant Charles Head posted sentries as the men relaxed and prepared their food. Durnford-Slater remembered:

I found that Charlesworth had already got his spirit stove into action and, having obtained some eggs from a nearby farm, soon had a first-class breakfast ready for me. Everybody else also did themselves well. As we were finishing breakfast, we heard another Italian battery firing from a position two miles away. I said to Charlie [Lieutenant Head] 'Come on we'll go and deal with that one too.' As we moved off, we heard the beginning of a tremendous bombardment of this battery by the ships of the fleet, so decided to leave well alone.[19]

In the early hours of 10 July, the victorious commandos and their prisoners were picked up from George Beach and returned to their mother ship, the *Prince Albert*.

17   J. Durnford-Slater, *Commando, Memoirs of a fighting Commando in World War Two* (London: Greenhill Books, 2002), p. 135.
18   Ibid., p. 136.
19   J. Durnford-Slater, *Commando, Memoirs of a fighting Commando in WW2* (London: Greenhill Books, 2002), p. 135.

The Special Raiding Squadron at *Capo Burro di Porco*, 9-10 July

On 4 July, the converted infantry landing ship HMS *Ulster Monarch* sailed into the Mediterranean carrying the men of the Special Raiding Squadron (SRS) and the landing-craft they would use to get ashore. During the afternoon, each officer was handed a box full of blue booklets entitled *A Soldier's Guide to Sicily*. All officers were then summoned to the briefing room by the ship's loud hailer. Maps and aerial photographs were issued as the great ship rolled in the heavy swell. In the cabin of Major Paddy Maine, DSO – the squadron's commanding officer – was a large wall map of Sicily, on which the officers studied the position of all enemy forces on the island. Questions were asked and all eventualities covered, and each officer then returned to his troop to explain their particular role.

In the initial assault on Sicily, the SRS – which numbered 270 men of all ranks – was to capture and destroy the coastal battery named Lamb Doria (named after an Italian naval hero) at *Capo Burro di Porco*. The battery was on the 5th Division's front south of Syracuse and was 300 yards from the cliff edge. Paddy Maine was ordered to take the battery and then play it by ear as to what he did next, depending on the circumstances on the ground. Re-embarkation on the *Ulster Monarch* was also an option.

Lieutenant Derick Harrison, of the SRS recalled the calmness of the sea on 9 July and the warm sunshine. However, things were about to change drastically:

> As midday approached the White Ensign at our stern, till then listlessly flapping round the mast, bestirred itself as the freshening breeze jerked it into life. Before long a half gale was blowing and towering waves, white crested with spume, gave way to sickening troughs into which the ship lurched and twisted dizzily. All that afternoon the rising wind lashed the seas into an angry maelstrom. As we drew nearer to our destination the moon came up, silhouetting the other ships in the convoy. Silently and fiercely, they butted their way through the still mountainous waves. In the ward room a meal of bacon and eggs was being served, but my stomach, already sorely tried by the storm, jibbed at it. I went below to get my equipment on before the ship switched to invasion lighting, and then went back on deck.[20]

On deck, Harrison's eyes became accustomed to the darkness and the dim outline of the island could be made out. Men's minds now became focussed as they moved closer to the area of operations, while on the shore, fires were burning fiercely. Bombs burst in the distance and flak climbed lazily in the night sky, trying to hit the British bombers that were attacking towns and airfields. Overhead came a loud drone that got louder by the minute as fleets of bombers joined in the attack on identified targets. Searchlights from Italian coastal units scanned the sky and the sea hoping to pick up on some unfortunate victim. The Allied flotilla crept closer and closer to the coastline

---

20   D.I. Harrison, *These Men are Dangerous* (London: Cassel, 1957), p. 36.

as the wind continued to howl. Flares burst in the sky, lighting everything up like day, and slowly fell into the sea to leave the night blacker than ever.

On board the ships carrying the SRS, loud hailers broke the silence: "SRS stand by!" The fully loaded men moved to their positions on the troop deck. Lieutenant Harrison came up from the mess deck and led his men to their allocated craft:

> Down there the scene was satanic. In the light of the red invasion lamps everything seemed to glow with fire, while long shadows darted and danced across the mess decks where we were assembled. Outside the landing-craft bumped and crashed against the sides of the ship as she tossed and lurched while, every few minutes, a wave higher than its fellows poured through the open oiling doors through which we were to embark. The voice spoke again 'SRS embark'. Slowly the head of the column moved forward to where the craft were swinging madly to and fro."[21]

As the landing-craft swung wildly, it would take only one misjudgement by an individual loaded with weapons and equipment to find himself plunged into the rolling sea. When the first craft was fully loaded, it was lowered into the waters and cast off into the darkness. The second craft was then quickly loaded up with men and equipment and similarly lowered into the sea. Harrison, who was on the second landing-craft, recalled:

> Up and down and round-about we went. Giddily the stars whirled by as we were tossed to and fro by wind and sea. With monotonous regularity wave after wave crashed over us squatting in the bows and I was soaked to the skin. Over most of the craft was stretched an awning but it availed us little. Water swirled round our feet, but the motor pump chugging away gave us a certain amount of comfort.[22]

As the landing-craft came into the lee of the land, the sea became somewhat calmer. An aircraft flying overhead dropped a cluster of flares and at once everything was as bright as day. The men approaching the beach felt their hearts sink as they suddenly became visible, their cloak of darkness stripped away. The flares hung in the sky before falling to earth, but still nothing happened. As they carried on their journey to the beach, Lieutenant Harrison saw strange shapes in the sea:

> Ahead and to starboard a British submarine rode on the surface, a small blue lamp pointing seaward to guide in the assault craft. In a matter of minutes, we had left her astern. Suddenly over the water came the cries of men. Hearts in mouths we strained our eyes and ears. Could it be German E-Boats? Out of the darkness floated a dim shape and with it came the voices again. A torch was

---

21 Ibid., p. 37.
22 Ibid., p. 38.

flashed frantically through the darkness. Someone shouted, 'Put that bloody light out!' It seemed impossible that the enemy sentries could fail to hear the shouting and see the light. Now we recognized the outline of a partially wrecked and submerged glider. Time had no meaning till at last we had them on the stern of the LCA[23] shivering with exposure and shock.[24]

The engines of the landing-craft roared as they made the final run-in to the beach. At 3:20 a.m., the Special Raiding Squadron landed unopposed on the correct beach. Slipping and sliding over weed-covered wet rocks, the commandos headed for the cliff face and, in single file, began to scramble up it. At the top, the men prepared their weapons as they hid in the darkness among the rocks and foliage. The last of the commandos joined their comrades; taking up their positions, they watched and listened for the enemy, who never appeared. The silence was unnerving, every shape ominous. In open formation, the men rose up and pressed on, some straight into the Italian battery without knowing it. There was a deafening roar and a blinding flash as the attacking troops fired mortar bombs into the battery position. Harrison's section came under fire:

> On the right a light machine-gun opened up on us as we scurried across the open ground between the battery and the farm. Bending low we made for the wall ahead as fast as we could and on the other-side we were safe for the time being. We were behind the battery now and most of the buildings were blazing. In the light of the flames, we could see the guns. I had to get the engineers in there fast. There came a sharp rattle of machine-gun fire and streams of green tracer cut through our ranks and as we dived for cover our Bren gunners swung round firing from the hip in the direction of the tracer. From our right front came a stream of red tracer and I yelled the challenge at the top of my voice 'Desert Rats'. Back came the answer 'Kill Italians'. We breathed again.[25]

The troops stormed into the battery position, firing as they went. The battle was short-lived, Italian troops beginning to surrender rather than die at their posts. The engineers who were with the commandos prepared the guns for demolition as the attacking force rounded up the Italian garrison. Among those taken prisoner were 20 women and children who had sought safety in the battery from what they thought was a raid by the RAF. They were terrified and numb, having been told that the British would treat them badly if they were captured. Wounded Italians were cared for as the engineers laid their charges, and all personnel – British, Italians and civilians – were shepherded to safety as the order was shouted out, "Stand clear!" This was followed by a great explosion that shattered the guns, sending large chunks of

---

23   LCA: Landing-craft Assault.
24   D.I. Harrison, *These Men are Dangerous* (London: Cassell, 1957), p. 39.
25   Ibid., p. 40.

steel flying through the air. Rockets were sent soaring into the night air as a signal of success.

The commandos prepared for an expected counter-attack that never came. Out to sea, the dark shapes of the Allied flotilla could be made out, drifting listlessly on the heavy swell, reminding them of the drama being played out below them as, 30 miles down the coast, the Eighth Army was coming ashore. Sentries were posted, and the officers organised their men and took stock of the situation. Mercifully, no casualties had been incurred. Planes roared above the commandos, and shortly after 6:00 a.m., heavy guns opened fired at the fleet from another battery further inland, their shells sending up great plumes of water around the Allied ships. The commando officers then met at the Damerio farmhouse and worked out the position of this previously unknown battery some 2½ miles distant. The troops advanced towards their new target, but as they did so they came under sniper fire from various locations. From beyond a belt of trees came the boom of heavy artillery; the troops had found the outer perimeter of the new gun battery, but the approach to it was impeded by six defended farms. Lieutenant Harrison recalled a chaotic situation:

> From a tree shrouded farmhouse on our left came a ragged volley of fire and lying in the open across a farm track we returned the fire. As we jumped to our feet to rush the place a white hankerchief tied to a rifle muzzle was waved to and fro among the trees. Our prisoners were some of the glider boys who, landing in the wrong place during the night, had decided to hold the farm till our arrival. We had not come ashore in khaki drill trousers and blue grey shirts, [so] not unnaturally they had taken us for Italians. We now came under fire from yet another farmhouse further over to the left.[26]

Paddy Maine now decided to attack a third battery located at *Punta Della Mola*, sending 1 Troop to make the assault, while the 3-inch mortars engaged a fourth battery at Faro Mas Solivieri. In all, three batteries were knocked out and large amounts of weapons and equipment were captured before the squadron linked up with the 5th Division, which had landed at Cassibile. Lieutenant Harrison settled down with his men for a well-earned meal:

> We were now overlooking Syracuse and it was suggested that we might turn the captured guns on the town. But we were in the dark as to the position of our own troops. For all we knew they might have reached Syracuse already. Reluctantly we destroyed the guns and settled down to eat our meagre rations, our first meal since leaving the *Ulster Monarch*. Meanwhile 1 Troop were still busy and, by the time we finished our meal, two neighbouring gun positions had fallen to them.[27]

---

26 Harrison D I *These Men are Dangerous* (London. Cassell 1957) p. 43.
27 D.I. Harrison, *These Men are Dangerous* (London: Cassel, 1957), p. 47.

These operations saved many lives, but few of the attacking forces of the Eighth Army were ever aware of the feats of bravery performed by the men of 3 Commando and the SRS and the debt the landing troops owed to them.

Disaster at the *Ponte Grande*, 9-10 July, 1st Air Landing Brigade

On the night of 9 July, the British 1st Airborne Division's 1st Air Landing Brigade[28] arrived off the coast of Sicily at Cape Passero in a massive aerial armada. As the men of Brigadier Phillip Hicks' brigade sat in their gliders and looked at the sea below them, they saw the Allied fleet off the Sicilian coast waiting for H-Hour. The 2,075 glider troops were to land near Syracuse to seize and hold the important *Ponte Grande* that crosses the Anapo River. They were due to be relieved the following day by the 5th Division as it advanced inland. The *Ponte Grande* was a major obstacle to the capture of Syracuse and its vital port; if the bridge was left in enemy hands, the movement of Allied vehicular traffic would be severely curtailed, impeding the 5th Division's drive to capture the port of Syracuse and ruining Montgomery's carefully timed plans. Montgomery's staff were shocked to hear about the proposed use of glider troops in advance of the main body of the Eighth Army; the capabilities of this new airborne force were not known, and the resources for such a plan were few. To expect an assault to be successfully made by gliders at such short notice made the outcome highly doubtful.

When the glider officers examined aerial photographs of Sicily, they found the terrain highly unsuitable for a glider landing operation. The Sicilian beaches were rock-strewn and fenced in by high cliffs. The drop zone was intersected by stone walls, and to make matters worse, the glider pilots were totally unprepared for night flying. Lieutenant Colonel George Chatterton, CO of the 1st Battalion Glider Pilot Regiment, voiced his objections loudly, but was told by his superior, Major General George Frederick Hopkinson,[29] that if he was not prepared to take part he would find a man who was. Chatterton backed down. Having secured Montgomery's acceptance for a massed glider landing at night as part of the plan to capture Syracuse, Hopkinson simply pulled rank on Chatterton and ensured that no one could thwart his ambitions to lead the first Allied attack on Europe. Staff Sergeant Alec Waldron, a pilot with the 1st Glider Pilot Regiment, commented on the weakness of Hopkinson's plan:

---

28 The 1st Air Landing Brigade was made up of the 1st Battalion Glider Pilot Regiment, 1st Battalion Border Regiment, 2nd Battalion South Staffordshire Regiment and 9th Field Company, Royal Engineers.

29 Major General George Frederick Hopkinson, OBE, MC, CO of 1st Airborne Division, General Staff (North Staffordshire Regiment), was killed in action on 12 September 1943, aged 47. He is buried in Bari War Cemetery in southern Italy.

The cautionary advice from both Army and RAF airborne specialists was rebutted, to the despair of these experienced and dedicated personnel, who were relegated to the role of helpless observers as the inevitable fiasco unfolded. The unforeseen wind conditions of 9th July, sufficient to justify cancellation, would be the final nail in the coffin.[30]

Fellow 1st Glider Pilot Regiment pilot Sergeant Victor Miller spent the day before the attack getting the right equipment from a stressed storeman who was beset with men claiming rations and other items from his stores. Sergeant Miller recalled:

> I had learned the evening before that we were due to take part in an airborne operation against Sicily on the night of 9/10th July, now that was tomorrow. The time left to us to re-equip was fantastically little. Normally at least one week was allowed for the stores to be passed down from the divisional dumps and in turn issued to the men, and here we were with less than 24 hours before take-off with most of us deficient of some type of equipment, arms or ammunition. To add to my confusion, I had missed all the detailed briefings that had been going on for the last few days.[31]

So it was that this fatally flawed, dangerous and bold plan, given the name Operation *Ladbroke*, was to be enacted, despite objections from various senior officers. The entire force was to arrive at the three landing zones at 10:00 p.m. and fight in battalion groups. The main focus of the operation was the *Ponte Grande*. On both sides of the bridge, eight Horsa gliders would land, then one company of the 2nd Battalion South Staffordshire Regiment were to seize the bridge before the defenders could react. The 1st Battalion Border Regiment, meanwhile, was to seize and hold the city of Syracuse until relieved by the 5th Division. In the days before the operation, the training given to the tug and glider pilots was inadequate. Lieutenant Colonel Chatterton had pleaded that his men be given night training but was ignored. Chatterton and others knew that despite their best endeavours, the force that took off from dusty airstrips in Tunisia on 9 July was ill-prepared to land over 2,000 men in a hostile landscape, in the dark and in winds of up to 35 miles per hour. The stage was set for tragedy.

Flight Officer Bob Wilson became bored waiting for his turn to take off and was curious as to the load his glider was carrying. He entered his Waco glider and examined the jeep and trailer inside. Lifting the canvas covering the trailer, he came across a grim reminder of what lay in store:

---

30   A. Waldron, *Operation Ladbroke. From Dream to Disaster* (Sussex: Woodfield Publishers, 2003), p. 34.
31   V. Miller, *Nothing is Impossible* (Kent: Spellmount, 1994), p. 53.

It really gave me a shock as it was full of material for marking graves, canvas bags and wooden crosses. Somebody already knew that we would not all be coming back.[32]

Sergeant Victor Miller sat in his glider's cockpit, drinking tea in the terrific heat and waiting for take-off:

A coughing roar broke out from the first tug to warm up its engines and everyone suddenly went quiet. I felt my heart beat a little faster as I glanced at my watch, it was 6:45 p.m., only 15 minutes to take-off. Behind the Albemarle a cloud of dust was swirling steadily across the sparse grass covered airfield. The Albemarle trembled against the chocks and brakes like a dog straining at its leash. The roar of the engines worked up to a crescendo of thunder. Another plane took up the cacophony of sound and yet another until the very air vibrated with the defiant thunder of scores of motors raising their voices, a swirling maelstrom of dust was everywhere. A fog of dust increased behind the tug as she slowly moved forward and the Waco slid forward. From out of the pall of dust the first combination emerged at the end of the runway climbing slowly. Ahead the faint outline of the Albemarle was discernible.[33]

The 1st Air Landing Brigade embarked from various airfields around Kairouan, Tunisia, on the evening of 9 July. They travelled in 137 Waco and 10 Horsa gliders piloted by men from the 1st Battalion the Glider Pilot Regiment, led by Lieutenant Colonel Chatterton. The bulk of the gliders were towed by C-47s belonging to the 51st USAAF Troop Carrier Wing, the remainder by RAF Albemarles and Halifaxes.

As this massive force approached Sicily, winds were running at 30–40 miles per hour. Heavy concentrations of flak from the coastal defences caught the leading aircraft, forcing them to take evasive action away from their original flight paths. Planes and gliders broke formation and the smoke from the flak batteries was blown inland by the winds, cloaking the landing zones and making them virtually impossible to be seen by the pilots. Italian flares rose in the night sky and ruined the night vision of the pilots, some of whom panicked and released their gliders far too soon, resulting in them crashing into the sea.

The vessels of the Allied fleet were under orders not to open fire as the glider force passed overhead, but near Cape Passero one nervous gunner fired on a C-47, leading to others doing the same. The aerial convoy now disintegrated as towing aircraft and their gliders flew off in various directions. Once out of formation at night, with no visual landmarks, it was virtually impossible for the pilots to regain cohesion. As the eyewitness testimonies below reveal, numerous factors came together to ensure that Operation *Ladbroke* was a disaster: inexperience, strong winds and accurate enemy flak were a fatal combination.

---

32   M. Peters, *Glider Pilots over Sicily* (Barnsley: Pen & Sword, 2012), p. 133.
33   V. Miller, *Nothing is Impossible* (Kent: Spellmount, 1994), p. 57.

Staff Sergeant Alec Waldron, piloting his glider, was having trouble keeping control of his flight path as they approached the coastline at 1,400ft. The moon was hardly visible, and below he could see white capped waves, indicating winds far in excess of what he had planned for in all of his calculations. A non-swimmer, the thought of ditching in the sea terrified him:

> Our final checkpoint of Cape Ognina was barely visible, thus precluding a posi-tive fix. The shore some 3,000 yards away was barely discernible, so as my tug began turning to starboard to head eastwards and clear of Cape di Porco I cast off and headed for the distant shore. In my anxiety I was guilty of premature or late release, I shall never know. It was soon obvious that we would ditch, [so] I told George to go aft and prepare our live load for a sea landing and to cut an escape hatch through the upper canvas of the fuselage. Meanwhile I glided as close to the shore as possible, maintained adequate flying speed and then managed to put the tail in first, thus reducing the impact, which neverthe-less felt like hitting a concrete wall. The [cockpit] Perspex burst open and the cockpit filled rapidly. In a frenzy born of survival instincts I forced my way through the broken Perspex onto the floating port wing, where I established that everyone else had exited safely. The shore, now dimly visible, was not that far distant, enabling all but myself to swim ashore and survive a most unpleasant experience.[34]

Lance Corporal Reginald Brown, from A Company of the 2nd Battalion South Staffordshire Regiment, was getting quite fed up with the journey to Sicily, wishing he could get back on solid ground:

> By now I was in the mood and was quite willing to fight the whole Axis army alone – if only I could get my feet 'on the deck'! ... Land fighting held no terrors for us, but for God's sake lets [sic] hurry and get there. Time was dragging like hell. ... We weren't flying very high, only just clearing the waves. Then we climbed to our casting off altitude ... [and] were told to black out the windows and the pilot put the lights on, which was better. Then there was a definite crack and a decided steadying of the Horsa. Now there was no doubt about it, we were alone gliding down to who knows what. We sat tight staring across at each other unseeingly in the dark and linked arms ready to take the strain of the landing. I heard a noise up-front, the lights came on and Lt Barrett was smashing away at the roof with a hand axe. The lights went off again and I slipped off my equip-ment in double quick time, as I could tell we were losing height rapidly and I knew the land or sea wasn't far away.[35]

34   A. Waldron, *Operation Ladbroke, from Dream to Disaster* (Sussex: Woodfield Publishers, 2003), p. 61.
35   *Pegasus Archive* <www.pegasusarchive.org> (accessed 2 April 2020).

Lance Corporal Brown's glider hit the water as someone shouted, "Hold Tight!", the jolt flinging him forward as the sea came pouring in, which terrified him as he couldn't swim. As he rose to his feet in a panic, he made for the hole in the fuselage and was pulled through it by one of his comrades:

> I was now standing on one of the wings and pulling myself together I started blowing up my rubber life jacket. Then I noticed how close we were to the land and by now the glider's wings were not as far out of the water as they had been, the old wreck was going down. A searchlight on the land switched on as though searching the waves for us, then bursts of machine-gun fire whistled around us, we thought we were spotted but the light continued its sweep and we were left in the dark again.[36]

Lieutenant Arthur Robert Royall, of B Company, 1st Battalion Border Regiment, was approaching Sicily under fire when the glider he was in was released far too early:

> As we approached Sicily Ack-ack fire could be seen ahead of us and the glider rocked badly. I felt the glider being released and although I could not see clearly, we were over the sea and there was no sight of land. In what seemed a very short time a call came down from the pilot 'Equipment off, prepare for ditching!' We hit the water with the most tremendous thump. Because of the metal framework the Waco glider sank to wing level very quickly. I must have been momentarily stunned as when I woke up the water was up to my shoulders. I was alone, it was dark and I still had my equipment on. I suddenly remembered I had a commando dagger on my belt, I took it out, pushed it through the canvas above my head, cut a large hole and pushed my head through. My appearance was greeted with a shout of 'Here he is!' I was hauled out through the hole, leaving my equipment behind. No sooner had I been extricated from the fuselage, which was now full of water, than Cpl Betts reported he had lost his glasses, he couldn't see and his lifebelt wouldn't blow up. He was still with us in the morning due to his mates holding on to him whenever he was in danger of being washed away.[37]

Lieutenant Royall could see the coast was a long way off. Nevertheless, two men asked for permission to swim ashore and set of in the stormy sea. Neither of them made it to land, and their bodies were picked up by the Royal Navy the next morning. The majority of Royall's colleagues remained on the glider all night in the heavy swell. Royall remembered that "It was much colder than ever I thought the Med could be." As dawn broke, a vessel pulled alongside the stricken glider, but as the men looked up they could see the boat was not English. They assumed they were being taken into captivity by an Italian ship. However, their luck was in as they heard an English voice

36 Ibid.
37 *Pegasus Archive* <www.pegasusarchive.org> (accessed 2 April 2020).

informing them that it was a Greek vessel.

Lance Corporal John James Bird, from the Support Company of the 2nd Battalion South Staffordshire Regiment, was in a glider as it approached the Sicilian coast. He recalled that a stiff breeze made conditions uncomfortable for the men as it buffeted the glider:

Lance Corporal John James Bird, 2nd Battalion South Staffordshire Regiment. (Author's collection)

> The bloody glider was going up and down like a yo-yo behind the tug and as we were flying not more than 100 feet above the sea, the waves were clearly visible from the glider. After a couple of hours, we sighted the Sicilian coast and could see searchlights, tracer fire and flak. We were still some distance from the coast when we felt the tow rope being released by the tug. Our glider pilot, a Scotsman, shouted we were coming down in the sea. To this day I wonder how the pilot landed that glider as he did, it was entirely down to him that we survived, for with the gale blowing and the roughness of the waves it was a miraculous feat. The water came in and in no time at all it was up to our knees. My first thoughts were to get out and I soon smashed through the fuselage and emerged under the wing. Fortunately, the main wings stayed afloat so I scrambled onto one and found five others already there. The main body of the glider, containing the jeep and trailers, had broken off and must have gone straight down and the remaining four occupants had been drowned as we never saw them again.[38]

Lance Corporal Bird and his comrades sat on the wings in the storm and darkness as the hours passed by slowly. When dawn broke, they looked out to sea. "It was a fantastic sight," said Bird. "There was a huge fleet of ships at anchor in the bay." In the misty morning light, they saw a line of landing-craft approaching, with a gun-boat leading. Bird continued:

> It was evident they were heading for the beach and we thought they wouldn't bother with us. But the last assault craft pulled alongside and we were hailed by megaphone 'Who are you?' Quick as a flash an officer shouted back 'We're

38   Ibid.

bloody British' and to our great relief they stopped and took us on board. As the boat picked up speed a commando said to me 'What mob do you blokes belong to?' and I replied 'We're airborne troops.' He said 'Fuck that for a lark.' Then he pulled out a flask and gave it to me, I felt the warmth of it as I took a drink and it was very welcome. The assault boat reached the shore and dropped off the commandos ... it turned and took us aboard the *Ulster Queen* [*sic*: *Ulster Monarch*].[39]

Corporal William Halliwell, of H Company of the 2nd Battalion South Staffordshire Regiment, was a long way off Avola when his glider was forced to ditch in the sea because of the concentrated flak coming their way. His friend, Lance Corporal Crossman, was trapped in the glider when it hit the water and his thigh had been split open. Halliwell applied a tourniquet and his shell dressing (a gauze pad and bandage). The salt water helped to congeal the flow of blood, and together they reached land in a very exhausted and unarmed condition. Italian troops took them both prisoner, and the pair came in for some rough treatment from one Italian officer who took great pleasure in physically assaulting them. Halliwell recalled:

I received a rifle butt to my head which forced me to fall back into the water. With my head throbbing and bleeding I was unable to help myself and would probably have drowned but for another Italian who pulled me out. A couple of Italians then hauled and carried us up the cliff and then dumped me unceremoniously on the filthy ground. I tried to get up to help Crossman, earning myself another bashing. An English-speaking Italian corporal told me my friend was being cared for so I asked him if he could get a doctor. Shortly an Italian officer ordered me to help Crossman and that both of us should start walking, even though they had taken away our boots. With Crossman, who was now delirious, on my shoulders I hobbled along for about three miles with my feet sore and bleeding. Once I stopped to rest from fatigue but the Italian lieutenant hit me, poked his pistol in my face and threatened to shoot me. Crossman still had not received any treatment for his wounds and I was sure he was going to die on my shoulders.... but still no doctor was available."[40]

They eventually arrived at a barracks near Syracuse and could plainly see from their vantage point a British unit making an attack on nearby Italian positions. The Italian colonel in charge then ordered Halliwell to approach the British under a white flag and inform them of the colonel's willingness to surrender. Halliwell was provided with a white rag and approached the British position, crawling for the last 50 yards in case they opened fire. From behind a low wall, hearing the noise of battle decrease, he called out as loud as he could that he was British. After what seemed an eternity,

39   Ibid.
40   *Pegasus Archive* <www.pegasusarchive.org> (accessed 2 April 2020).

A crashed Waco glider that managed to get down in one piece. (Author's collection)

a voice demanded that he stand up with his hands on his head. Halliwell was naked but for a blanket:

> Unable, with my hands on my head, to cover myself with the blanket, I stood there naked. Confronted by a seemingly empty expanse of barbed wire, as I stood there, 6 or so British soldiers slowly rose up into view. They cut through the barbed wire and identified me by means of my identity discs. The Italian colonel and his officers duly surrendered, all except for the pig who had been torturing me. The Italians all filed past me and two of their soldiers seized one of their number and brought him to me. It was the bastard who had so viciously interrogated me and denied Crossman medical aid. He was now dressed as a rank-and-file soldier. The British sergeant major was informed as to what had happened and said 'Leave him to me!' He had him escorted to the back of the building and I heard a burst of fire from a Sten gun. The sergeant major, on returning, said 'He tried to escape'.[41]

Despite pilot Lieutenant Bernard Halsall, of the Glider Pilot Regiment, having studied aerial photographs of the Sicilian coastline, when it came into view he could see nothing he recognised:

> The tug was anxious to return home as we had seen firing on the ground as well as flak coming up at us. We released at about 800 feet. At about 700 feet we crossed the shoreline and flew on into the darkness. We hit the first tree of an olive grove at about 80 miles per hour. Several minutes later, after we had all regained consciousness and gathered ourselves together, we moved off in the direction of the firing. It took us four hours to reach the bridge, picking up stragglers and having to fight through several enemy positions.[42]

41   Ibid. (accessed 20 March 2020).
42   Ibid.

Sergeant Wallace J. Mackenzie, of the 2nd Battalion South Wales Borderers, recalled being cut loose and the tug turning for home as his glider made for the landing zone:

> There was a certain amount of anti-aircraft fire and some small arms fire from the ground. We came in at full flap, but the light was not good at this point and it was not possible to see exactly where the ground was, so as we pulled back, we were more or less feeling our way to the ground. I knew we were very close and our speed was about right, but then we hit something that could have been a simple undulation in the ground. I went through the nose and was unconscious for some time. Robin Walchi was the lucky one who walked away. But the four men we had met for the first time a few hours earlier all died in the crash. I was picked up and carried to a small barn for the night.[43]

Staff Sergeant T.R. Moore, of the Glider Pilot Regiment, flew from Tunisia in his Waco glider, carrying 12 infantrymen, four handcarts of ammunition and a Bangalore torpedo. Shortly after take-off, the Perspex panel at the front blew out, sending a stream of cold air through the glider, much to the discomfort of all on board. The noise from the blast of air made radio contact with the tugs very difficult. As they reached the Sicilian coast, they were caught in a searchlight beam and the tug pilot dived with Moore's glider in tow. The landing zone drew ever closer and the men prepared to hit the ground, as Moore remembered:

> We cast of at about 2,300 feet, a mile and a half from the coast, the wheels were smashed on landing and the glider came to an abrupt stop as the nose hit a large rock. This penetrated the nose of the machine, broke my ankle and pinned my legs under the cockpit seat. [Co-pilot] Garret was unhurt and he kicked his way through the side of the cockpit. Within a few seconds of landing the fabric top of the fuselage was in flames caused by grenades thrown by the Italians. Flaming patches of fabric fell into the handcarts of ammunition in the centre of the glider and before all the troops could escape there was a series of explosions, caused by the ignition of phosphorous grenades and mortar bombs. Six of the airborne-infantry managed to get out but the remainder perished. Those who did escape took cover among the rocks and shrubs, but the explosions were so violent that one man was killed well over 100 yards away.[44]

While Staff Sergeant Moore was pinned in the glider seat by his legs, his friend Garret was seen to help one man from the blazing wreckage. A piece of shrapnel then struck Garret, tearing away the whole of his left elbow joint, and he fell. Unable to move, Moore was horrified as the seat he was on began to burn. However, Garret struggled back to the stricken glider and, with his uninjured right arm, lifted the nose a little to help Moore escape. Moore continued:

---

43   Ibid.
44   M. Arthur, *Men of the Red Beret* (London: Hutchinson, 1990), p. 86.

I knew this was my last chance, I threw myself forward and wrenched my leg free and as I did so I felt my leg break. Once I was free Garret and I tried without success to pull another man from the wreckage. He was unconscious and already burnt. We scrambled about 30 yards away and took cover in the rocks from the explosions which continued for about two hours, until one particularly violent one scattered the blazing skeleton of the glider far and wide.[45]

Lieutenant Joseph Stephenson Davidson Hardy, with the Signals Platoon of HQ Company, 1st Battalion the Border Regiment, watched with interest the scene below him:

Lieutenant Joseph Stephenson Davidson Hardy, 1st Battalion the Border Regiment. (Author's collection)

As tracer bullets, so elegant in their upward trajectory but so deadly in their impact, greeted our approach, we were cast off too early. We landed in the sea about 200 yards from the shore and in the dark. The weather was stormy and the main fuselage of my glider sank immediately below the water level but was kept close to the surface only by the span of the wings. Somehow, I managed to force open the door and releasing my equipment pulled myself out. The trapped men inside tore the canvas and exited the aircraft. Three of the survivors and I were able to swim to the shore, minus our equipment and our boots, [but] I did however manage to hang onto my revolver. Once ashore we were confronted with a high, virtually perpendicular, cliff, which was impossible for us to climb in the darkness."[46]

Lieutenant Hardy and his men sat in the darkness, cold, wet and shivering, and waited for the dawn. As the darkness faded, they began to make their way up the cliff face, reaching the top. Here they came across an Italian machine-gun post manned by three men, who immediately surrendered to them. The glidermen stole their weapons

45   Ibid., p. 87.
46   *Pegasus Archive* <www.pegasusarchive.org> (accessed 2 April 2020).

and boots, and leaving one man to guard the prisoners, they moved inland but never made it to the *Ponte Grande* in time.

Sergeant Victor Miller passed over Syracuse as lines of red tracer climbed up towards his glider through the darkness. The rush of air past the glider drowned out the noise of bursting flak as he approached their destination. He recalled:

> The next minute we were among the hungry fingers of the flashing tracers and at the same time a purplish coloured searchlight burst forth and pinpointed us squarely in its blinding beam. The interior of the cabin became like daylight and I fought to pick out the lights of the tug in front. Then the light went out and the sudden transition back to darkness was almost too much for my eyes. Red and yellow tracers streaked past the side window of the cockpit.[47]

Private Walter Collings, of the 1st Battalion the Border Regiment, sat in his glider as flak and tracer fire erupted all around him. The pilot tried to take evasive action but was forced lower and lower to nearly sea level until the glider ditched. Collings remembered their crash landing:

> As we hit the water I was forced through the top of the glider and found myself outside on the wing. I reached back inside and caught hold of Pte Arkwright and pulled him out onto the wing, then a couple more [of the men]. During this time others were also emerging. It was not long before the glider started to break up and the only thing keeping the wrecked parts from drifting away was the wire frame attached to them all. During the night search-lights from the shore were searching the sea for gliders. When one was

Private Walter Collings, 1st Battalion the Border Regiment. (Courtesy of M. Denney)

found other lights joined in and then we could hear machine guns open fire at the unfortunate lads in the water. We were lucky to be too far away. I laid on the glider wing and held on as best I could as I had no lifebelt, nor could I swim.[48]

47 V. Miller, *Nothing is Impossible* (Kent: Spellmount, 1994), p. 63.
48 *Pegasus Bridge* <www.pegasusarchive.org> (accessed 2 April 2020).

The next morning, as dawn broke, Private Collings and his comrades saw many landing-craft approaching the shore, carrying the men of 3 Commando. A naval rating shouted to them, "Sorry lads, can't stop." A little later, a gunboat appeared and the under-tow of the propellers began to suck the wrecked glider beneath the waves. Collings fell off and started to sink but managed to grab a piece of wreckage that kept him afloat. The gunboat lowered a small rowing boat into the sea to try to save the stricken glidermen. The men in the water shouted and pointed to one of their number who was in a bad way and needed urgent attention, whereupon one of the naval ratings, without hesitation, dived into the sea fully clothed to assist him. They were all eventually rescued.

In the 1st Air Landing Brigade's War Diary, the following anonymous accounts are recorded:

> Glider number 99: Waco: Glider landed in sea four miles off shore, hitting water hard and filled up immediately. 13 missing believed drowned.
> Glider number 39: Waco: Glider unable to make land and came down in the sea 1 to 2 miles off the coast. 1st Pilot alright, all others believed drowned.
> Glider 93: Waco: Glider just cleared cliff and hit a wall. Crew surrounded by Italians after a few minutes. 2 pilots killed, six wounded.[49]
> Rough flight, glider subjected to AA fire after release, heavy tracer, left wing hit. Flew over landing zone and landed 16 miles south-west of Syracuse. Hit a six-foot wall, left wing burning, also 77 grenades ignited inside glider. Thick smoke inside glider and men trapped by ammunition paniers which began to explode, intense heat and small arms fire made extrication of men difficult, two pilots and 12 other ranks killed, seven wounded.[50]

Royal Navy Captain Lord Ashbourne was stationed off the beaches aboard the *Keren* when he saw a body in the water and made an amazing discovery:

> I saw a body floating in the sea, almost alongside and evidently alive. I told the captain of the *Keren* to pick him up. A few minutes later a dripping soldier arrived on the bridge. He turned out to be Major General G.F. Hopkinson commanding 1st British Airborne Division. We rung out his clothes and gave him a plate of eggs and bacon, and then sent him off ashore to catch up with the rest of his soldiers.[51]

Lieutenant Eric Charles O'Callaghan, of the 9th Field Company, Royal Engineers, attached to the 2nd Battalion South Staffordshire Regiment, approached the Sicilian coast when his towing aircraft caught fire. However, the flames were extinguished

49   C. D'Este, *Bitter Victory, the Battle for Sicily 1943* (Glasgow: William Collins, 1989), p. 232.
50   HMSO, *By Air to Battle* (London: HMSO, 1945), p. 94.
51   S.W.C. Pack, *Operation Husky* (London: David and Charles, 1977), p. 87.

by the pilot once their heavy weapons and stores had been jettisoned. O'Callaghan remembered:

> When we landed the glider struck a wall and broke in half, skidding over the ground until it hit some trees and stopped. Three men were injured, Cpt Weiss and two other ranks. We made the injured as comfortable as possible and left them in the glider.[52]

Lieutenant O'Callaghan realised he was a long way from his drop zone and began to head north-east with the remainder of his men. As they marched, flares dropped by the RAF over Syracuse lit up the area; snipers took advantage of this artificial light and shot at the advancing glider troops. As they crossed a bridge at dawn, fire was also directed onto O'Callaghan and his men from the high ground in front:

> The platoon worked its way around the right flank, whilst myself and another man stalked and killed three snipers who were shooting at us from the rear. We assaulted the high ground taking three prisoners and killing several of the enemy. At this point six other ranks of the Border Regiment joined us and we advanced over the main road. Throughout the day we worked our way to Waterloo [code name for the *Ponte Grande*] fighting various small actions.[53]

O'Callaghan led his small band to an orchard 800 yards from the bridge, but before he could make plans to attack, he was met by a Captain Holmes and a group of sappers, who informed him the bridge had been taken.

Sergeant Victor Miller flew towards his objective through flak, tracer and search-lights. His co-pilot had one hand poised over the release lever as yet another search-light caught the glider in its beam, and he decided it was time to go:

> The tow rope dropped away, [and] there was a loud bang and a rush of air as the field telephone was pulled through the canopy. We had not disconnected it before release. We were riding free and I instinctively eased back on the wheel to lose excessive flying speed and in automatic reaction to climb clear of the search-light beam that was swinging towards us. Now the thump of exploding shells drummed through the sides of the cabin in muffled grunts. Directly ahead a fountain of tracers seemed to float up slowly towards our nose and a split second later were flashing past. BG [Captain Boucher-Giles] called out 'Ok turn in'. I needed no second bidding and wheeled into a sharp turn to port while the frightening tracers slid off to the right.[54]

---

52   *Pegasus Archive* <www.pegasusarchive.org> (accessed 2 April 2020).
53   Ibid.
54   V. Miller, *Nothing is Impossible* (Kent: Spellmount, 1994), p. 63.

Sergeant Miller could just see the outline of the coast as he swung the nose round and straightened out, the flying tracer and searchlights now behind him. The edge of the cliffs came into view, and fires were burning inland. His glider was travelling far too fast and too high, and his co-pilot took the controls as they slipped over cultivated fields. Miller recalled the impact of landing:

> Once more I called out the reading of 100 mph; it was the last thing I remembered for a while, for the next second there came an exploding crash and a brilliant red flash seemed to tear my head apart. A noise like thunder filled my ears and blackness descended as I was hurled into oblivion. I came to with the smell of burnt metal in my nostrils and shocking stabs of pain passing through my head. I pulled my head out of the remains of the dashboard and fought to draw air into my tortured lungs. I could not move and in an agony of pain I pushed against the remains of the nose. A haze of dust filled the cockpit and I heard BG calling out to me. There was a crack of something ripping through the fabric of the wrecked glider, followed instantaneously by the loud report of a rifle. We were being fired on and another shot snapped through the body of the glider. I crawled out the other side where BG was half crouched over one of the gunners sprawled out on the ground groaning in pain. Another man had pulled the injured man under the wings in the shadows, for the moon had now burst forth in all its revealing light. A strong wind was blowing and the torn and tattered fabric was fluttering and slapping on the glider. It lay like some grotesque monster of the pre-historic age, the nose tilted up in the air.[55]

Part of the glider body had been ripped away and pieces of it were scattered in a 50-yard gouge in the earth it had made as it hit the ground. The undercarriage had been completely destroyed and one wing was smashed and hanging off. Sergeant Miller heard another shot hit the earth nearby, and suddenly remembered he had a Sten gun in the glider. Painfully, he crawled into the black interior and, after clambering around in the dark, he found his weapon and ammunition. He crept back to the group huddled under the glider wing and looked up into the slightly cloudy night sky; stars shone brightly in the open areas between the clouds that scudded quickly by in the high wind, while the moon appeared and disappeared at intervals. Miller continued:

> Out towards the coast searchlights and tracers were combing the night sky and gliders were still coming in. I listened to the gentle whine of a glider that seemed to be circling rather fast. Searchlight beams swept the sky and suddenly one caught the glider in its revealing light. A second searchlight darted across the sky, pinning the glider in its beam also. Golden tracers arched swiftly up, at first from one point and then another and yet another, until the wheeling glider was caught in the cross-fire of at least four streams of tracers. I watched

55   Ibid., p. 69.

in fascination as the pilot threw the glider almost up on one wing in a vertical turn while the whistle of the slip-stream rose higher and higher. The dull thud of anti-aircraft guns echoed across the field. Then the glider fell into a steep diving turn and in a second had slipped out of the hungry fingers of the hot steel that played upon its body. I could still follow the flight of the glider by the ugly high-pitched shrill whine that told me the pilot was coming in much too fast. The noise grew louder and something flickered past overhead, momentarily silhouetted against the star-studded sky. With a last rush of sound, the machine disappeared over the far end of the field and for a moment silence reigned, to be followed by the sound of a terrible rending crash. The flak had claimed its victim after all. Before the sound of the crash had fully died away, I was aware of another machine slicing down out of the dark with a softer wail. With my ears I followed the course of the glider coming lower and lower until that too faded out of earshot, [then] again came the sound of a shocking impact followed by an uncanny silence, broken only by the sounds of distant firing from several directions.[56]

Of the 147 gliders that had taken off from Tunisia, no less than 69 crashed into the sea, drowning 252 men. Fifty-nine gliders were scattered over a 25-mile area outside Syracuse, two gliders were shot down by flak and 10 turned back to Tunisia. Only 12 landed on their intended drop zones, one within 300 yards of the *Ponte Grande*. But despite the catastrophic turn of events, the troops that did manage to land on or near their drop zones immediately went into action, cutting telephone lines and ambushing any patrols that came their way.

Sergeant Miller followed Captain Boucher-Giles and his men through orchards and over walls as they headed for the bridge. Just after 2:00 a.m., a steady droning came from the sky and suddenly a Vickers Wellington bomber roared overhead, with other bombers following closely. A vibrating roar filled the air as flares appeared, hanging in the sky in the direction of Syracuse, while flak fire opened up from the town and port as searchlights were turned on. The British bombers continued towards their target, and amid the throb of powerful engines the first whistle of falling bombs could be heard. After a short pause, the earth shook and vibrated with the concussion of high explosive, a red glare lighting up the night as the airborne troops looked on. The explosions ceased, the sound of aircraft engines faded away, tracer fire stopped and the searchlights were turned off. Quiet once more settled on the Sicilian countryside. Sergeant Miller recalled: "We waited until the last flare had flickered out and then emerged from our shelter and set off again, hugging the wall and hedge. The field was slightly illuminated by some fires that burned away in the direction of Syracuse, which helped us to pick our way along." The group Sergeant Miller was with came across a column of Tommies and joined them in their quest to reach the bridge. Daylight was approaching, and as Spitfires roared low overhead the men continued along a road that suddenly turned in a sharp bend. Machine-gun

56   V. Miller, *Nothing is Impossible* (Kent: Spellmount, 1994), p. 67.

fire suddenly ripped down the centre of the road, causing the men to jump into the ditches on either side, but the group by-passed a German post and continued on their way. More stragglers joined them, and ahead the sounds of firing were becoming clearer. Miller found himself looking over a valley where, about a mile away, the outline of the *Ponte Grande* came into view. Several men wearing the distinctive red beret could be seen on the bridge; some airborne troops had obviously managed to reach the target and take it.

Bert Holt, DFC, of the Glider Pilot Regiment, carrying men of the 1st Battalion Border Regiment, was one of the few glider pilots to land exactly where he was supposed to, close to the bridge:

> After much confusion we made our way to the bridge. I got there by crawling through a big tomato field. When we finally arrived, we took up our positions on the bridge with the Borderers and other glider pilots.[57]

Lieutenant Louis Withers sat in his 30-seater Horsa glider, number 133, with his 26-man platoon of C Company, the 2nd Battalion South Staffordshire Regiment as they were cut loose from their tow plane. The glider pilot, Lieutenant Dennis Patten Galpin,[58] tried desperately to get his bearings in the dark, without any success. But his luck was to change when an Italian searchlight suddenly lit up the scene around *Ponte Grande*, illuminating the landing zone and the bridge itself. After he had landed, Withers soon realised that the other gliders of his company were not going to arrive and that the task of taking the bridge was now left to his platoon.

Lieutenant Withers' original task had been to neutralise one of the pillboxes protecting the bridge, but he wasted no time in understanding what he must do

Lieutenant Dennis Patten Galpin, DFM, Glider Pilot Regiment. (Courtesy of P. Kendrick)

Lieutenant Lewis Withers, MC, 2nd Battalion South Staffordshire Regiment. (Courtesy of G. Kendrick)

---

57   *Para Data* <(accessed 20 March 2020).
58   Lieutenant Dennis Patten Galpin of the Glider Pilot Regiment was awarded the Distinguished Flying Medal for his bravery.

now. The glider troops listened intently to their commander as he issued orders for the attack in hushed tones. The company plan for this attack had been thoroughly practised and Withers was very familiar with it. Withers and five of his men swam the cold canal and the Apana River that both ran under the bridge. Soaked through and shivering, Withers and his small group edged towards a menacing looking pillbox, and it was not long before they were spotted. The harsh crackle of small-arms fire from automatic weapons and the explosions of hand grenades echoed around the rocky countryside as they attacked the pillbox guarding the northern end of the bridge. Meanwhile, the remainder of the platoon attacked from the south, and after a short, sharp fight, the bridge was taken intact.[59] The Italians' demolition charges were removed and thrown into the river. This important primary target was now in the possession of a tiny section of the 1st Air Landing Brigade. During the remaining hours of darkness, other British troops and glider pilots (one American) slowly made their way to the bridge, guided by the noise of battle and the flashes of explosions. The Italian defenders melted into the night, leaving behind two dead comrades.

Withers' 28-strong force of glider troops had achieved what 1,200 had set out to do, but they knew this had only been the opening shots of the engagement and that the enemy would soon be back in strength. During the night, a nervous vigil was kept as the men strained their eyes peering into the darkness for signs of movement, but none came as the grey light of dawn began to break. The Italians now knew of the presence of the British airborne troops, and the commander of the Italian XVI Corps, General Enrico Rossi, promptly ordered the movement of four combat groups to the area. Any one of these groups had the firepower to take out the small band holding the *Ponte Grande*, but fortunately for the bridge's defenders, Rossi's orders were never received: the British airborne troops that had been scattered around the island had been busy cutting telephone wires and creating confusion among the Axis forces. Italian Army communications had been disrupted to the point that General Rossi was unable to organise a major assault on the *Ponte Grande*. Despite Rossi's failure to move strong forces to the bridge to take back control of the crossing, local Italian commanders began to act on their own initiative. Several armoured cars and numerous infantry were sent against the outnumbered and lightly armed glidermen. The Italian troops began working their way to the bridge, firing wildly as they progressed.

Sergeant Victor Miller and his comrades eventually reached the bridge after a hazardous journey over rough terrain, approaching a Lieutenant Withers who was holding the position:

> Our party was warmly welcomed by the officer in charge, [but] he had very few men and was extremely worried. Our arrival helped a lot but it was not enough.[60]

---

59 Lieutenant Louis Withers was awarded the Military Cross for this action. He died in 2015 at the age of 93, and his obituary appeared in the *Telegraph* on 18 January of that year.

60 V. Miller, *Nothing is Impossible* (Kent: Spellmount, 1994), p. 78.

The cry went up, "This looks like it." The bridge's defenders could see lorries full of Italian troops leaving Syracuse, and soon enough the Italian infantry began to deploy. The first volley of bullets arrived, thudding into the earth and ricocheting off the structure of the bridge and the trees around it. The British replied with rifle and Bren-gun fire. A lorry approached the bridge, with two Italian soldiers sitting in the cab alongside the driver, an elderly civilian. The British held their fire as the lorry came closer, its occupants seemingly unaware of the events unfolding before them. Just before the bridge, the lorry stopped. Sergeant Miller recalled:

> There came a shattering roar from the bridge end and the windscreen dissolved into a thousand fragments. The engine roared for a moment then died and the lorry jerked to a halt. Again, spiteful cracks and the crash of rifle fire, screams rent the air from the lorry and I saw one man topple over. The old man's arms thrust skyward, as cries of fear poured from his lips. Another short burst and his old battered civilian hat flew off at a tangent while he fell forward inside the truck. The firing stopped and for a moment I felt sickened by this wanton killing of what seemed to be an old harmless civilian, who had probably hitch-hiked a lift.[61]

Private Rodney Albert Hall, MM, of the Support Company, 2nd Battalion South Staffordshire Regiment, remembered the accurate shelling they had to endure as he and his comrades sheltered in a shallow ditch that ran parallel with the road:

> On the bridge there appeared to be a small delivery lorry with an old Italian, long dead, sprawled over the front. A bend in the ditch brought us directly in line of fire with a block-house. Lt Reynolds decided that our force of five was not sufficient to mount an attack and he sent two men back to the safety of the canal bank. The shelling had become very accurate but unfortunately the missiles would arrive and explode before we knew it was coming. Pte Blakemore, Lt Reynolds' batman, and another man were the last to

Private Rodney Albert Hall, MM, Support Company, 2nd Battalion South Staffordshire Regiment. (Courtesy of H. Miller)

61   Ibid., p. 80.

leave and had to run 50 yards down the ditch, [but] as they did so the second shell arrived killing them both.[62] We were now under intense small arms fire as well as shellfire. I then jumped the canal and took up a position facing the enemy who were by this time engaging us with heavy gunfire.[63]

The attacking Italian troops sprayed the bridge with automatic gunfire, the vastly outnumbered defenders crouching low to avoid the bullets that bounced and ricocheted off the rocks that littered the area. Italian mortar teams were brought up, and it was not long before their bombs were exploding on and around the bridge. The mortar barrage was accurate and deadly, and at the same time machine-gunners and riflemen kept up a steady stream of fire on the British troops, whose numbers were dwindling fast. Sergeant Miller never forgot the effects of the accurate mortar fire on his position:

A new sound arrived like a clap of thunder that twisted my nerves, it was the noise of the first mortar bomb I had ever heard being fired in my direction. The bomb screamed over the bridge and burst 200 yards away, [and] the sharp rending explosion and the stab of crimson-tinged flame through the swirling grey smoke caused me to cringe well down on the unyielding earth. The next mortar bomb was on target; it came with a shattering suddenness, there was a short sharp scream and the next second a shocking steel tearing explosion filled the air. Earth and grey smoke spewed skyward and moments later the spine-chilling whirr of falling red hot shrapnel filled the air. I flattened myself out along the ground as the searing metal smacked into the earth and cracked against a tree. A number of cries and groans fell upon my ears. Again, the harsh rending scream through the air and again the ground shook with the impact of the bombs. I buried my head a second before the impact while my body twisted up tautly in horrible anticipation. Immediately after the explosion I looked up and saw a similar pall of smoke rising from the trees on the far bank. I thought 'Oh God, how much longer before they raise the range to our side?'[64]

Mortar bombs continued to fall around the bridge with monotonous regularity, and the defenders could only crouch down and take their punishment. Occasionally, the Italian spotters would see groups of men running to other positions and would redirect the mortar fire onto them. Machine-gun fire also swept the area and casualties began to mount, but the British managed to hold the bridge. When the Italian infantry closed in, the defenders could at last see a target to fire at. Two Italian fighter aircraft roared over the bridge without firing a shot as they returned to Syracuse. The enemy fire increased as that of the defenders decreased through lack of ammunition.

---

62   Private Norman Blakemore, 2nd Battalion South Staffordshire Regiment, was killed in action at the *Ponte Grande* on 9 July 1943, aged 29. He is buried in Syracuse War Cemetery.

63   *Pegasus Archive* <www.pegasusarchive.org> (accessed 2 April 2020).

64   V. Miller, *Nothing is Impossible* (Kent: Spellmount, 1994), p. 81.

At this point, the Italians brought forward a field gun that began firing over open sights at the British troops. Through sheer weight of numbers and superior firepower, the men on the north bank were overrun by the middle of the afternoon, having run out of ammunition and grenades. Several men tried to escape by swimming for it, but some were killed in the water by automatic weapons fire. Sergeant Miller met one survivor as he emerged from the river:

> The enemy fire seemed to be increasing and the whine of bullets became almost continuous. My attention was suddenly dragged away by the sound of splashing in the river. Swiftly I turned and crawled up the bank while I trained my Sten in the direction of the noise. Sgt Cawood did likewise. A dripping figure carrying a rifle appeared over the crest and I instantly recognised him as one of our men. Another man with water running down his clothes followed closely on his heels. Together they slipped over the brink while bullets snapped past. They dropped down alongside and I noticed that the first man was a sergeant from one of the regiments we had carried in. He seemed agitated and was panting from his exertions. He struggled for breath and said that he had been ordered over this side as the front could not be held much longer. He stated that the rest of the men were following him over at intervals. We were to move under the bridge and then back up alongside the road until we reached the crest of the hill where we would take up new positions.[65]

The Italians then turned their attention to the 13 defenders holding out in a ditch on the south bank of the canal, firing machine guns at point-blank range into the British position. The defenders fought so long as they had ammunition, but this did not last long; they tossed their empty weapons into the canal and, with arms raised, emerged from the ditch to surrender.

Pte Rodney Hall recalled the end of their heroic defence:

> In this dire situation, surrounded by dead and wounded men, an officer came along and said that the position was untenable and wished everyone good luck. He suggested that we should surrender. The remaining 10 or so men that were left alive stood up and surrendered to the enemy.[66]

For nearly 12 hours, a mere handful of British troops and four glider pilots had held the bridge against overwhelming odds,but had eventually been overrun. Over a third of their number had been killed and another third wounded and captured. At 3:15 p.m., the bridge was once again in Italian hands. Pilot Bert Holt remembered the moment of defeat well:

---

65   V. Miller, *Nothing is Impossible* (Kent: Spellmount, 1994), p. 84.
66   *Pegasus Archive* <www.pegasusarchive.org> (accessed 2 April 2020).

> When it was all over the Italians lined us up and asked us questions in Italian
> which we didn't understand, so they went through our pockets and our gear,
> taking anything useful to them.[67]

Other glider troops who had not reached the bridge made their way to friendly lines
as best they could. The night had been icy cold, but when the sun rose the next day,
hope once again took hold. When the sea mist cleared, the vast Allied armada off the
coast was clearly visible as it nosed towards Avola 5 miles to the south.

Sergeant Miller and his comrades had retreated to positions on the hillside overlooking the bridge:

> I lay at the bottom of the trench, my eyes closed, seeking a place where I could
> rest my aching body. I felt despondent, everything seemed to have gone wrong,
> and where would it end? I lay there in a half daze of exhaustion. I must have
> dozed off when suddenly I was roused by the sound of bullets thudding and
> cracking into the parapet of the trench. My body felt like lead. Dimly I saw
> the sergeant who had led us up here pull himself up sharply and peer over the
> edge of the trench. The next second his head jerked back and he spun round to
> topple down in the trench, his lifeless body half doubled up and jammed down
> in between the trench sides. With a body that did not seem to belong to me I
> pushed myself off the ledge I had been leaning on and slowly straightened up. As
> I did so the whole trench seemed to erupt in smoke and flame while a stunning
> concussion smashed through it. I felt a blow like a hammer hit my left thigh
> but felt no pain. My ears rang with the explosions while my eyes were blurred.[68]

Miller, straining to see through the murk, could not move and watched silently as
the men still standing climbed out of the trench above him and disappeared. He lay
with the dead sergeant as rifle fire cracked around him. Voices could be heard as he
stood and pulled himself over the parapet. Bullets swept around him as he staggered
away, one leg giving way as he lapsed temporarily into unconsciousness. Waking, he
found it agony to breathe but desperation drove him on. He came across a wounded
man and dressed his wound, a towel acting as a makeshift dressing. A shot from an
enemy soldier tore away half the moustache from his lip as the bullet flew past. With
the enemy seeming to be taking no prisoners, Miller fell back in panic. He recalled:
"I felt no pain, only the deep agony of despair, [and] my thoughts welled up inside
me as this seemed to me to be the end. In those seconds I died a thousand deaths."
Machine-gun fire flew around him, and nearby ancient stone columns sent chips of
stone flying in all directions. Running as only a man in fear of his life could run, an
Italian grenade rolled under him and exploded. "The explosion seemed to burst my
head apart and I hit the ground in an oblivion of grey black smoke. I could feel a

67   Ibid. (accessed 19 March 2020).
68   V. Miller, *Nothing is Impossible* (Kent: Spellmount, 1994), p. 87.

terrible pain tearing at my face and couldn't feel my mouth. I felt certain it had been blown clean off."

Miller lay numb on the ground, tensing himself up for the anticipated final bayonet thrust that would end his suffering. Angry Italian soldiers gathered around him, their bayonets pointing close to his face, but they spared his life. Sitting up as he regained his senses, he saw unfriendly faces all around him but was elated to still be alive. Getting to his feet, he staggered forward, encouraged to do so by the prodding bayonets. On the far side of the field he was being marched over, he saw a number of freshly dug holes and assumed he was being taken there to be shot. But as he got closer, he saw they were trenches with men occupying them. After a long journey, Miller ended up in a hospital at Syracuse.

Meanwhile, glider pilot Staff Sergeant Moore was struggling to get his wounded comrade, Garret, to the coast. He held out little hope of being found by friendly forces:

> During the night Garret had lost a lot of blood and he suffered from the intense cold. I used a puttee as a tourniquet to control the bleeding but by morning his forearm was completely black. In the morning we heard a cry and saw someone propelling himself towards us on his back by the use of his elbows. We recognised him as the corporal from our glider, he had been struck between the knees by an exploding grenade. I ripped the legs off his trousers and tried to dress his wounds but it was hopeless. The hole in each knee was larger than the field dressing. I dragged myself to the wreck of our Waco and came across a dead Italian. I took his carbine and bayonet and found they served well as a crutch. Eventually I heard voices so I hid, then I heard the sound of approaching footsteps and someone stood before me silhouetted against the evening sky. For a few anxious moments there was silence and then I realised that the visitor was wearing a British steel helmet.[69]

The British prisoners taken at the *Ponte Grande* were force-marched under armed guard in the direction of Syracuse, but they would not remain prisoners for long as the group was ambushed by an airborne officer and a gliderman who opened fire on the Italians. Those not killed in the initial burst surrendered, and the British troops were free once again.

Rodney Hall and the other defenders taken prisoner at the *Ponte Grande* were marched to a small hut adjacent to the bridge, where they were searched. Anything the Italians took a shine to – whether watches or kit – they took. They were then marched towards Syracuse, as Hall recalled:

> Our Italian captors were decidedly jumpy and after two or three miles over rough terrain we began to walk along a tarmac road. We came to a clearing at the side of the road close to a maize field and while sitting, standing and

---

69   M. Arthur, *Men of the Red Beret* (London: Hutchinson, 1990), pp. 87–88.

sprawling in this very small lay-by there was a sudden burst of firing from the road some 10 feet above us. A section of the British army came into view. One or two of our Italian captors attempted to engage the British soldiers and were immediately shot for their trouble. We persuaded the remaining Italians to hand over their weapons which they did and the captors became the captives as we were handed over to the British troops.[70]

Later in the afternoon, advanced elements of the British 17th Brigade, 5th Division, had reached the bridge and launched an attack on the Italian forces now holding the position. The armoured troop carriers of the 2nd Battalion Royal Scots Fusiliers were soon in possession of the vital and mercifully undamaged *Ponte Grande*, and as night closed in, the primary target of Operation *Ladbroke* was back in British hands. Infantry and tanks of the 5th Division could now stream across the *Ponte Grande* thanks to the airborne troops having removed the demolition charges. But they had paid a fearful price in lives: only 19 glidermen and two pilots survived the encounter unscathed.

The badly wounded Sergeant Victor Miller, now in a hospital ward where several nuns tended to the men, remembered the noise of distant gunfire as the Eighth Army drew closer:

> We lay back and listened to the sound of the guns, light and heavy, rumbling and barking in the distance. Perhaps it was the Eighth Army advancing on Syracuse at last. We hoped so, although we were afraid that we might be evacuated if they came too close. Towards evening there came the roar of low flying aircraft, [as] they thundered down over the roof of the hospital. Machine-gun fire and light AA fire broke forth and we cringed down in our beds. A window was blown in as the planes zoomed down. The thundering concussion of bombs falling about half a mile away rocked the building and another machine skimmed low over the roof. I never heard the bomb come, there was a mushroom of dirty grey black smoke rising up outside the window. The thunder of the explosion was deafening and a wave of concussion beat across the room. I heard glass crashing to the floor.[71]

Later in the afternoon, a German officer, accompanied by Italian medics, came to the ward to inspect the patients. Anyone able to walk would be evacuated as prisoners of war. Miller, removing his bandages to expose his leg wound, lay back feigning semi-consciousness. His luck held and he was left behind to be rescued by the advancing Allied forces.[72]

---

70 *Pegasus Archive* <www.pegasusarchive.org> (accessed 6 April 2020).
71 V. Miller, *Nothing is Impossible* (Kent: Spellmount, 1994), p. 102.
72 Sergeant Victor Miller was sent home to recover from his wounds. He later re-joined his regiment to take part in the Battle of Arnhem and the assault crossing of the Rhine, then on into Germany.

The stand by the British airborne troops at the *Ponte Grande* and its later recapture caused panic among the Axis forces in the region. German anti-aircraft batteries in Syracuse and Augusta pulled out to the north, followed by Italian flak batteries. As more British troops crossed the bridge, Italian commanders gave the order that defensive positions in Syracuse should be demolished, and the major city was abandoned to the Allies.

2

The Main Landings
XIII Corps, 10 July

On the morning of 10 July, the Italian and German troops defending Sicily's coast looked out to sea, and before them was a vast array of Allied ships that filled the view to the horizon. The ships were crammed with fighting men ready to launch the invasion, each of whom carried their own hopes and fears.

Among them was Lieutenant Peter Lewis of the 8th Battalion Durham Light Infantry, who had found that the time past quite quickly on his Dutch ship the *Ruys* on the morning of 9 July. The daily positions of the other convoys that were approaching Sicily from North Africa, Malta and the United Kingdom were being marked on a map in the board room. His convoy had come from Port Said in Egypt, carrying the 5th and 50th Divisions, and did not appear to him to be particularly large:

> This was to change soon after mid-day on the 9th, our last day at sea, [when] the other convoys rendezvoused with us from Port Said and it was an amazing sight. As far as the eye could see there were hundreds of ships of all shapes and sizes ahead of, astern of and on either side of the *Ruys*. The naval liaison officer pointed out to me a trio of American built LCIs [landing craft infantry] on the starboard beam pitching and rolling like small rowing boats. 'They're yours for the show,' he said. 'They've only crossed the Atlantic a few weeks ago.' I was at a loss for words, they looked as if they were going to sink at any minute. I made a mental note to see that all my men took their anti-seasick medicine before we boarded such an unstable looking craft that night. Beyond the LCI the Tank Landing Craft, in company with MT ships and flak ships [anti-aircraft ships] ploughed their way through the sea that had suddenly become angry. Almost on the horizon were the cruisers and battleships that formed the heavy escort, while closer in destroyers fussed about in and out the convoy. As I looked on a Greek destroyer surged past, her crew waving to our chaps on the upper deck. To look at this vast array of shipping it hardly seemed possible that there was room for it all to lie off the coast of Sicily.[1]

---

1   P. Lewis, *The Price of Freedom* (Durham: Pentland Books, 2001), p. 5.

Meanwhile, just off Malta, Captain Peter Young of 3 Commando watched with interest as the convoy of ships carrying the assault troops to Sicily crept slowly by:

> Some of the tank landing craft were having a rough time in the heavy swell which had now begun to trouble us. By the afternoon the sea had risen so much that we wondered if the operation would have to be postponed. Lowering landing craft from heavily rolling ships would be a hazardous business. As night fell the wind began to drop and we could see nothing ahead in the darkness but the red glow from the top of Mount Etna, impressive but forbidding.[2]

Able Seaman Leonard S. Thacker, serving with the Royal Navy, sat and watched events unfold with an avid interest:

> The night before the landing I was strangely thrilled. We crept forward in the inky blackness and could see the flashes as our bombers went in, [and] the enemy flak was going up in a vain attempt to stop them. The heavy detonations of the bombs [inland] were so powerful that they could be felt as well as heard.[3]

Lance Corporal Denis March, who was with the 6th Battalion Seaforth Highlanders, recalled all the last-minute instructions given to the men on 9 July regarding their kit and what they would have to carry with them as they went ashore:

> Tomorrow was the big day and we had received instructions about our kit. We had to take with us our assault respirators, our rifles, spare boots and socks with flashes, one blanket, one housewife [mending kit], gaiters, one towel, a mosquito veil, shaving kit, mosquito cream, spare laces, cardigan, balmoral, water puri-fying tablets, pouches full of ammunition and steel helmet. The weather was sweltering.[4]

Lieutenant David Cole of the 2nd Battalion Royal Inniskilling Fusiliers took his platoon to the ship's lounge to view the maps that were laid out across the tables:

> The lounges of the ship were filled with maps, models, timetables and air photo-graphs, all intended to concentrate our minds on that tiny portion of history in whose manufacture we were to assist. I had led my platoon round this feast of operational intelligence to the accompaniment of shrewd questions like 'Where are the Germans?' and 'When can we have a smoke?' We all enjoyed ourselves hugely. On 9th July the sun slipped beneath the horizon in a last blaze of crimson. The wind had risen sharply and white spray was dancing on the darkening waves. The sea had become unfriendly and the ship was lurching

2   P. Young, *Storm from the Sea* (Northamptonshire: Wren's Park Publishing, 2002), p. 80.
3   Correspondence with author, L.S. Thacker, 1991.
4   Correspondence with author, D. March, 1989.

uncomfortably. The stream of instructions which had been flowing all day from the ship's loudspeakers had ceased for a moment and the operator was once more able to play his favourite and it seemed only record. Here it came again: The Boogie Woogie Bugle Boy of Company B, echoing up and down the passage ways and resounding across the decks. Soon the curtain of night had been drawn and the rest of the convoy had disappeared in the blackness. The sea was shuddering and pitching angrily and, with the rolling of the ship, the spray that swept the decks had lost their charm. I went inside where instantly the throbbing of the ship's engines commanded my attention. 'We're almost there, we're almost there,' they said.[5]

Lieutenant Colonel William I. Watson, who commanded the 6th Battalion Durham Light Infantry, stood alone on deck on the evening of 9 July, prepared himself mentally for the trials to come:

At 8pm, against a stormy looking sunset, with the gale still blowing but with not quite the same force, we got our first distant views of Sicily. Very low on the horizon we could just see the outline of Mount Etna towering above it all, Europe. Then darkness fell and everyone was very quiet. Got up shortly before 11pm, ship proceeded slowly. Went out on deck, the wind still blowing in the rigging, and an unpleasant looking sea stirred around us. All very dark except for flak from the shore against the bombers and gliders of the airborne division. They passed over about 10pm. Nobody on deck, [and] certainly the black oily waters looked far from comforting. The moon had gone down, perhaps the sea would be a little calmer when we got a little nearer to land but it was not too good now. Some of the thoughts that passed through my mind, I can remember, were whether we would get to the right place and

Lieutenant Colonel William Innes Watson, CO 6th Battalion Durham Light Infantry. (Courtesy of William Ridley)

5   D. Cole, *Rough Road to Rome* (London: William Kimber, 1983), pp. 14-16.

what our reception would be. Would it be a terribly wet landing and would we survive the storm.[6]

Trooper Walter Sandifer, serving with A Squadron of the Royals, remembered that the night before the landing, the sea was rough as he stood guard, his ship pitching and tossing about in the storm:

Some of the [armoured] cars broke loose from their chains and as the ship moved from side to side the cars ran backwards and forwards, what a night. Then we heard the drone of planes and a fleet of transports and gliders came low overhead, one was so low it touched a balloon and took it with it. Then away to our left we saw flares and the flashes of gunfire and soon the whole sky was lit up with fire. Flares hung like great chandeliers and tracer bullets darted across the sky until it looked like a Crystal Palace firework display. This was about 3am and we must have been about 10 miles out. Come the dawn and what a sight met our eyes, [as] lying about a mile offshore were hundreds of ships of all sizes. Destroyers and battle-ships were pounding away at the enemy defences to the north."[7]

Lieutenant David Fenner of the 6th Battalion Durham Light Infantry recalled the preparations as they left the relative safety of their transport ship and climbed aboard the landing craft:

We had our final meal on board on the evening of the 9th, one wag called it 'The Last Supper' and the Padre gave communion. At midnight the assault troops paraded on the mess decks and we were called forward by LCA [landing craft assault] loads to our boat stations. I had my platoon, 25 of us plus 3 sappers from 505 Field Coy, RE; the sappers carried packs containing two anti-tank mines in sandbags, equipped with pull igniters and a short fuse. This equipment was for blowing gaps in barbed wire defences. We were to be very grateful for someone's foresight.

Lieutenant David Fenner, 6th Battalion Durham Light Infantry.
(Courtesy of William Ridley)

6   H. Moses, *The Faithful Sixth* (Durham: County Durham Books, 1995), p. 241.
7   Correspondence with author from W. Sandifer, 1990.

The move to our boat stations was smooth and quiet, the fruits of much training. We reached our LCA and the heavily laden soldiers climbed aboard. The ship's engine stopped and the assault craft were lowered into the heaving sea. The craft were released and we pitched off into the black night.[8]

Lieutenant Peter Lewis, who was with the 8th Battalion Durham Light Infantry, moved with his men to the boat deck along a prearranged route led by the company commander, Captain P.J. Lucas. Twenty-three men climbed into each of the landing craft that were hanging on the davits before being lowered into the sea:

Being swiftly lowered she hit the water with a splash and immediately the boat became remarkably unsteady. By this time the wind had blown up very rough, [and] the watchers on the troop ship could see that the small boats were making heavy weather of it and were being buffeted unmercifully by the rough seas. To make things worse it was a pitch-black night and the men were heavily laden with kit. Each man went down the side of the *Ruys* by an iron ladder, waited on the last rung until the LCI lifted on the crest of a wave and then jumped. It was a miracle that no one was lost in the surging waters between the LCI and the troopship. The two company commanders, company NCOs and crew members of the American LCI caught the men as they jumped and helped break their fall as they landed on the iron deck. Eventually we were ready to go and we glided away from the ship that had been our home since we left Port Said.[9]

The 50th Northumbrian Division lands at Avola

Off Avola, Able Seaman Ernest Mansell, Royal Navy, manned an LCT carrying tanks and troops of the Durham Light Infantry, which formed part of the 50th Northumbrian Division:

As we approached the shore the guns opened up on us and one craft [LCA] was hit by two shells. I don't think there were any survivors. By this time, we were at the beach and were unloading our cargo, [when] five shells dropped pretty close but we were lucky. We then went alongside a troop ship and loaded up with troops [Durham Light Infantry] and back we went to the beach. This time there was no resistance as the lads had pushed in off the beach. We had not finished yet as three German fighters machine-gunned the beach. I saw at least ten ships sunk and consider myself lucky to have survived.[10]

8   H. Moses, *The Faithful Sixth* (Durham: County Durham Books, 1995), p. 242.
9   P. Lewis, *The Price of Freedom* (Durham: Pentland Books, 2001), p. 8.
10   Letter to the author from E. Mansell, 1991.

Men of the 50th Northumbrian Division come ashore at Avola, 10 July 1943.
(Author's collection)

As the numerous landing craft loaded with men and equipment made their way to the coast, many of them became scattered by the rough sea and lost touch with their neighbours. On the 50th Division's front, A and B Company of the 6th Battalion Durham Light Infantry should have landed at 2:45 a.m., C Company at 3:00 a.m. and D Company at 3:15 a.m. In the event, the first Durhams ashore were the men of B Company, who landed less one platoon some 90 minutes late and some 3,000 yards from their planned landing position. The remaining companies landed at 4:30 a.m. some 4,500 yards south of their intended positions.

Captain Reginald Atkinson, serving with the 6th Battalion Durham Light Infantry, thought the rough sea so bad he wondered if they would ever reach land:

> I happened to be allocated a position near the front of the craft. I had more or less accepted the fact that I was bound to get my feet wet in the landing but I hadn't bargained for the soaking I got every time the bows of the craft rose then went through the top of the waves. We appeared to be meeting the waves head-on and the result, in addition to getting extremely wet, was that we were subjected to a continual and very pronounced see-saw action. The bows would rise up, hover a second in mid-air and then plunge down into the trough between the waves, making a loud thud as the flat bottom hit the water. I seriously began to wonder if we would ever reach land. Conditions like these made it impossible for the

coxswains to maintain position and soon there was a lot of shouting between the crafts as they tried to check up on their positions. Teddy Worral was standing up in the bows looking extremely well, but as I glanced round the boat, I saw many doleful faces. I had never been sea-sick in my life before, but this eternal motion of up and down, up and down, was beginning to do peculiar things to my tummy. I grabbed my pint mug and was violently sick into it.[11]

The 9th Battalion Durham Light Infantry was a little more fortunate, but not much. Two companies landed within 500 yards of their allotted beach, but the remainder came ashore in scattered parties 4,000 yards too far south. Despite these setbacks, the main beach was cleared of the enemy relatively easily, though shell fire continued for quite some time. Once ashore, the troops quickly reorganised themselves and, as it was now daylight, a number of clearly discernible landmarks enabled companies to redeploy, mopping up any enemy resistance as they went. At dawn, the 8th Battalion Durham Light Infantry landed some 3,000 yards north of their allocated beach, coming under heavy shell fire and being attacked by enemy aircraft.

Lieutenant John Erskine of 3 Commando had just returned with news of his mission inland to destroy an enemy gun battery (see Chapter 1) when Axis aircraft attacked the ships that were unloading stores and equipment for the beaches:

As we climbed aboard our mother ship fighter bombers were attacking the merchant ships being unloaded for the transfer of stores by lighters to the beach. One of the enemy aircraft dropped a line of three small bombs, the last of which just clipped the bow of a large merchantman being unloaded by a working party and [which] was full of four-gallon tins of petrol. These particular tins were of a brand notorious in the army for being too thin walled and constantly leaking [these tins were nick-named flimsies]. In this case I saw a small flame flicker for a moment up on the bow and then the whole petrol filled ship erupted in a fire ball killing everyone on it. Even though we were several hundred metres away on the *Prince Albert* I was slightly scorched.[12]

One man who could clearly recall the difficult passage to the beach was Private Ralph Hymer, who was with C Company, 8th Battalion Durham Light Infantry,:

The sea was very rough and the landing craft was blown all over the bloody place, so when we landed on the beach we weren't in our own battalions. We joined anything [any unit] to go forward and the Germans were there waiting for us. We had a struggle on the beaches, there was that many craft so close together, the German aircraft couldn't miss them. There was a lot of casualties lying about and lots of shells dropping around us.[13]

11   Interview with the author, R Atkinson, Durham, 1992.
12   *Commando Veterans* <www.commandoveterans.org> (accessed 20 December 2018).
13   Correspondence with author, Ralph Hymer, 1992.

Lieutenant Peter Lewis, with the 8th Battalion Durham Light Infantry, followed the two assault battalions and looked on as Spitfires roared overhead and warships blasted away at the coastal batteries:

> It seemed the assault waves had been successful, [as] crews of landing craft returning from the beaches gave the thumbs up signal as they swept past on their way back to pick up more passengers. It all looked deceptively peaceful in the morning sunlight. The illusion was soon shattered when three Messerschmitts swooped low over the beaches, raking them with deadly machine-gun fire.[14]

Lieutenant Lewis' landing craft was blown from its original course by the strong winds, ending up on the 5th Division's front near Cassabile. He remembered warships out to sea blasting away, but shells were still dropping all around them as the enemy guns had not been silenced:

> There was a roar and a sheet of flame as another landing craft received a direct hit on the stern just as she was about to beach. She turned lazily round broadside on, a thin wisp of smoke curling out of the aft troop hatch. It could so easily have been our LCI. Tragically there was nothing we could do.[15]

When Sapper William Astle of the Royal Engineers landed with the 50th Division, he and his comrades were tasked with dealing with any minefields encountered by the infantry:

> We landed at a place called Avola with the infantry and our first job was to sort the mines out. I stepped off the landing craft into the water and there must have been a [shell] hole, [as] this poor little blighter who went in with me went down into the hole and disappeared. I had to grab him and pull him out. We carried our steel helmet, pack and rifle and the whole shoot. We used our bayonets to prod for mines and didn't always use a detector, in fact around Mount Etna you can forget detectors because of the lode stone that was in the ground from the volcano. They were magnetic and rendered a mine detector useless.[16]

Private John Harold Clark of the 8th Battalion Durham Light Infantry was in a neighbouring landing-craft, and remembered the run in being a tricky one:

> We were tossed about quite a bit in the swell and as we were approaching the beach, we picked up quite a few parachutists who had missed the land and dropped into the sea. There was a good bit of opposition and our landing-craft stuck fast on a sand bank. The officer in charge told people to get off and

14   P. Lewis, *The Price of Freedom* (Durham: Pentland Books, 2001), p. 10.
15   Ibid..
16   Letter to the author from W. Astle, 1988.

about half a dozen stepped off into 20 feet of water and were drowned. The landing-craft alongside us got a direct hit and was set on fire. There were quite a few casualties that day."[17]

Trooper Walter Sandifer, serving with A Squadron of the Royals, approached the beach in a heavily laden Landing-Craft Tank which became stuck on a sandbank because of its heavy load. They had to begin unloading their vehicles in the shallow waters:

Private John Harold Clark, 8th Battalion Durham Light Infantry.
(Courtesy of J.H. Clark)

When you realise we had on board 30 tanks, 10 armoured cars and scores of other vehicles, you will understand that it was going to take some time to empty the ship. Jerry aircraft soon put in an appearance and about 10 enemy aircraft came strafing, and what a barrage of fire met them. The ships threw up everything they had at them. One bomb hit the stern of a ship on our left and it was soon a mass of flames. Beside ammunition she carried petrol, and as black smoke was pouring from her, we pulled away from her just as the flames were reaching the ammunition. She soon sank, leaving a great patch of burning oil on the water. After nightfall, Jerry visited again and the noise of the guns and bombs was past description. A big four-funnelled hospital ship was lying about three miles out and was deliberately attacked. She had all her lights on and the Red Crosses were illuminated. She sank quickly with very few survivors. I hoped I would never have another day and night like that.[18]

A New Zealand reporter, Lieutenant R.J. Gilmour, described the scene on the beach as he watched men and equipment from the 50th Division spilling into the beachhead:

Once ashore in an LCA we passed three different types of amphibious vehicles driving ashore under their own steam. Beach as busy as a country fair. From dozens of landing craft with their fronts let down, trucks, carriers, quads, and jeeps previously waterproofed, bounce into four and five feet of water. With sea water gushing from the driving cabs and tool boxes they roar up on to the beach in first gear. Wire mesh track leads across the soft sand and up a wadi

17 Correspondence with author, John H. Clark, 1991.
18 Correspondence with author, W. Sandifer, 1990.

to a de-waterproofing park where REME [Royal Electrical and Mechanical Engineers] specialists strip adhesive tape, grease and water-proof cloth from ignition and induction systems. Down on the beach clanking bull-dozers splash into the sea to extract one vehicle in twenty that stalls in the big splash. Without the bull-dozers and their drivers there would be chaos. Through a loud speaker the Navy's beach-master harangues the tardy, abuses the odd fool and stage manages the whole incredibly efficient show. 'LCT 33 come on in now, come on hurry there's ample depth, what are you waiting for. Come on that Dodge truck in LCT 198 and give her everything you've got. LCA 190 get the hell out of here, get to your proper place along the beach. Party loafing near the wire track get in the water and push that jeep. Party landing from LCI 786 double off the beach and get inland. Enemy aircraft approaching from the west, come on double up, at any moment you are likely to be dive-bombed and machine-gunned.'[19]

As soon as 151st Brigade of the 50th Division had begun to move inland to their concentration area, its sister 69th Brigade was ordered ashore and, expecting the worst, got a pleasant surprise at the lack of opposition. However, Private Harry Forth, with the 5th Battalion East Yorkshire Regiment, saw his first casualties before he reached the beach:

Private Harry Forth, MID, 5th Battalion East Yorkshire Regiment, and his wife Renee. (Courtesy of H. Forth)

> We clambered down the ropes into the landing craft. On the approach the matelot [sailor] dropped us into 12 feet of water, the ramp goes down and you're off. The boat was still moving as the lads at the front stepped off and it carried on over them – they were drowned. Myself and some of the lads got wise and jumped off the side. I had my Bren gun, my Mae West [life vest], three or four bandoliers of ammunition, grenades and all my other equipment. You floated thanks to your Mae West but when a boat goes over the top you have no chance. The landing after that was simple – the Italians were there with their suitcases waiting to come off the island! We had very little opposition until we got further inland. We knew then we were meeting the Germans again.[20]

---

19   *Middle East Weekly Parade* magazine, 1943. Cutting given to author by Norman Hardy, 1989.
20   Interview with the author, Harry Forth, 1991.

Private Norman Hardy, of the 5th Battalion East Yorkshire Regiment, looked at Sicily from his landing ship before taking his turn to make the run in to the beach. He had never been abroad until war broke out and thought the island looked beautiful, with the odd tell-tale blemish:

> I was on one of the big ships in the mess-deck on the morning of 10 July and one of the lads said, 'Come on deck and take a look at the island.' It was beautiful. You could see shells bursting and smoke coming up from blazing fires, but otherwise it was perfect. The landing was quite easy. We had 2lb bombs with fuses ready to be lit to blow a gap in the barbed wire, but we just walked up the beach.[21]

Private Norman Hardy, 5th Battalion East Yorkshire Regiment. (Courtesy of N. Hardy)

Due to his past experience of combat, Lance Sergeant Ken Rutherford of the 5th Battalion East Yorkshire Regiment felt uneasy about the initial lack of resistance on the beach:

> "We expected everything to be shot at us and we got practically nothing. It was like being on a picnic until the night came. It was that quiet we thought we were walking into a trap. It was uncanny. There was dogfighting above us. We were under a tree when an Italian pilot came down on a parachute. He was alright but he'd lost the bag of his testicles and all he could say was 'No bambino, no bambino'."[22]

Lance Sergeant Ken Rutherford, 5th Battalion East Yorkshire Regiment. (Courtesy of K. Rutherford)

21   Interview with author, Norman Hardy, 1990.
22   Interview with author, Ken Rutherford, 1992.

The follow-up troops of the 50th Northumbrian Division landing at Avola.
(Courtesy of D. King)

Private Thomas Atkinson, serving with the 5th Battalion East Yorkshire Regiment, had expected the worst when he landed with his unit, but found the going easy to start with:

> We'd had a few days' rest on our journey from Port Said along the Med, apart from daily PT and lectures on the attack at Avola Lido, Sicily. We had seen models of the coastline and photographs of the beaches. We had been told that it would be a piece of cake because the Italian home-guard was defending the beach, but we'd heard that tale before. We assembled on the boat-deck loaded like pack mules and boarded our allocated assault craft, which then swung out in the davits as this armada closed in on the shoreline, still unseen in the darkness. We heard the engines of aircraft passing over as they took the paratroops for the first assault, or so we were told. Later we heard that some had been dropped short in the sea. Then as the sky lightened and we could see other landing-craft scattered around us we were lowered into the sea for our journey ashore. As dawn broke so did the air attacks and shellfire from the land. The naval escort put up a good show in knocking out enemy guns, so it was only the occasional shell that dropped on the beach as we laid mesh tracking for the half-tracks and Bren-carriers. We had no trouble with mines or small-arms fire so in effect it was a piece of cake. We had landed and formed a beachhead, and the rest of the company advanced with the Green Howards along the coast eastwards. This campaign introduced us to compo-rations, which were a great improvement on what we were used to. Having handed over the beach track maintenance to support troops, we rejoined our company heading towards Augusta with the 5th Division. So far resistance had been slight and our advance steady.[23]

23   Interview with author, Thomas Atkinson, 1991.

Troops of 69 Brigade inspect a knocked-out German half-track. (Courtesy of J. Betts)

When Captain D.L.C. Price of the Royal Artillery made landfall, he found little resistance as he left his landing-craft:

> I was one of the advanced-party of 124th Field Regiment in the 50th Division. We soon got ashore in our armoured carrier and our first act was to cook break-fast. Happily, there was little local resistance, but I was conscious that the army was not fully alive to the absolute necessity to move inland quickly, for our toe hold would not save us in the event of a counter-attack. On a sunny afternoon I went on a reconnaissance with Major Paul Parberry,[24] O/C 288 Battery, and was disturbed to hear a loud explosion in front, his half-track vehicle had gone over a land-mine and I think all the occupants were killed.[25]

The 5th Division lands at Cassabile

The 5th Division landed south of Syracuse, with the 15th and 17th Brigades in the first wave and 13th Brigade following. Powerful air and naval bombardments rained down on the coastal defences and the roads leading to the bridgehead as the men of the 5th Division scrambled down their landing nets and into the landing-craft that pitched and rolled in the heavy sea.

24   Major Paul Parberry is not recorded as a war casualty, so he must have survived the blast.
25   S.W.C. Pack, *Operation Husky* (London: David and Charles, 1977), p. 141.

A 19-year-old Royal Navy midshipman, R.D. Butt, found himself in charge of three landing-craft carrying troops of the 5th Division:

> That evening [the 9th] I was sitting in the [HMS] *Reina* listening to Highland Light Infantry pipers playing warlike music when the summit of Mount Etna appeared on the horizon. We felt naked, [as] if we could see land, then an observer there must see us. The landing-craft had been rising and falling several feet in the middle of the night and with about 33 fully armed soldiers on board each one, launching and disengagement would be an alarming operation with every risk of severed fingers and cracked skulls. To my relief LCA 275 achieved a faultless launch and we proceeded about 400 yards ahead of the *Reina*. The sea was so rough that soon we were shipping seas over the bow ramp and had to reduce our speed to 3 knots with about 18 inches of water milling about on the bottom of the boat.[26]

Lance Corporal Denis March, of the 6th Battalion Seaforth Highlanders, was also preparing to leave his mother ship and climb into a landing-craft:

> We were ready by midnight and zero hour was 3:00 a.m. Everything went well as we boarded the landing-craft and set off into the night. We had not gone far when we heard a cry for help coming from the sea. We had arrived near an airborne soldier who had been dropped off target and was struggling to stay afloat. Anyway we dragged him on board looking like a drowned rat, all equipment gone.[27]

Lieutenant David Cole, serving with the 2nd Royal Inniskillings, sweated in the stifling heat as he and his men prepared to board their landing-craft. A loud explosion shook the ship as a shell landed not 100 yards away, followed by two more. Cole recalled that the ship's loudspeaker then boomed out the order to disembark:

> The landing-craft were drawn up close to the ship's side and men were swarming down scrambling nets into them. Soon we ourselves were clambering down, one eye on the net and the other on the craft bobbing around below us. An unpleasant gap yawned and closed between the ship and the landing-craft. I held my breath and jumped, landing with all my equipment as gracefully as a lump of concrete. The sea breeze was like a tonic after the moist heat of the ship's entrails. A few final instructions, laced with four letter words, were shouted up to the deck above and then we were away.[28]

---

26 Correspondence with author, R.D. Butt, 1990.
27   Correspondence with author, D. March, 1989.
28 D. Cole, *Rough Road to Rome* (London: William Kimber, 1983), p. 22.

Able Seaman Leslie Harris was aboard the Royal Navy's landing ship HMS *Prince Albert* and was one of a party that took it in turns to go out in small boats to lay smoke canisters in the water, giving the stationary larger vessels some cover:

> Going out on one occasion George was sat at the back of the boat between two smoke canisters amongst all the noise, guns blazing and tracer fire lighting up the sky. He shouted to me 'I would not have missed this for the world.' One after another American Liberty Ships were being hit in the same place, just in front of the bridge. We picked up survivors and took them to the hospital ship. These merchant seamen were in a dreadful state, covered in oil, and many were burnt.[29]

As they neared the shore, Midshipman Butt looked out for the beacon directing him to the beach, with machine-gun fire coming from Italian coastal positions. His landing-craft was a mile too far towards Avola, but the infantry officer with him was eager to get ashore:

> The craft grounded a few yards offshore due to the amount of water we had shipped. The soldiers waded out in single file behind their officer, fortunately on dead ground that the Italian opposition could not reach from their gun emplacements. We then heard a few shots and screams away to the left, followed by cheers and the skirl of the bagpipes, and knew that the Highland Light Infantry had hit their target and our chaps were not alone.[30]

Lieutenant Cole's craft heaved and bumped through the waves, some men retching and suffering the discomfort of seasickness. Their mother ship faded into the darkness as they progressed, while the sound of gunfire became ever more distinct. There was a bump as the ramp went down, throwing all the waiting men forward, and they moved quickly onto the beach in knee-deep water, boots crunching in the sand. This would be a summer's day at the beach they would never forget. Being part of the second wave, the sight that greeted Cole as he led his platoon up the beach was chaotic:

> We moved swiftly up the beach, guided by white tapes and beach landing officers with megaphones, along a strip of matting like a tropical cricket pitch, through barbed wire which had been cut and wrenched aside and past little boards marked 'Mines'. Sappers were working delicately with their detectors in coarse grass littered with ammunition cases, and the remains of a wrecked glider. [There was] a devastated gun emplacement, shell craters, telephone poles at drunken angles and a group of cottages battered by gun fire. Then the beach was behind us and we began filing up a dusty lane flanked by high walls. A

---

29   Correspondence with author, L. Harris, 1990.
30   S.W.C. Pack, *Operation Husky* (London: David and Charles, 1977), p. 96.

crowd of Italian prisoners [were] coming up the other way. Could these be the men we were fighting? Was this what an Italian coastal division, so formidable on the map, looked like in reality? Slovenly and unshaven. Behind them came a party of Sicilian women and children, brown as Arabs and dressed in dusty black clothing. An old woman hissed *Viva Inglesi* and held her hand out hopefully. I thought uncomfortably of the Eighth Army challenge 'Desert Rats' for which the password was 'Kill Italians.'[31]

It was imperative that the troops of the 5th Division move forward as quickly as possible to relieve the paratroopers of the Special Raiding Squadron who had taken and were holding the *Ponte Grande* over the River Anapo. The 6th Battalion Seaforth Highlanders of 17th Brigade capture *Casa Nuove* after the initial bridgehead had been formed around Cassabile. Clashes with small parties of enemy troops and shell-fire from coastal artillery had not prevented the capture of Cassabile by 10:00 a.m. The 17th Brigade advanced towards the hard-pressed glidermen at the *Ponte Grande*, but transport was scarce and numerous forms of local transport, including donkeys and horses, were commandeered to compensate for this deficit.

Lance Corporal March looked on as barbed-wire beach defences were demolished by the use of Bangalore torpedoes, enabling his fellow troops of the 6th Seaforth Highlanders to move off the beach:

> As we scaled a stile, we heard a metallic ring beneath our feet and found we were walking near Teller Mines, but I expect the Italians who had laid them were more scared of them than us because they hadn't sunk the fuses into the ground sufficiently. I was stood taking orders from the company commander [Major Waylen][32] when he was shot through the head from a burst of machine-gun fire and died immediately.[33]

The Move Inland

All beach defences were quickly overrun, and the discomfort of seasickness suffered by many of the attacking troops was more than offset by the low casualties from enemy fire when getting ashore. The Italian coastal divisions largely disintegrated without firing a shot, and the field divisions were soon also driven back. Mass surrenders of dispirited Italian troops were not uncommon. The first day had been singularly successful, in spite of early mishaps, and Montgomery was jubilant as his Eighth Army seized all of its initial objectives.

---

31   D. Cole, *Rough Road to Rome* (London: William Kimber, 1983), p. 23.
32   Major Francis Roy Waylen, MC, 6th Battalion Seaforth Highlanders, was killed in action on 10 July 1943, aged 28 years. He is buried in Syracuse War Cemetery, Sicily.
33   Correspondence with author, D. March, 1989.

Troops of the 5th Division move off the beaches and push inland. (Author's collection)

Once assured of the success of the Eighth Army's landing, Montgomery exhorted both corps commanders – Dempsey of XIII Corps and Lieutenant General Oliver Leese of XXX Corps – to push inland with great haste. Major General Sidney Kirkman (50th Division) was ordered to advance on Noto and Avola, while Major General Horatio Berney-Ficklin (5th Division) was to head for Syracuse and then on to Augusta. Montgomery landed on 11 July to find Syracuse had fallen to the 5th Division and that its important port had been seized undamaged. During the critical period before the invading troops were firmly established, there was a dangerous counter-attack by the German *Panzer* Division Hermann Göring, which was equipped with the formidable new 56-ton Tiger tanks. This unit had been stationed at Caltagirone overlooking the Gela Plain where the American 1st Infantry Division had landed. On 11 July, only a few American tanks were ashore owing to the congested state of the beaches and unloading problems caused by the heavy surf. This also led to a shortage of anti-tank guns and artillery pieces. The *panzers* and *panzer* grenadiers of the Herman Göring Division launched their attack, and in the first rush overran many American outposts. It was not long before the Germans had reached the sand dunes bordering the beaches and were preparing to drive the invaders back into the sea. However, accurate naval fire saved the day and broke up the attack, heavy-calibre shells targeting the German forces and destroying many tanks. Another German thrust on the left flank of the US 45th Infantry Division was broken up in the same manner.

Within three days, the Eighth Army had taken all of south-eastern Sicily, but despite their early success the British and Americans were soon to learn that this was to become a hard-fought infantryman's war. The troops had spent many months fighting in the open spaces of the deserts of North Africa, but now they were among green fields and olive groves lined with drystone walls that criss-crossed the land in every direction and offered superb defensive cover. The easy landing gave many the hope of a short and painless campaign, but things did not turn out that way. After visiting the front, Montgomery decided to attempt to break through north into the plain of Catania from the Lentini area. He wrote in his diary:

> I was confirmed in my view that the Battle of Sicily would primarily be a matter of securing the main centres of road communication. Movement off the roads and tracks was very difficult and often impossible, so that if the nodal points were gained it was clear that the enemy would be unable to operate. On the flank of XIII Corps, I decided that we should make a great effort to break through into the plain of Catania from the Lentini area and ordered an attack for the night of 13th/14th July. A parachute brigade and a commando brigade were made available for the operation, in which the main problems were to force the bottle-neck through the difficult country between Carlentini and Lentini and secure two bridges, one north of the Lentini Ridge, the Malati Bridge, and the other the Primosole Bridge over the River Simeto.[34]

The plan involved landing the 1st Parachute Brigade during the night near or on Primosole Bridge over the Simeto River, with orders to capture and hold it, establishing a bridgehead on the north bank. Contact would then be made with 3 Commando, which would land west of Agnone and capture the Malati Bridge over the Leonardo River. The main thrust directed at Catania would be led by the 50th Northumbrian Division. The 50th Division prepared itself for the push north through the foothills of Lentini at the southern edge of the plain of Catania. Its 151st Brigade moved into the area around Floridia and Solarino, positions vacated by 13th Brigade of the 5th Division. Troops here were in heavy contact with the enemy, who were very active with artillery, mortar fire and machine guns. The 69th Brigade, meanwhile, concentrated south-east of Floridia in preparation for an advance on Lentini; it prepared a mobile column consisting of a squadron of tanks, carriers and self-propelled guns, which were to advance through Canicattini Bagni with the intention of cutting the Solarino–Palazzolo road, then attack the enemy's rear at Solarino.

The fighting advance along the coastal road – 50th Northumbrian Division

The 69th Brigade's mobile column, however, was late in assembling and was hindered in its progress by the difficult terrain it had to advance over. Contact with the enemy was made west of Solarino, and after a brief fight and the taking of several prisoners the column withdrew the way it had come. The Italian troops west of Solarino made

---

34   N. Hamilton, *Monty* (London: Hodder and Stoughton, 1981), p. 265.

two abortive attempts to break through the British lines, once with an infantry attack and then with infantry supported by six captured French R35 tanks; five of the tanks were knocked out on the Palazzolo road as they headed for Solarino, while the fifth carried on through Solarino and Floridia, shooting up anything that moved. As a British 15cwt ammunition truck exploded, the advancing troops of the 5th Battalion East Yorkshire Regiment and 6th Battalion Durham Light Infantry scattered into the roadside ditches and behind stone walls. Private Harry Forth, of the 5th East Yorkshires, couldn't get out of the way fast enough:

> In the distance we could hear explosions as these tanks were hit and bullets were flying all over the place. Me and my mates looked for the nearest ditch and dived in, [as] we had nothing that would stop a tank. One kept on going and it flew past us with its engine roaring and its machine gun firing at anything and everything. I thought they must be brave men to keep going. Most would have made their escape and felt lucky to be alive. Trucks exploded to our rear and I was told later that the tank was knocked out. I often wondered if the crew survived.[35]

The commanding officer of the 5th Battalion East Yorkshire Regiment, Lieutenant Colonel R.B. James,[36] was driving a motorbike accompanied by his intelligence officer in a carrier as the rogue Italian tank came into view. Both bike and carrier immediately spun round and beat a hasty retreat, but the tank hit the carrier and blew off its track, the vehicle ending up in a ditch. It then pursued Colonel James for another half a mile, firing bursts from its machine gun, until it was knocked out by a British 105mm self-propelled gun near Floridia. The Italian infantry bravely advanced but were met by heavy concentrations of artillery fire and were soon broken up and the attack petered out. Later in the evening, 69th Brigade Headquarters received orders from division to continue the advance through Sortino and Lentini. The 151st Brigade was to follow up and occupy Sortino once it was in the hands of 69th Brigade, then concentrate in that area and contact XXX Corps. The 151st Brigade sent out patrols east of the Sortino road with the intention of clearing up any isolated pockets of Italians still present.

The transport situation for the British troops in Sicily was still acute, and the nature of the country often made matters worse for them. A brief description of the landscape at this point will give some idea of the problems the British had to overcome. In south-east Sicily, a coastal plain 7 miles wide runs between Cassibile and Syracuse, while north of the road that links Syracuse, Floridia and Solarino lies a great mass of broken hilly country which runs all the way to the plain of Catania. Of the two roads running northwards, one was a good coastal road used by the 5th Division for

35   Interview with author, Harry Forth, 1991.
36   Lieutenant Colonel Robert Brian James, DSO and two bars, Essex Regiment, commanding the 5th Battalion East Yorkshire Regiment, was killed in action in France on 3 August 1944, aged 31. He is buried in Hottot-le-Bagues War Cemetery, France.

A carrier of the Durham Light Infantry is held up as a fallen tree blocks the road.
(Courtesy of J.H. Clark)

their advance. The other inland road ran through the hills from Floridia to Sortino. Both converged on Lentini on the edge of the Catania plain, from where one main road crossed the Leonardo River, running along a low commanding ridge until it dropped again to the Primosole Bridge over the Simeto River. Past this point the road ran over very flat terrain, overlooked by Mount Etna in the distance, to Catania itself. The 50th Northumbrian Division was about to advance along the inland road, which ran for much of its length along valleys dominated on both sides by steep hills rising some 300ft above it. As it approached Sortino, the hills were closer to the road until they formed a gorge with its sides covered with trees and shrubs. About a mile-and-a-half from Sortino, the road climbed in a series of sharp bends to the town on top of the ridge. Beyond Sortino, halfway between Floridia and Lentini, the nature of the land was more open as the road dropped to Carlentini and Lentini. Every inch of the way was winding, dust-covered and narrow, not at all made to accommodate two-way traffic of the military kind. Stone walls and olive trees border the roadsides, and bends in the road were often of the hairpin variety.

The men of 69th Brigade, expecting to find enemy stragglers, searched buildings for German troops. Private Bill Cheale and his mates in the 6th Battalion Green Howards came across an old shed and approached it with great care, only to find a shocking scene inside:

During our march to our objective, I vividly remember searching a shed for the enemy and what did I find? Four naked men lying on tables. The corpses were starting to decompose and were being eaten by maggots. The bodies showed evidence of torture. It was beyond my comprehension how anybody could do this kind of thing to another human being and I hoped they would perish in hell.[37]

The 5th Battalion East Yorkshire Regiment, with an advanced guard comprising C Company, made for Sortino. Little opposition was expected and the troops pressed on along the dusty road, but just east of Sortino, German and Italian troops lay in wait for them in well-concealed positions on both sides of the gorge. As Sortino came into view, C Company came under fire. A universal carrier had moved too quickly up the attacking column and as it reached the head of D Company and was turning a sharp bend in the road, it was met by a deadly hail of Spandau fire. C and D Companies deployed and a heavy fire fight ensued as the Tommies pressed up the slopes to find their ambushers.

Major J.K, Harrison described the action as seen from the rear of his 5th East Yorkshires column:

Sudden and exciting, I heard from my position in B Company the unmistakeable purr of Spandau fire. Bren-guns replied from our leading companies and then the heavy thumps of German mortar bombs echoed down the valley. We halted for a while hoping that C and D Companies might soon overrun the enemy. But the noises of battle continued spasmodically and without knowing much about the situation B Company was told to advance further down the narrow valley. Further ahead at the road junction we were ordered to establish ourselves on a hill to our right. The enemy could not see to fire its Spandaus at us as we were still climbing the slopes and hidden by stone walls and trees, but a regular procession of mortar bombs hit the valley bellow near the road junction we had just left. Dusk was rapidly approaching and in my platoon area I found the CO with my company commander. The CO's plan was that B Company should occupy one of the enemy hills during darkness while C and D Companies were given similar assignments. Although the men were tired, hungry and thirsty after the long march in the tropical sun they welcomed the move and set off with a good heart. The CO led us in the darkness, [the] company commander with him. I was immediately behind with my platoon but the exceedingly rough ground and many stone walls made it hard going for my men with their rifles, Brens and other platoon weapons.[38]

B Company arrived at the foot of a hill criss-crossed with stone walls at 02:30 a.m. Everything was quiet, and the moon made a welcome appearance to help illuminate

37   Manuscript forwarded to author by Bill Cheale, 1995.
38   Manuscript forwarded to author, J.K. Harrison, 1991.

the way for the East Yorkshire Regiment. The troops scrambled up the sides of the steep hill, only to find the enemy had withdrawn. Sentries were posted and the men were able to have a couple of hours' precious sleep. The East Yorkshiremen had achieved all of their objectives during the early hours of the day, with any enemy stragglers rounded up and sent to the rear. By dawn on 13 July, 69th Brigade was firmly established on the high ground beyond Sortino but had lost contact with the retreating Axis forces. The tired and hungry troops of the 50th Division pressed on in the heat and dust, fighting periodically as they went. It now became imperative that the high ground overlooking the Plain of Catania should be taken before the enemy could regroup and co-ordinate any serious opposition in this difficult terrain.

On 12 July, 151st Brigade had moved out in the direction of Solarino to relieve the 2nd Battalion Wiltshire Regiment (13th Brigade, 5th Division), which was in contact with the Italian Napoli Division at Solarino. The Italians held the high ground and could observe every movement of the British troops below them. At 5:30 p.m., the relief by the 151st was complete; this was at the same moment that Italian tanks had broken through the East Yorkshire Regiment positions, as stated above. Lieutenant Colonel James, CO of their 5th Battalion, came racing down the road on his motor-bike shouting, "Look out, tanks are coming." The Durhams' anti-tank guns were quickly put into position among the houses and across the road, and any civilians who were still around swiftly disappeared. The solitary French-made tank and its Italian crew then raced into Floridia with all guns blazing, smashing down a telegraph pole and finally crashing into a Sherman tank, after which the crew were taken prisoner. The Durhams then came under attack from the Napoli Division, and it was decided that the 6th Battalion Durham Light Infantry would counter-attack the Italian positions at 4:45 a.m. on 13 July, preceded by a heavy six-minute artillery barrage.

Lieutenant David Fenner led the battalion's 13 Platoon into the subsequent battle:

> The sounds of pre-attack preparations were going on all around in the dark, [with] magazines clicking on to Bren-guns and the snick of bayonets fixing. We deployed on the start line waiting for H hour and I gave out the last of the rum. I recall the men puffing away at cigarettes as they advanced with rifles at the high port. The guns had stopped firing and as we approached the objective (some farm buildings on a ridge) we saw the enemy. The two leading platoons swept forward whooping until our progress was stopped by a low stone wall across our front. Beyond this were three lorries and a lot of Italians shooting at us, [so] we stopped and returned fire. Dominic [Parker] came up to speak to me and was hit in the chest, [and] L/Cpl Montgomery, our company stretcher bearer (a splendid man) ran up to attend to him and some other casualties. We were shooting back at these Italians. Cummings who was standing next to me was firing his Bren from the shoulder, [and] I could see the tracer passing over one of the trucks. I said, 'shoot the truck', [and] his first burst (more by luck than by judgement) started an explosion followed by a fire with burning debris showering over the Italians lying by the vehicles. We broke through the dry-stone wall and I found myself amongst a bunch of Italian soldiers. I started shooting at them with my

Men of the 6th Battalion Durham Light Infantry take General Porcinari, commander of the Napoli Division, and most of his staff into captivity. (Courtesy of G. Worthington)

revolver when I realised that they were surrendering and offering me cigarettes. I remember saying 'no thanks I smoke a pipe' before realising how stupid it sounded. The fighting here was over and we settled on our objective and made some protection for ourselves building up sangars by pulling down the drystone walls. Tea was brewed, prisoners carrying casualties moved to the rear and the dead were buried."[39]

By 5:30 a.m. the Durhams had taken the Italian positions, finding a very demoralised enemy. The action resulted in the destruction of the Napoli Division and the capture of several hundred troops. As the Durhams rounded a corner in the road at Casa Rossa, they came upon an Italian staff car that contained General Julius Cesare Gott-Porcinari, the commander of the Napoli Division, together with most of his staff, who were taken prisoner.

Sergeant Thomas Cairns, who was with the 6th Durhams, described the scene along the road:

Two wrecked and abandoned 88s cover the road, a 75 hit by a shell heels over into a road-side ditch. Motor cycles and tricycles, some smashed, others

---

39   H. Moses, *The Faithful Sixth*. (Durham: County Durham Books, 1995), p. 248.

burning, are strewn across the road making passage difficult. Abandoned machine-guns, mortars and anti-tank guns are thrown along the walls and hedges bordering the road. Cartridges, bombs and shells are heaped amid the cactus. In the fields more guns, more trucks and more cycles stand unattended, left behind in the rush of a headlong retreat. An ammunition carrier, set alight by Bren tracer, blazes on the road, its cargo popping and whizzing into the neighbouring fields. Italian corpses charred and mangled, some headless, some legless, are everywhere. Three dead Italians lie huddled around an anti-tank gun. In the roadside ditch a few yards away lies one of our lance corporals.[40]

The 5th Division advance on Syracuse and Augusta

On 10th July, the 5th Division continued its march on Syracuse and relieved the glider troops at the *Ponte Grande*. Four miles from Syracuse, the 2nd Battalion Northamptonshire Regiment met a group of 400 Italian soldiers forming up for a counter-attack. However, it did not take long to persuade the Italians to surrender; they had with them prisoners from the 1st Airborne Division who had been dropped wide of their landing zone. By the evening of the 10th, the men of the 2nd Northamptonshires and the 2nd Battalion Royal Scots Fusiliers entered Syracuse, accompanied by the B Squadron Sherman tanks of the County of London Yeomanry. The town of Syracuse had been severely bombed, but the port was found to be intact. Troops of the 5th Division remembered spending their first evening there drinking Italian wine. Men of the Royal Scots Fusiliers liberated a silk-stocking factory, throwing away the contents of their packs to make room for as many pairs of stockings as they could cram in.

Lieutenant David Cole of the 2nd Royal Inniskillings recalled the terrible heat of the march and the opposition his battalion met as they moved to block the main route to Syracuse:

> Towards mid-day on the 10thJuly we reached our first holding position some six miles inland. Our immediate task was to hold the bridge over the Cavadonna River just ahead and to block the road into Syracuse from the south-west that ran across it. We began to dig in and hardly had we started when, with a roar that burst the sky open, a plane streaked over us skimming the tree tops. Fast as it was, we caught a glimpse for the first time of the black German crosses on its wings. It flew past us, and as we could hear from the crunch of exploding bombs, it had found easier targets on the beach. We could see only the heat shimmering above the distant walls and fields and a few inquisitive butterflies meandering from shrub to shrub. It all had the sleepy look of a hot and peaceful

---

40   Ibid., p. 249.

summer's day. Only the distant thud of the guns and the occasional glint of metal in the grass suggested that the world was not at peace.[41]

Cole's battalion set up a road block and waited astride the road to Syracuse. They did not have long to wait, as a group of Italian soldiers on bicycles came round the bend in the road as though on an afternoon jaunt:

> The finger of one of our hidden Bren-gunners squeezed the trigger for a brief moment and a stream of bullets zipped through the cyclists who jumped and fell off their bicycles into ditches. The bicycles lay crumpled in the middle of the road, then from the grass and scrub timid hands slowly appeared. Some of the Italians were slightly wounded, [and with] their rifles discarded and arms raised, [they] scrambled to their feet and walked down the road to our positions. They were quickly searched, bandaged and hustled back to the rear. In a moment the scene had lapsed again into rustic tranquillity.[42]

The tranquillity was not to last long. The Italians had no idea the British had got so far inland, and quite substantial forces were still trying to get to Syracuse via the road being held by the Inniskillings. A large Italian armoured car appeared round a bend in the road and edged forward suspiciously up to the Inniskillings' road block. The British troops, who had been told to hold their fire, watched quietly as a convoy of more Italian armoured cars, supply trucks, a staff car, a light field gun and other assorted vehicles pulled up in front of the road block. With the congested convoy at a standstill, the Inniskillings finally opened fire. Lieutenant Cole continued:

> The Italians immediately leapt from their vehicles and dived into the hedges and ditches, some of them scattering into the orchards and beyond. What had looked a moment before like an Italian traffic jam now seemed more like a battle-field, with some limp forms lying lifeless between the deserted vehicles and the sound of wounded men calling and groaning from the ditches. In the middle of their column several Italian soldiers had succeeded in extricating a Breda machine-gun from a lorry and had set it up in a ditch. With this they began to fire back fiercely at Johnny's leading section for several minutes until the section commander, Bogle, crawled forward and then charged the Breda single handed, killing its crew with his Tommy-gun. In the fields and orchards ahead of us Italians walked forward with their hands up, [and] the prisoners were herded together, about a hundred of them including six officers. The latter, unlike their men, were well groomed and appeared to be in their best uniforms. I can recall even now, how I walked past the blood-stained bodies sprawled on the road.[43]

---

41   D. Cole, *Rough Road to Rome* (London: William Kimber, 1983), p. 25.
42   Ibid., p. 27.
43   Ibid., p. 28.

As dawn broke on Sunday, 11 July, Floridia was in the hands of the 5th Division. For the rest of that day and most of the 12th, the 2nd Battalion Cameronians were in reserve around the town. The barracks in Syracuse had been the last position to hold out, but the troops there surrendered to the Royal Scots Fusiliers. Naval experts then moved into the docks to maintain them so they could be used by the Royal Navy. During the afternoon of 11 July, the 5th Division had made plans for a battalion-strong morning attack the following day, supported by the divisional artillery which had moved into new positions between Syracuse and Priolo. The Germans forestalled this plan by withdrawing from Priolo during the night. A platoon of the 2nd Northamptonshire Regiment quickly established itself at the northern end of the town as British bombers plastered the southern section.

George Nolan Johnson, a driver with the Royal Artillery, entered Syracuse after the infantry of the 5th Division. He remembered:

> The road was strewn with burnt-out Italian vehicles and there were a few Italian corpses in the ditches. As we neared Syracuse a long column of Italian prisoners was being escorted along by a cocky British infantryman. The Italians tried to scrounge cigarettes from us. Bob and I drove into Syracuse in our water truck. Our instructions were to rendezvous at the Piazza Archimedes. Here we parked our truck outside a large building and washed and shaved. What seemed to be two annoying wasps whizzed past our ears and disturbed us, [and] in astonishment we realised we were under sniper fire. The infantry dashed off to deal with it.[44]

After Syracuse had been secured, Johnson looked down onto the port, which was now full of ships flying the 'Red Duster'. The Royal Navy had installed a boom across the harbour mouth to prevent Axis submarines from entering and taking the ships there by surprise. Johnson looked on with avid interest as an Italian submarine came into view:

> Into this arena arrived an Italian submarine with colours flying and the crew on the deck cheering. The navy obligingly opened the boom and in came the boys. Halfway across the harbour they must have realised their mistake – you can imagine the conference on the bridge – and tried to turn for the open sea. As they neared the boom a battery fired a shell across their bow, and down came their flag. Redcaps [Military Police] arrived in a motor-boat to arrest them.[45]

The fall of the ancient port of Syracuse, along with its massive defensive works, came quickly. Behind the enemy lines, confusion reigned. Desertions from troops based around Syracuse had been heavy, but worse was to come. The fortifications here were probably the best on the whole island: heavy coastal guns were housed in reinforced bunkers, anti-aircraft batteries were numerous and in prepared positions,

---

44   Correspondence with author, G.N. Johnson, 1989.
45   Ibid.

and the approaches to the town were strewn liberally with minefields and barbed-wire. Apart from naval and artillery fire, no direct threat had appeared, but still the Italians commenced to blow up these sound defences. The British wasted no time in preparing the port for use by mine-sweeping the approaches. Captain A. Patience, Royal Navy, watched events unfold:

> As we closed with the enemy coast we could hear and see gun-fire and our prayers were with those brave soldiers. We reached our allotted position and continued to sweep [for mines] all night and morning as the troops were still landing. They quickly moved inland and the sound of gunfire got fainter. We encountered consistent air attacks, having a few near misses, as the main convoy of ships was about a mile south of us, and if the Itie or Gerry planes had any bombs left, we were always presented with the leavings. When Syracuse fell, we were the first ship to be sent in, as we had to sweep the area for safety. On the way we saw the sickly sight of a stranded hospital ship [the *Aba*] that had been bombed.[46]

Harry Wood, a gunner with the Royal Artillery, entered Syracuse harbour on 11 July and was shocked at the scene he encountered:

> As we approached the harbour at Syracuse it was obvious that the bombers and naval guns had been active. A hospital ship lay on its side by the quay, other ships had been sunk and the sky was alive with planes and ack-ack fire. As we left the town, following the 5th Division, we saw a number of crashed gliders scattered around. News came that the ship carrying our guns had been dive-bombed and sunk with the loss of everyone on board. How close I had come to being one of that number, but driver Spinks had taken my place. We all felt depressed at such a heavy loss of life.[47]

Conditions for the civilian population of Syracuse were deplorable, with many of the people starving. Lieutenant John Picken, serving with the Royal Navy, noted the poor conditions the locals had to live in:

> We were billeted on the top floor of what had once been a government office in Syracuse. I have vivid recollections of the desperate hunger of the civilian population who eagerly assailed the waste bins containing the left overs of our own diet.[48]

Gunner Harry Wood also noticed the poor situation the Italian civilians were in, especially the children. Eventually, his battery was supplied with new replacement artillery pieces, and Wood and his comrades settled down for the evening:

---

46   S.W.C. Pack, *Operation Husky* (London: David and Charles, 1977), p. 120.
47   Correspondence with author, H. Wood, 1993.
48   Conversation with author, J. Picken, 1991.

We moved through this poverty-stricken land and as we were unloading our new equipment, I noticed two children descending some stone steps from a farm building. They came down on all fours as their legs were not strong enough to support themselves. It was the worst case of malnutrition I had seen and my first sight of rickets. Soldiers of all nations never let kids go hungry, so we fed them. But it was Wilkie, the battery hardman, who excelled himself. Out of his large pack came the much-prized chocolate that he had been saving for months. He put this in his empty kitbag and went round the troop asking for donations of anything edible. An hour later he was in the town square giving goodies to these poor kids. Grown-ups came clamouring round shouting for food but he just clipped them round the ear-hole and concentrated on the youngsters. He came back with an empty kitbag and a rare thing for Wilkie, a smile on his face.[49]

Augusta falls and Battle Group Schmalz makes a stand, 11-12 July

The next task for the 5th Division was to take the port of Augusta. The coastal road that led to it ran through the small town of Priolo, which was surrounded by thick woods and could only be reached via a meandering narrow road with stone walls on either side. On a bright and sunny day, a mixed force from the 5th Division advanced without incident until their progress was sharply checked. In the wooded area around Priolo, men and anti-tank guns of Battle Group Schmalz waited in well-prepared positions. They would prove once again the Germans' ability to fight effective defensive battles. Above the roar of the British tanks there could now be heard the crack of anti-tank guns and the rattle of machine-gun fire as Battle Group Schmalz, from the Hermann Göring Division, opened fire from its skilfully concealed positions. Three tanks of the County of London Yeomanry exploded as they were hit by 88mm armour-piercing shells, and two more were put out of action. This was bad country for armour, with the British tanks unable to get off the road to deploy. The regimental history of the County of London Yeomanry has left a brief account of this action:

> In a very bloody affray Guy J. Caunce was among half a dozen wounded, unfortunately very severely. He lost his sight in one eye and, although at first, he insisted on not going back, he had to be evacuated later that evening. Captain Woods now re-assumed command south of Priolo.[50]

In the early hours of 12 July, Colonel Wilhelm Schmalz was driven into Augusta to assess the situation. All seemed to be quiet at that time, and he remembered watching as a battery of German anti-aircraft gunners engaged Allied ships off the coast

---

49   Correspondence with author, H. Wood, 1993.
50   A. Graham, *Sharpshooters at War* (London: The Sharpshooters Regimental Association, 1964), p. 115.

and then switched to target bombers coming in from the sea:

> After an incredibly short time the officer was ready to fire his four huge guns and they blasted off at the vessels. The ships retaliated and were soon obscured in clouds of smoke. The gunners' faces were beaming, they were convinced they had hit one of the destroyers. Then a new alarm, bombers were flying in from the sea. In a twinkling the barrels turned upwards and shooting began again into the sky.[51]

Colonel Wilhelm Schmalz, commander of Battle Group Schmalz, Sicily, July 1943. (Author's collection)

Battle Group Schmalz was the only reliable fighting force left in the Eighth Army's sector, but it was too weak to take the offensive and had to content itself with fighting delaying actions, which it did very successfully. Colonel Schmalz[52] was an intelligent, tough and resilient commander, and used his task force to prevent a breakthrough to the Plain of Catania and certain disaster for the Axis forces in Sicily. While the Italian defenders were crumbling at Augusta, Schmalz's force was blocking the advance of the 5th Division north of Syracuse. The main obstacle for the Eighth Army, sitting astride the coast road, was the town of Lentini, which hindered Montgomery's march towards Messina – the part of Sicily closest to southern Italy – and a quick victory. The task of holding back the British, and therefore the fate of the Axis forces in Sicily, rested in the capable hands of Colonel Schmalz. He had created a defensive line before the British arrived, and then held them off without any reserves to call upon. In such a situation, even Schmalz could not hold out forever, but the lack of any large-scale attack by the British enabled him to hang on to his positions south of Lentini.

Private Ronald Alfred Marson, who was with the 2nd Battalion the Cameronians, was moving up the coast road with his unit when they came under fire:

---

51   H. Pond, *Sicily* (London: William Kimber, 1962), p. 114.

52   Battle Group Schmalz was named after its commander, Colonel (later Lieutenant General) Wilhelm Schmalz, and consisted of an infantry battalion and two artillery batteries of the Hermann Göring Division and the 115th *Panzer* Grenadier Regiment of the *15th Panzer Division*. Wilhelm Schmalz survived the war and died on 14 March 1983. He is buried with his wife in the municipal cemetery at Weilmunster, Laimbach, Germany.

For most of us it was to be our first time in action. We moved in convoy along the road and as we did so we were strafed by enemy planes. A truck in front of ours was hit and set on fire and a friend of mine was killed. A line of bullets hit the road just ahead of our truck, kicking up the dust. The rear of the truck was hit, wounding two of the occupants, although the driver and I sitting in the cab were unaware of this at the time. My clearest recollection of this time was of the heat, the dust and the smells. Here the Germans were putting up a fierce rear-guard action and we came across many of the dead of both sides. I remember vividly finding many dead airborne soldiers still hanging in their parachute harnesses in the trees. They must have been helpless when the Germans shot them.[53]

Lieutenant David Cole reached his allotted place in the line with the 2nd Royal Inniskillings near Augusta:

Having thus reached our objective we dug in astride the main road to the west of Augusta, sited our anti-tank guns, machine-guns and mortars, laid our telephone cables, ate our hard rations and awaited events. Indeed, it was good to be alive, especially when we could smell the alternative option from some shallow graves beside the road.[54]

Lance Corporal Denis March came under shell-fire for the first time as the 6th Seaforth Highlanders approached Augusta:

As we moved towards Augusta we came under accurate shell-fire. One shell scored a direct hit on C Company Headquarters. I was nearby and got covered in earth and dust, but I wasn't injured thank God. The lad who had taken over the duties of company clerk, Jackie Cowie,[55] was killed.[56]

The scattered landings of numerous gliders all around Augusta had given the impression that a massive airborne attack had been launched, and Axis units in the town decided withdrawal was their best option. A German naval garrison demolished their positions in Augusta's harbour and pulled back, while the Italian holding positions in the same vicinity did the same. However, the Italian garrison was shaky at the best of times, and as defending infantry units disappeared, the coastal batteries spiked their guns rather than let them fall into enemy hands. As the troops of the 5th Division reached the heights overlooking Augusta Bay, orders were issued to the remaining Augusta garrison to destroy their fuel supplies and the radio station.

---

53   Correspondence with author, A.R. Marson, 1990.
54   D. Cole, *Rough Road to Rome* (London: William Kimber, 1983), pp. 42-43.
55   Private John Cowie died of his wounds on 16 July 1943, aged 23. He is buried in Syracuse War Cemetery, Sicily.
56   Correspondence with author, D. Marsh, 1991.

As Schmalz held up the British, Italian forces launched a counter-attack at dawn on 11 July, with tanks and infantry supported by an artillery barrage. The attack was made near Solarino on the 13th Brigade sector, but was repulsed with heavy casualties.

On the afternoon of 12 July, a white flag was reported to be flying from the citadel in Augusta. The *Ulster Monarch* entered the harbour that afternoon, accompanied by three Royal Navy destroyers. Italian coastal batteries still in operation on Santo Croce to the north bombarded the British ships, but were soon silenced by the destroyers. The SAS troops on board the *Ulster Monarch* disembarked from landing craft and found the port deserted for the most part. Patrols from Battle Group Schmalz were encountered on the outskirts of Augusta, but the Germans were now pulling back as the columns of 17th Brigade approached.

The town of Augusta was entered on 12 July by troops of the 1st Battalion Green Howards and 2nd Battalion Seaforth Highlanders. Sergeant Alfred Hinds of the Seaforths recalled the events of the day:

> On the 12th we advanced with a couple of tanks to a small town on a hillside to the north of Priolo, which dominated the main road to Lentini. The Italian garrison there had been severely bombarded by our ships in Augusta Bay and had not the will to fight any more. The town was a pile of rubble but for the church and there had been lots of civilian casualties. We felt sorry for the poor devils.[57]

Tanks of the County of London Yeomanry accompanied the Seaforths as they entered Augusta. The history of the CLY describes the scene:

> At the earnest request of Brigadier Tarleton, commanding 17 Brigade, the squadron leader agreed to do all he could to assist the leading battalion, the Seaforths, to get into Augusta that night. He took with him two tanks, his own and 2/Lt John Crews.[58] After a time, he got out and walked ahead of the tanks with the leading company commander. It was a nerve-wracking march as the two tanks and the infantry nosed their way forward in the half-darkness past pill-boxes and buildings which were presumably garrisoned. Whenever there was any trouble or suspicion of trouble, Captain Woods climbed into his tank and let fly with all available weapons, [and] about 70 Italians surrendered. The moon went down and the Seaforths halted, the Royal Scots Fusiliers came through them to continue the advance. Captain Woods[59] put Lt Crews into the turret of his tank and himself sat on the front of it. A 2.8cm anti-tank gun opened up firing explosive bullets, [and] it scored a hit on the leading tank and

---

57   Correspondence with author, A. Hinds, 1989.
58   2nd Lieutenant John Nicholas Crews, 3rd Battalion County of London Yeomanry, was killed in action on 12 July 1943, aged 26. He is buried in Syracuse War Cemetery, Sicily.
59   Captain Woods was awarded the Military Cross for this action.

killed Lt Crews. The Lowlanders went forward with the bayonet and before dawn Augusta was in Allied hands.[60]

At dawn on 13 July, men of the 168th Brigade, which was now part of the 50th Northumbrian Division, had landed at Syracuse and moved to a concentration area east of Floridia, and from there to the north of Melilli. Montgomery was now very keen to push his troops forward into the heart of Sicily. He issued a personal message which was to be read out to all of his divisions, with the intention of spurring them on in their quest for victory:

> The beginning has been very good, thanks to your splendid fighting qualities and to the hard work and devotion to duty of all those who work in the ports, on the roads and in the rear areas. We must not forget to give thanks to The Lord Mighty in Battle for giving us such a good beginning towards the attainment of our objective and now let us get on with the job. Together with our American allies we have knocked Mussolini off his perch. We will now drive the Germans out of Sicily. Into battle with stout hearts and good luck to you all."[61]

The 50th Northumbrian Division at Mount Pancali

The troops of the 69th and 151st Brigades, 50th Northumbrian Division, pressed on remorselessly up the coastal road to the Plain of Catania against constant opposition. Ahead of the 151st Brigade, 69th Brigade was encountering stiffening resistance as it ran into German troops of Battle Group Schmalz. The rough terrain made the going hard, the sun was merciless and the fighting bitter.

By midnight on 13 July, the 6th Battalion Green Howards had captured part of the approach to Mount Pancali but could advance no further because of the heavy fire coming from this feature. At 5:00 a.m. on 14 July, the 7th Battalion Green Howards made an attack on Mount Pancali's slopes, supported by an artillery barrage and machine guns of the 2nd Battalion Cheshire Regiment.

Captain K.A. Nash, of A Company of the 7th Green Howards, took part in the assault and later wrote:

> We are to attack Mount Pancali, a high hill on our left alive with machine-guns. A Company goes left and we make the frontal assault. I can see the objective rising suddenly about 2,000 yards away, with a flat plain between us. This waiting for an attack is bloody, the men don't like it and neither do I. The guns open up and we move forward, [arriving] at the foot of the hill at last and it looks bloody steep from here. There are big boulders as we climb, [but] the men

---

60   A. Graham, *The Sharpshooters at War* (London: The Sharpshooters Regimental Association, 1964), pp. 115–16.

61   B.L. Montgomery, *Memoirs* (London: Companion Book Club, 1960), p. 217.

are splendid climbing up grimly, not knowing what to expect at the top. We reach a ledge just before the summit and pause for breath. I hear a shout 'follow me 11 Platoon' and I find myself on the top. Now machine-guns open up all around, [then] a miserable Boche crawls from behind a boulder with the inevitable shout of '*Kamerad*'. He could have killed me twenty times over as I stood there but he is too shaken to press the trigger. I ran past him and bullets are whining everywhere but our blood is up, we are shouting, swearing, cheering, it's easy, they're giving themselves up, they've had it. Except that on our right there's no sign of Nigel and a lot of fire is coming from behind that wall. The rest of the company has swept forward and I can hear the CSM yelling encouragement to them. Geoff is quiet and looks bad. He was hit in the thigh but staggered on to the top and collapsed in a hail of bullets. I am excited as hell now and get a Bren to open up towards the enemy, and Jerry quietens down now. I must be excited now as I do a darned silly thing: I zig-zag forward under cover of the Bren. Two blokes say 'good luck sir' and one voice says 'I'm coming with you sir'. Grand troops, it was Corporal Kendrick. We dash forward among the Spandau lead, [and] our Bren silences one machine-gun. Another 20 yards then more Spandau and a dash for cover behind a boulder, [and] I turn round to see Kendrick shot clean through the throat. I grab his tommy-gun and loose off the magazine. Poor Kendrick.[62] Courage evaporates and I hug the ground and pray. Then Jerry starts shelling us. I shout back for a smoke screen on the copse only to find the mortar crews have been knocked out. I lay there nearly half an hour sweating. Presently the Boche gets browned off and come out with their hands up. What a morning.[63]

By 10:00 a.m., the objective was captured, German forces leaving the area littered with their dead and wounded. Some 29 German machine guns were found on top of the hill. The fatigue of the British troops and the stubborn rearguard actions delayed the advance, and the landscape they passed through south of Carlentini and Lentini bore witness to the grim struggle that had taken place there. Burning vehicles obstructed the roads, and during the morning of 14 July Axis aircraft roared in to strafe and harass the slow-moving columns.

Private Ernest Kerens, serving with the 9th Battalion Durham Light Infantry, described the scene:

The battalion was on the road in single file each side of the road, [and] the only action was provided by two low flying ME 109s [Messerschmitts], as we marched both sides of the road. At the first sign of the two planes everybody shouted at once and vanished as if by magic, into the fields that edged the road and behind any cover there was. From it they sent a shower of bullets at the

---

62 Corporal Arthur James Kendrick, 7th Battalion Green Howards, was killed in action on 17 July 1943, aged 22. He has no known grave and is commemorated on the Cassino Memorial.
63 Manuscript sent to the author by K.A. Nash, 1989.

Troops of 69th Brigade pass through a street in Carlentini. (Author's collection)

aircraft. The Bren carriers and ammunition trucks were not always so lucky. An ammo truck was hit and was a danger to everyone in the area as it exploded. I suppose the driver could have jumped off and run like hell but instead he drove it up the hillside as far as he could before it exploded killing him, poor blighter. We marched on and on, mile after mile over dusty rough Sicilian roads nursing the precious contents of our water bottles.[64]

By early afternoon on 14 July, the men of 69th Brigade had secured Carlentini and Lentini. The 5th Battalion East Yorkshire Regiment made contact with 3 Commando north of Lentini, and the bridge over the river was found to be intact. The 4th Armoured Brigade passed through Lentini with the objective of pressing on to the Primosole Bridge to relieve the hard-pressed airborne forces there.

Captain D.L.C. Price of the 124th Field Regiment, Royal Artillery, entered Carlentini and had his men set to work immediately to relieve the sufferings of the townsfolk. He recalled:

---

64   H. Moses, *The Gateshead Gurkhas* (Durham: County Durham Books, 2001), p. 246.

The battle was now taking shape and I remember shelling Carlentini, a suburb of Lentini, and then an hour later using up all our dressings bandaging up civilian wounded after entering the town. They were very understanding and all the church bells were ringing, so I didn't feel too badly, and in any case, nobody was seriously hurt. But the futility of war was brought to mind by that incident.[65]

Private Kerens and his comrades followed the tanks into Lentini:

Tanks went through to deal with the Germans and we followed them down into Lentini. Italy was still at war with us but while we waited in the town the villagers lined the main street cheering and clapping and plying us with water, *vino*, oranges and of all things pickled olives. One old chap kissed me on both cheeks and hugged me like a long-lost son. It was very noticeable that the only females were either very old or very young, but fluttering bedroom curtains showed where they hid the others. We were off again down to the bottom of the hill and along the road to Primosole Bridge. There was a hell of a long way to go and no transport. Darkness fell but still we marched. The column strag- gled, [and] the strong carried the rifles of the weak, less than two miles from our objective, the Primosole Bridge. Nobby [Colonel Clark] had to call a halt to his weary column and said food would be provided and we would sleep here.[66]

Lieutenant Colonel Schmalz, realising the bulk of the coastal defences had capitu- lated, made the decision to withdraw his battle group to positions on the Plain of Catania in order to prevent the Eighth Army from capturing the port at Catania and advancing on Messina. His forces fought a brilliant fighting retreat from Floridia, through Sortino and Lentini. He was waiting to be joined by the Napoli Division, but by now they had been virtually destroyed as a fighting unit and their commander captured. A young Italian officer and his battalion arrived from Syracuse and asked for permission to join the battle group. This unit fought enthusiastically alongside the Germans, earning the respect of their new commander, Schmalz, who said:

If every man of the coastal batteries had only fired one shot, the English landing would have been considerably hindered, [but] as it was, they landed unopposed."[67]

During the first three days of the advance, Eighth Army had met only minimal opposition, but Montgomery's bold plan now focussed the success of the Sicilian campaign upon an ugly 400ft-long structure of steel girders called the Primosole Bridge. Highway 114 passes over it, leading to the city of Catania 7 miles to the

65   S.W.C. Pack, *Operation Husky* (London: David and Charles, 1977), p. 142.
66   Manuscript forwarded to author by E. Kerens, 1991.
67   H. Pond, *Sicily* (London: William Kimber, 1962), p. 118.

north. At this point, the River Simeto winds its muddy way in a series of loops through marshland devoid of cover, its banks overgrown with tall reeds. A concrete blockhouse stood at each end of the bridge, and close to the northern end was a series of farm buildings. To the east and west of Highway 114, to a width of over 1,000 yards in each direction, were lines of vineyards and olive trees that extended to 500 yards in depth. Along the northern edge of the vineyards ran a sunken track, while further north the plain opened out, devoid of cover. Treacherous gullies and other natural obstacles would impede progress further. Nearly 3 miles north of the bridge, Highway 114 passed over a dry irrigation canal, the *Fosso Bottaceto*, which outlined the southern defences of Catania airfield. During the planning of the campaign, Montgomery had realised that the Primosole Bridge was the key to securing the Plain of Catania and the city, though in the event of a successful British advance it could turn out to be a dangerous bottleneck. This structure would now become the focus of attention for the British and German forces in a deadly game that would alter the course of the whole campaign.

3

The Battle for the Bridges

The ease of Eighth Army's advance in the first 48 hours led Montgomery to believe erroneously that he could successfully attack on two fronts. The first thrust was to drive along the coast, cut through to the Plain of Catania and take the city. The second thrust inland by what was known as Harpoon Force[1] would capture Vizzini, Caltagirone, Enna and Leonforte. Patton's US Seventh Army would hold off counter-attacks from Gela while Harpoon Force swept around the rear of the Hermann Göring Division, trapping the German forces between Lieutenant General Omar Bradley's American II Corps and Leese's British XXX Corps. However, the thrust by Harpoon Force failed as it ran into unexpected stiff resistance from the Hermann Göring Division, which held Vizzini until 15 July, stopping the inland thrust in its tracks. After this setback, Montgomery turned his attention to the primary coastal thrust. The 1st British Airborne Brigade was alerted to take Primosole Bridge on the night of the 13/14 July. Montgomery's audacious plan was straightforward: the 1st Parachute Brigade was to be dropped around Primosole Bridge, followed by a small glider force carrying 10 light artillery pieces. Simultaneously, 3 Commando would land by sea and take the bridge at Malati which crossed the Leonardo River 3 miles to the north of the city of Lentini. While these bridges were being held, the 50th Northumbrian Division– reinforced by the 4th Armoured Brigade commanded by Brigadier John Currie – would drive north, take Carlentini and Lentini, relieve the commandos, press on to Primosole Bridge to relieve the airborne troops there and establish a bridgehead by nightfall on 14 July. This combined infantry, airborne and armoured force would then advance and seize the city of Catania.

The troops of the 1st Parachute Brigade, led by Brigadier Gerald Lathbury, prepared themselves for the trial ahead. The brigade was to drop north and south of Primosole Bridge (code name Marston), capturing it from both sides of the river. During the late afternoon of 13 July, trucks carrying the 2,000 British paratroopers who would launch the assault began to arrive at their dusty airstrips in North Africa. The American aircrews who would transport them to Sicily allotted groups of men to the aircraft that would carry them. The Douglas C-47s had been in action many

---

1   Harpoon Force consisted of the 23rd Armoured Brigade, the 51st Highland Division and the 1st Canadian Division.

A view of Primosole Bridge and its surrounding area from the air. (Author's collection)

times in North Africa and showed the scars of battle on their fuselage; numerous flak holes had been patched up, black soot from explosions coloured the underside of their wings and the original paintwork was peeling. Laden down with equipment, weapons and rations, the paratroopers started to clamber aboard their transports. Many of these young men were inexperienced recruits, having just arrived to make good the losses of previous actions. This lack of experience would prove fatal for many. As the sun went down, the aircraft lumbered slowly forward and, one by one, took off and headed for Sicily.

Montgomery summoned General Sidney Kirkman, CO of the 50th Northumbrian Division, to attend a briefing on 13 July with Lieutenant General Dempsey, commander of XIII Corps. Kirkman was told that it would be his responsibility to ensure that the 50th Division got forward as speedily as possible, breaking through all German opposition so that the paratroopers at Primosole could be relieved on 14 July. This meant a fighting advance of over 30 miles, through territory that favoured the defenders, in less than 24 hours. At the same time, the 5th Division was to advance along the coastal strip from Augusta, to link up with the 50th at Carlentini and occupy the high ground to the west to prevent any enemy interference on the flanks.

The battalions of the 1st British Parachute Brigade were allotted individual tasks. The 3rd Battalion, under the command of Lieutenant Colonel E.C. Yeldham, was to land 1,000 yards north of the bridge, where the river ran to the sea, establish a bridgehead and counter any enemy moves from the direction of Catania. The 2nd Battalion, commanded by Lieutenant Colonel John Frost, was to capture the vital high ground south of the river, which consisted of three small hills, code named Johnny 1, Johnny 2 and Johnny 3. From these hills, all access to the bridge from the south could be controlled. The 1st Battalion, under Lieutenant Colonel Alastair Pearson, was to drop north and south of the river and seize the bridge itself.

German reinforcements arrive

As the British airborne troops made ready, the German High Command at last responded to calls to relieve the beleaguered Battle Group Schmalz holding the line in Sicily. Lieutenant General Richard Heidrich left his headquarters at Avignon in southern France and flew to Rome to meet with Field Marshal Kesselring, commander of all German troops in the Mediterranean, to be informed that his 1st *Fallschirmjäger* Division was soon to deploy to Sicily. The following day, Hermann Göring himself sent a message to Heidrich ordering the immediate dispatch of one parachute regiment to bolster the troops of the hard-pressed Herman Göring Division.

Lieutenant Colonel Ludwig Heilmann's 3rd Parachute Regiment was to be the advanced guard, followed by the division's machine-gun battalion and a signal company. These forces would shortly be joined by anti-tank units and finally by the 4th Parachute Regiment. These men were mostly veterans, having seen action in Poland, the Netherlands, Crete and Russia. They were young and tough, believing themselves to be the cream of the *Wehrmacht*, which they proved by their actions throughout the war.

Heilmann was contacted by telephone on 11 July by Heidrich, and was told his regiment would spearhead the drop into Sicily by the 1st *Fallschirmjäger* Division. He was ordered to personally reconnoitre the drop zone, as the German High Command had little idea of the true situation. Heilmann was to leave Avignon at 5:00 a.m. on 12 July and fly direct to Sicily. He took with him a small advanced party consisting of Captain Specht and Captain Strangenberg. As the plane carrying the German officers approached Catania, great black clouds of smoke from the combat below rose into the morning air. To prevent them from being spotted, the pilot flew at very low altitude in the hills around Mount Etna. Heilmann later recorded his thoughts:

> The pilot acted like an infantryman as he wove into Catania whose airport still had fresh smoking craters from the recent air attack. High above the airfield the RAF Spitfires circled as the pilot landed. His landing was a work of art, as was

his take-off. We saw for the first time the face of the hot ground of Sicily and felt more than before that we are actually only bits of dust on this earth.[2]

The transport that Heilmann's troops would need on their arrival was organised by Specht, while Heilmann and Strangenberg went south of Catania to reconnoitre a suitable drop zone. Allied air raids were constant in and around Catania, and on more than one occasion the officers had to take cover in the rocky landscape as Allied airmen marauded overhead. To the east of Highway 114, Heilmann selected some open ground for his regiment's drop zone. Unbeknown to him, this was very close to the area where Lieutenant Colonel Frost's British 2nd Parachute Battalion was to land. The coordinates of the selected drop zone were transmitted by Strangenberg to the German paratroopers of the advanced guard, and it was not long before they were on their way.

Lieutenant Martin Poppel of the 1st *Fallschirmjäger* Regiment watched the airfield at Avignon with interest as the air vibrated with the noise of dozens of engines, churning up the dust and blotting out the sun. One aircraft after another thundered up the cement runway and slowly rose into the clear blue sky:

> Then it's our turn, up into the morning air, past Vesuvius and out over the open sea. Our tired old crate hasn't been able to keep up and we are alone in the sky yet again. We pass the Straits of Messina and now there will be an increasing danger of British fighters. Tension mounts though many men still manage to fall asleep. The monotonous humming of the engines induces drowsiness but the danger of fighter attacks doesn't bother experienced men. We must be near our objective now because we can see three [Heinkel] He 111s from our wing, recognisable by their squadron markings and colours. Then Catania lies beneath us and we glide in to land at 8:14 a.m. on an excellent runway. There had been a raid just before we got there and two of our aircraft are ablaze on the airfield, our tired old crate brought us luck after all. We hadn't even stopped rolling when a lorry shoots out and orders us to be quick, [and] at top speed we fetch our heavy weapons containers, throw the rucksacks onto the lorry and unload the bags of supplies. Then off the airfield at top speed because of the fear of fresh air attacks.[3]

Heilmann's first impressions of his new posting were not encouraging. As soon as he landed, he had seen long streams of Italian soldiers fleeing towards Catania, and there was a noticeable lack of air cover on the island. He feared for his men as they flew in slow transports that would be easy targets for the Allied fighter-bombers. Fires were lit marking the drop zones, and by a great stroke of luck for the Germans the Allied airmen disappeared from the skies and an opportunity was lost. The 1,400 men of the

---

2   C. D'Este, *Bitter Victory, The Battle for Sicily 1943* (Glasgow: William Collins, 1988), p. 354.
3   M. Poppel, *Heaven and Hell: The War Diary of a German Paratrooper* (Kent: Spellmount, 1988), pp. 120–21.

Men of the 3rd German Parachute Battalion dropping onto their landing zones. (Author's collection)

3rd Battalion *Fallschirmjäger* Regiment dropped out of their Heinkel He 111 troop carriers unmolested, and within less than an hour had been picked up by the transport organised by Specht. Heilmann and his paratroopers were taken to the area north of Lentini, where they came under the command of Battle Group Schmalz, with the 2nd Battalion sent to Francoforte to help plug the gap between Schmalz's troops and the Hermann Göring Division defending Vizzini. The remainder of Heilmann's force took up defensive positions between Carlentini and the coast on 12 July.

Lieutenant Martin Poppel moved to his new positions and began to unload all the equipment they had brought, hiding the containers under trees and camouflaging them. The men made themselves at home and began to prepare for the fight ahead. As they did so, the Allies attacked the airfield at Catania where they had just landed. Poppel remembered:

> In the sky we see the first formation of four engine enemy bombers going over heading towards the airfield. I hope to God that the men over there see them in time and get under cover. Then the shock waves from the explosions reach us. Columns of smoke rise and spread out till they look like thick clouds and our thoughts are with our comrades who recently landed at the airfield. Soon

Hauptmann Laun arrives with others. Now for an assessment of our first casualties by going through the complement of each aircraft. Two aircraft are still
missing and we have had appalling casualties before the bloody operation has
even begun. All because they sent the formation off without a fighter escort,
what kind of people have we become?[4]

The next day, 13 July, saw the arrival of further German reinforcements. Members
of the 1st *Fallschirmjäger* Machine-gun Battalion air landed at Catania airfield in the
middle of another Allied raid and were ordered to move to a position 2,000 metres
south of Primosole Bridge. When they arrived at their new positions, they immediately dug-in on the edge of an orange grove to the west of Highway 114, which gave
them concealment from air observation. Captain Laun reported to Heilmann near
Carlentini that his troops were ready and dug-in. Heilmann told him:

> Something is bound to happen tonight: the enemy will try to sneak through to
> the Catania Plain and to do so he will send in more troops by sea or air. If he
> manages to land them in our rear and dig-in, then we are cut off for sure. Your
> battalion will remain south of Catania. Hold the bridge [Primosole] over the
> Simeto and put one company between there and the sea.[5]

Lieutenant Poppel and his comrades settled down for the night and wondered what
the new day would bring:

> Night comes slowly into the valley, our first night in Sicily and a beautiful
> one. The moon shines brightly through the olive trees and makes us dream.
> Dreaming of love at home and the happy hours we spent there. Our first night
> here and I wonder how many more will we watch through, how many sacrifices
> and how much anxiety, how much blood will be spilled here. Our guns are lying
> at hand, uniform complete. The sentries have been posted on elevated ground. I
> dream and doze the time away.[6]

A clash between the German and British airborne troops at Primosole Bridge was
now inevitable. Battle Group Schmalz had been given some extra muscle and would
make good use of these fresh elite fighters to slow down XIII Corps as it drove for
Lentini and the Plain of Catania.

On 13 July, the British 5th Division thrust towards Lentini ran straight into the
115th *Panzer* Regiment and two fresh battalions of German paratroopers. The 15th
Brigade was stalled all that day as they battled their way forward.

4   Ibid., pp. 121–122.
5   C. D'Este, *Bitter Victory, The Battle for Sicily 1943* (Glasgow: William Collins, 1988), p. 356.
6   M. Poppel, *Heaven and Hell, the War Diary of a German Paratrooper* (Kent: Spellmount,
     1988), p. 122.

Troops of the Green Howards pass through a Sicilian village. (Courtesy of J. Verity)

With Montgomery's audacious plan running into trouble he turned up the heat on General Kirkman, who drove up to his leading troops of the 50th Northumbrian Division to urge them on. He found them brewing up after a hard battle the night before. Kirkman told Brigadier Edward Cunliffe Cooke-Collis, the 69th Brigade commander:

> You are not going to sit down and rest, you go on now until you drop if necessary and occupy the ground you will have to fight for tomorrow. Get them all on the move, now is the time to go on.[7]

3 Commando at the Malati Bridge

On the morning of 13 July, Montgomery summoned the commanding officer of 3 Commando, Lieutenant Colonel John Durnford-Slater, from his base ship the *Prince Albert* to a meeting in Syracuse. In attendance at the meeting was the commander of XIII Corps, Major General Dempsey, and the commander of Naval Force B, Admiral Rhoderick McGrigor. Dempsey explained the situation and Durnford-Slater has left the following account:

7   E.W. Clay, *The Path of the 50th* (Aldershot: Gale and Polden, 1950), p. 181.

On 13th July I received a signal to go at once to Syracuse to meet Monty, General Dempsey, and Admiral McGrigor, to plan another operation. I had barely time to warn my men when I was whisked away on a fast motor launch, [and] as we left a Messerschmitt dive-bombed a tanker a few hundred yards away. The tanker went up with a roar, flames reaching several hundred feet in the air. The meeting took place on the quay at Syracuse, it was very hot and most of the buildings had been bombed. The battle was going favourably and the three senior officers present were in high spirits and Dempsey did most of the talking saying 'We've got a new operation for you tonight, it's an ambitious one but I think you'll like it'. Before I left Monty had the last word: 'Everybody is on the move now and the enemy is nicely on the move, we want to keep him that way and you can help us to do it. Good luck Slater'. I hurried back to the *Prince Albert* and we sailed at once.[8]

Captain Peter Young, serving with 4 Troop, 3 Commando, remembers the moment when Durnford-Slater returned to brief his men:

It was late in the afternoon when John returned to the *Prince Albert*. He arrived in the wardroom rather breathless with a roll of maps under his arm, summoned all officers and announced that we were going to do an operation that same night. This caused some consternation and I felt quite sorry for the troop commanders who were not go going to have much chance of briefing their men and little enough time to complete their administrative arrangements.[9]

This action would turn out to be one of the most perilous operations undertaken by 3 Commando during the whole Sicilian campaign. The hot-tempered Durnford-Slater accepted his task calmly but knew that his troops were tired out by other recent operations undertaken during and after the landings. The news that the Malati Bridge was only held by Italians was taken with a pinch of salt by this battle-wise old soldier, and he thought caution was needed here as he had an instinct for danger. The Malati Bridge crossed the only road linking the German and Italian forces with their bases in the Messina area, and it was likely that the Germans would make sure it was securely held. Montgomery wished the CO of 3 Commando luck as he left the meeting, but Dempsey was not so optimistic as he knew the 50th Northumbrian Division was having a hard time getting forward against strong enemy forces; he told Durnford-Slater that if the troops of the 50th Division had not reached the Malati Bridge by daybreak on 14 July, he was to move his men to the rear and hide up for the day.

No air reconnaissance photographs of the target area were available, and even if they had there would not have been enough time to study them in any depth. Durnford-Slater, who had only three hours to make plans for his attack, decided it

8   *3 Commando at Malati Bridge* <www.3commandoattheMalatiBridge.org> (accessed 15 December 2019).
9   P. Young, *Storm from the Sea* (Staffordshire: Wren's Park Publishing, 2002), pp. 88–89.

would be launched in two phases. The first would be to land and secure the beach, upon which other troops would pass through them and head for the Malati Bridge. After the bridge was taken, two patrols would be sent out: one would try to link up with the British paratroopers at Primosole Bridge to the north while the other moved south to meet the advanced troops of the 50th Division. The men of 3 Commando were quickly given their orders and prepared as best they could in the time left to them. All unnecessary equipment was discarded, including helmets – berets were preferred – and they would go into action carrying only their weapons, ammunition and iron rations. This operation was to be run on a shoestring and its success depended on the speedy advance of the 50th Division linking up with them before they ran out of ammunition.

At 7:00 p.m. on 13 July, the *Prince Albert* raised anchor and set sail. It was still light when a sleek grey shape was seen to be cutting through the water at high speed, heading for the *Prince Albert*. As soon as it was identified as a German E-Boat, the alarm was raised. Machine guns started to fire in its direction, sending a storm of tracer hurtling at the German torpedo boat as it weaved from side to side to avoid being hit. Two torpedoes were fired by the German vessel, their progress visible by the trail of bubbles they left in their wake. The *Prince Albert* turned to port and the first torpedo slid past, missing its mark. The helmsman then turned sharply in the other direction and the steel plates of the ship groaned under the strain. The second torpedo passed under the ship's hull without causing any damage. The skipper of the E-Boat then swung his craft round and headed for home at high speed before the British fighter-bombers could make an appearance. The crew of the *Prince Albert* and the commandos could relax for the moment.

The men of 3 Commando lined the rails watching the drama that was unfolding as the great ship approached the coast, with tracer rounds and very lights soaring into the night sky above Catania. Allied bombers were making another attack on Catania airfield, and flak shells could be seen exploding around them. The land mass to their immediate front, however, was in total darkness, with no sign of life visible. As the waiting commandos strained their eyes trying to see into the gloom, two planes came from behind them trailing smoke and fire as they crashed into the sea. The roar of other aircraft engines grew louder, followed by the eerie swishing of gliders being towed inland. The commandos looked up to see an airborne fleet passing overhead as the British 1st Airborne Brigade made their way to their drop zone at Primosole Bridge. But the men of 3 Commando now had their own worries as the moment of truth approached. A loudspeaker barked out orders, summoning the men to their various stations. They were going in.

The Bay of Agnone

On the evening of 13 July, 3 Commando were to be put ashore behind enemy lines in the Bay of Agnone. Once ashore, they were to make a forced march of 5 miles to the Malati Bridge and take it intact. This crucially important bridge spanned the River Leonardo 2 1/2 miles north of Lentini and was an important linchpin in Montgomery's strategy. The bridge carried about 300 yards of Highway 114, the main artery joining Lentini and Catania, the only direct road to Catania and Primosole Bridge that the 50th Northumbrian Division had to travel along. The first commandos landed at 10:00 p.m., led by Lieutenant Colonel Durnford-Slater.

Captain Peter Young looked inland as his craft headed for the shore, escorted closely by the destroyer HMS *Tetcott*. There was a great deal of activity in the vicinity of Catania, which was under constant bombardment from both sea and air. Explosions lit up the coastline momentarily, enabling the men to get their bearings. Over Syracuse, the night sky was illuminated with coloured tracer and exploding flak shells. As the landing-craft approached the coast, C-47 Dakota aircraft towing gliders passed overhead. About 100 yards from the beach, Italian machine gunners opened up on the small craft, but the *Tetcott* returned fire at once to silence the coastal defences. Meanwhile, tracer rounds from the commandos raked the pillboxes on the beach.

Durnford-Slater approached the beach in his landing-craft:

> Before we hit the beach a concentrated cross-fire was opened up on us from several pill-boxes. We returned the fire heavily but surprisingly the enemy continued his machine-gun attack, unlike the wilting fire during the earlier landing. The whole place was lit up with tracer bullets which passed angrily in the air from both directions. A sailor was shooting from just behind me so that the muzzle of his weapon was only a few inches from my head. Holt shouted, 'Don't shoot the Colonel's bloody head off!' I found it all most exhilarating, there was a bright moon and we could see men running about on the beach. Johnny Dowling was standing beside me firing magazine after magazine from the Vickers K gun. Streams of tracer were flying in all directions and the noise was too great for me to make myself heard, so I was slapping Johnny's face to indicate to him which way to switch his fire. We continued in good formation and hit the beach.[10]

Peter Young's landing-craft hit the beach and the ramps went down:

> The Colonel with the flotilla officer, Lt Holt, was in the fourth craft from the right and I was in the right-hand craft at least two lengths behind him, so he touched down first as was his custom. The ramps went down and there was a momentary lull in the enemy fire as we ran across the sandy beach not fifty yards wide. Lt Charley Head, in the left-hand craft, got ashore to find himself looking at an Italian machine-gun. He began to pull out his pistol, found it took too long, ran up to the emplacement and kicked the gun over to the astonishment of the crew who promptly surrendered.[11]

---

10   J. Durnford-Slater, *Commando, Memoir of a Fighting Commando in World War Two* (London: William Kimber, 1953), p. 140.
11   P. Young, *Storm from the Sea* (Staffordshire: Wren's Park Publishing, 2002), p. 90.

Once all the men were ashore, Lieutenant George Holt's flotilla headed back to the *Prince Albert* for the second wave of commandos, while the first wave struggled to get off the beach. Durnford-Slater passed through the wire on the beach and received a novel message from the advanced troop:

> Some men from 3 Troop brought me back a prisoner to view. 'Lieutenant Herbert has sent back this prisoner for you sir' a lance-corporal told me very correctly. I looked at the prisoner, he was in a German uniform. This was George's effective way of telling me there were Germans about. It also explained why the opposition on landing had been so stiff.[12]

Captain Young ordered his men to take cover while the wire defences were blown by Bangalore torpedoes. Grenades exploded continuously as fire from both sides created confu-

Lieutenant Charles Head, MC, 3 Commando. (Courtesy of M. Denney)

sion, forcing another troop to edge towards Young's position. Cursing and bawling, Young restored some sense of order when a voice from his left called out that a gap in the wire had been found. The Bangalore torpedoes were abandoned as the men followed Young's lead and filed through the gap. Italian grenades fell all around the commandos, causing many casualties, but they pressed on inland along the track. Italian prisoners were coming the other way, heading for the beach. Firing broke out ahead of the commandos when suddenly an enemy motorcycle and sidecar, with a mounted machine gun, appeared. Private Cox hurled a grenade at it and finished off the crew.

Lieutenant John Erskine of 3 Commando remembered the opposition that met them as they landed on the beach:

> The beach seemed to stretch for miles away to the right in the moonlight and it was surprisingly narrow with thick barbed wire lining the inland edge of

---

12   J. Durnford-Slater, *Commando: Memoir of a Fighting Commando in World War Two* (London: William Kimber, 1953), p. 141.

it. We had Bangalore Torpedoes with us to blow gaps in the wire. The boats moved us in slowly in the moonlight. Enemy fire bounced harmlessly off our armour plates as we crouched at each side of our landing craft. Three spare light machine-guns [Lewis guns of First World War vintage] were being aimed with full magazines from each of our eight boats [by our expert marksmen] and opened fire straight into the Italian pill-box loop holes. The slow firing Italian machine-guns were no match for our Lewis gunners and the enemy fire was stopped except for one gun. I was as usual carrying one end of a roll of wire netting to throw over the barbed wire as I was first out of the boat. My troop led the advance and after a few moments [of] confusion the whole commando was held up under the wire. One of my men pointed out a narrow gap just to our left alongside a pill-box just below a bit of cliff. I rushed through the gap with my section right behind me and with little Italian red devil grenades thrown from the cliff above bursting all around. Having run unscathed through the gap in the wire I was just about to run around behind the pill-box to deal with the enemy when my sergeant grabbed my shirt and pulled me to a halt as he threw one of our very effective '36' ['Mills bomb'] grenades behind the pill-box. After a very satisfactory explosion he pointed to one German and one Italian, both dead. He said smugly 'That's the way we do it in the commando, sir'. He was a fine young soldier and he saved my life, then we ran on into the night.[13]

The commandos came under fire from the railway line, and after a brief firefight the Italian defenders melted away into the night. Beyond the railway line could be heard the lilting tones of a hunting horn belonging to Captain Lincoln Leese[14] as his men outflanked the Italians. The troops surged forward and followed the general line of the railway. Captain Young reached Agnone railway station and found four Italian prisoners sat with a wounded British officer. Young saw it was Captain Leese, who said to him, "I can't see, I'm sorry but I've lost an eye. It was a grenade and my sergeant major [CSM Wareing] is dead."[15] Once past the railway station, the advance gained momentum, the men not now diving into ditches every time a shot was fired at them. Any houses passed were searched with great caution to make sure they were empty of any hostiles, and shortly a tunnel over the railway line was reached. At this point, Durnford-Slater took the opportunity to enquire about casualties and to confer with his troop commanders. The countryside was a tangle of massed undergrowth, 8ft-high reeds, walls, rocks and marshes. For the next five hours, the commandos fought their way forward over a rugged landscape. Durnford-Slater described the terrain:

13   *Commando Veterans* <www.commandoveterans.org> (accessed 20 December 2018).
14   Captain Lincoln Leese, Gloucestershire Regiment, attached to 3 Commando, lost an eye during the advance to the Malati Bridge and was killed in action on 5 October 1943. He is buried in the Sangro River War Cemetery, Italy.
15   Company Sergeant Major Nicholas Wareing, Royal Artillery, attached to 3 Commando, was killed during the advance to the Malati Bridge on 14 July 1943. He is buried in Catania War Cemetery, Sicily.

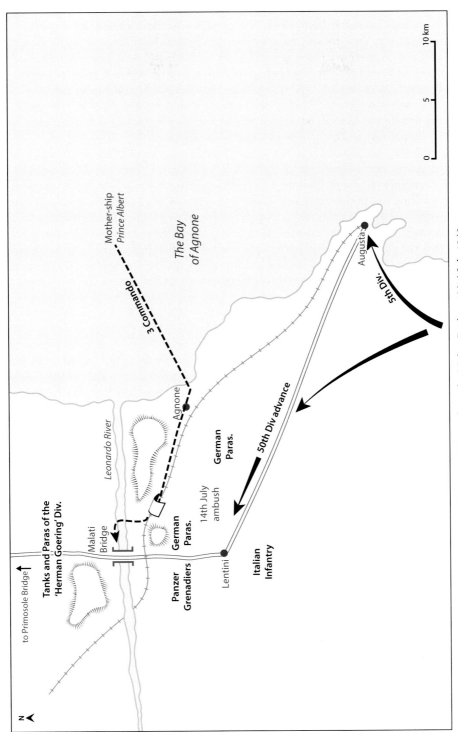

N

to Primosole Bridge

Tanks and Paras of the 'Herman Goering' Div.

Malati Bridge

Leonardo River

Panzer Grenadiers   **German Paras.**

14th July ambush

German Paras.

Lentini

Italian Infantry

Agnone

3 Commando

The Bay of Agnone

50th Div advance

5th Div.

Augusta

Mother-ship *Prince Albert*

0   5   10 km

3 Commando's attack on the Malati Bridge, 13/14 July 1943.

> We found ourselves in rocky low hills covered in bramble thickets and low stone walls. It was very difficult country even for commandos. Once through the village of Agnone we had a series of violent little battles and had to advance continually against machine-gun posts. In one foray George Herbert was knocked unconscious by an exploding grenade and was bleeding from one ear. 'How are you George?' I asked anxiously. 'Getting weaker' he said. George thought he was done for but fortunately he just had a temporary concussion. In ten-minutes he was on his feet and leading the advance.[16]

As the action petered out, the night became quiet apart from the drone of many aircraft engines overhead. Looking up, Durnford-Slater and his men saw white parachutes falling out of the night sky. These were some of the British paratroopers who were supposed to land at Primosole Bridge but had been dropped too soon. A corporal was brought before Durnford-Slater and told that his destination was a long way off, and that the paratroopers had better stick with the commandos. The young corporal thanked him for the offer but said he had his orders, and he and his men disappeared into the night as they headed for their objective many miles distant.

The Bridge

After numerous firefights, the Malati Bridge was finally in sight, and some of the commandos of 4 Troop crossed the Leonardo about a mile from the bridge, waist-deep in water. Durnford-Slater planned to cross the Leonardo River and surprise the defenders by attacking from the northern end of the bridge. The terrain on the northern side was a jungle of reeds that the commandos had to pass through before they came to a valley and a road that led to the bridge's northern end. The approach track was easy going, and before long the bridge could be seen, glowing white in the bright moonlight. Durnford-Slater commented on the scene before him as he walked towards the bridge: "The night was still, as it would have been in the heart of Cornwall."

Peter Young led his party to a hedge to the right of the approach road and saw an orchard just beyond it. The leading section of 4 Troop passed him and he advanced into the orchard, where he came face-to-face with a solid-looking pillbox:

> Everybody stopped and looked at it, whilst on all sides people began giving orders and calling for grenades. I had no grenades but seeing that there was no wire round the pill-box I ran up to the middle loophole and fired my rifle through it two or three times. Inside an Italian began shouting, evidently in a state of wild alarm, [and] almost at once he ran out into the road. Brian Butler, advancing at the head of his section, threw a Mills bomb at him and killed him. Craft came running up and gave me two grenades. There were more explosions

---

16   *Commando Veterans* <www.commandoveterans.org> (accessed 20 December 2018).

and then Brian Butler of Lloyd's troop dashed past shouting 'With me movement group!'[17]

About 30 yards past this pillbox, another concrete emplacement in the shape of an arrow head was spotted. The commandos ran to it but found it unoccupied.

Just before midnight, the commandos formed up near the bridge. Captain Lloyd of 4 Troop made sure his men were in position and, accompanied by Lieutenant Colonel Durnford-Slater, led the attack on the four pillboxes at the northern end of the bridge. Lloyd rushed forward at the head of his men, hurling grenades into the pillbox apertures and firing automatic weapons through the slits after the grenades exploded. Those who tried to escape were shot down, and within 10 minutes – by 3:00 a.m. – the commandos had overcome the troops defending the northern end and occupied the pillboxes. The commandos then removed most of the demolition charges from the structure. The ground around the bridge was like rock, making it impossible to dig proper defensive positions, so the men made the most of the cover provided by the concrete constructions made by the Italian engineers. The commandos now found themselves 10 miles in front of the advancing Eighth Army, straddling the only line of communication open to the German and Italian forces in the area.

After the whole position had been overrun, Durnford-Slater situated his troops in positions best placed to defend the bridge against the expected Axis counterattack. He later stated:

> Captain Lloyd[18] and 4 Troop occupied the road junction, George Herbert and 3 Troop were posted to secure the bridge and Veasey and 1 Troop covered the Catania Road. German troops and vehicles were parked in an orchard not far from the bridge and a party of commandos was sent under the bridge to secure the south west end. 3 Troop got half way over the river when they came under fire from German Paras lining the far bank who began to fire down on them. 3 Troop held out for an hour and were then ordered to withdraw at 04:00 a.m. Before they did so they managed to dismantle some of the demolition charges.[19]

Second flight: 5 and 6 Troops arrive

Back on board the *Prince Albert*, the men of 5 and 6 Troops were straining at the leash to get into the fight with their comrades. As they stood on deck, ready to go, they could make out the dim shapes of Lieutenant Holt's flotilla that was returning loaded up with wounded. It was now 1:00 a.m., and as the small craft came alongside, the

17   P. Young, *Storm from the Sea* (Nottinghamshire: Wren's Park Publishing, 2002), p. 98.
18   Captain William Eric Lloyd, Royal Berkshire Regiment, attached to 3 Commando, was killed in action attacking a machine-gun post during the attack on the Malati Bridge, 14 July 1943, aged 29. He is buried in Syracuse War Cemetery, Sicily.
19   *Commando Veterans* <www.commandoveterans.org> (accessed 23 December 2018).

air was heavily laden with the smell of cordite. They brought with them the news that the opposition the first wave had met was heavier than expected. The landing-craft were hauled out of the sea on the davits up to the deck, and the wounded were taken to the sickbay. The men of 5 and 6 Troops then embarked and slowly made their way to the beach. When they were several hundred yards from their landing point, the supporting HMS *Tetcott* opened fire on the cliff top with smoke shells, setting the dry vegetation ablaze. By now the enemy had been reinforced, and an anti-tank gun and numerous automatic weapons opened fire on the commandos. Luckily for them, the landing-craft had such a low silhouette that this fire did little serious damage. As the commandos looked back, they saw the looming shape of the *Tetcott* alongside and expected it to run aground as it was so far in to the shore, but at the last moment the ship pulled back out to sea. Most of the craft landed safely, but that commanded by Lieutenant Anthony Butler got stuck on some rocks and could not be extricated.

The craft which made it to shore dropped their ramps and the troops rushed out, machine-gun bullets splashing around them as they left the water. Those in the stranded craft jumped into deep water under heavy fire; of the 28 men, only nine made it through the defences. Others, cut off in small parties, scaled the cliff, capturing many prisoners and weapons. Once the second wave was ashore, Lieutenant Holt's craft and their brave crews pulled away for a second time, struggling through the heavy rolling sea under fire. However, when they thought they were far enough away to be safe, the courageous Holt was hit in the neck and mortally wounded.[20]

Lieutenant Donald Hopson and his men had been given the task of defending the gap in the wire on the beach and to signal to the second wave as it landed where to head for. This Hopson did, even though his small force had enemy troops on three sides. The defending Italians had now been reinforced by German troops, and on top of this Hopson had in his charge 30 Italian prisoners and a number of wounded commandos. The whole beach was still under fire when 6 Troop landed on the right, with grenades thudding into the soft sand. The beach was an unhealthy place to stay for long, so 5 and 6 Troops moved through the wire, formed up in column and advanced to the railway line. As the men advanced along the embankment, an Italian soldier sitting in a tree challenged the commandos and hurled a grenade at them. This elicited a burst of automatic fire, and the Italian's body crashed to the ground. This alerted the Germans in positions very close to the railway line, and as their commands were barked out, machine-gun fire began to rake the rails. The commandos returned fire and moved away into the night to their objective. The second wave found the railway tunnel and struck off along the route the first flight had used to get to the Malati Bridge. Lieutenan John Pooley, OC of the second wave, found Durnford-Slater and reported the arrival of 5 and 6 Troops.

---

20 Lieutenant George Wilfred Holt, DSC, Royal Naval Volunteer Reserve, was mortally wounded on 14 July 1943 during the action at Agnone, Sicily. He died of his wounds on 9 September 1943, aged 31, and is buried in Alexandria (Hadra) War Cemetery, Egypt.

Hold the bridge

Lieutenant Colonel Durnford-Slater was anticipating the arrival of numerous prisoners and needed a suitable place to keep them. Lieutenant Charles Head was given the task of finding a practical position where they could be kept and guarded. As the first Italian prisoners arrived, one of them was hysterical, his screaming and bawling giving away the commandos' position. "Knock him out," shouted Durnford-Slater and Lieutenant King silenced him with a swift uppercut. At this point, Durnford-Slater decided to snatch 40 winks, using his haversack as a pillow:

> I woke up very shortly to a loud explosion that was very close. 'What's that?' I asked Charlie. He said calmly 'a mortar bomb', 'don't be silly we haven't brought a mortar' I said. 'No but they have' he replied and for the next few hours they literally showered us with mortar bombs, inflicting many casualties. By the time John Pooley had arrived with the second flight the casualties were mounting. We had about 15 killed and wounded. The trouble was we didn't have enough cover as the pill-boxes could only take about a dozen men and now our strength was 350 officers and men.[21]

Lieutenant John Erskine of 3 Troop moved with his men onto the southern end of the captured bridge and was surprised to discover how close he was to the German paratroopers who were well dug-in on the far side of the river:

> I occupied a pill-box and placed two men in sniping positions nestled into the inner side of the south bank of the river, as well as a Bren-gunner lying on the parapet of the bridge. My senior sergeant quickly rearranged some of the positions as the Bren gunner was ridiculously exposed. I could see the quick movement of enemy German soldiers or paratroopers that were very close indeed. My 12 men were the only ones at the south end of the bridge, the rest were busily digging-in around the other end. There were in fact enemy soldiers, at least a hundred, dug into the area beyond the south end of the bridge, no doubt surprised to have us come at them from the wrong direction. Some of the enemy were within five metres of us just over the other bank but across the roadway. I scrambled across the shallow river and found the 2i/c [Peter Young] and told him my situation and that there seemed to be a good few Germans on the other side. He sent me back to expect an immediate counter-attack. We could also hear tanks clattering up the road [from the south] from the direction of Lentini.[22]

21   J. Durnford-Slater, *Commando: Memoirs of a Fighting Commando in World War Two* (London: William Kimber, 1953), p. 145.
22   *Commando Veterans* <www.commandoveterans.org> (accessed 20 December 2018).

After the confusion of the night, dawn broke and the commandos were shooting up any enemy who came into range, causing great confusion in their ranks. The main problem now was to hold the bridge until the 50th Northumbrian Division arrived, as Highway 114 was as important to the enemy as it was to the British. It was the main Axis supply route to all its units fighting to the south of Lentini, as well as their route of escape to the north.

A short lull in the fighting followed. Weary commandos fell asleep where they had slumped on the ground, only to be awoken by the sound of a tracked vehicle approaching the bridge. In the half-light of dawn, Captain Peter Young heard the rumble of a heavy vehicle slowly approaching from the south. On it came, the suspense of knowing it could be a tank stretching the men's nerves to breaking point. As the vehicle tried to cross the bridge, it was seen to be an ammunition truck towing a large trailer. The men manning the PIAT anti-tank guns at the northern end of the bridge held their fire. Young described what happened next:

> At last with a roar one of the Piat men struck the enemy vehicle amidships which blew up and went on exploding for many minutes. Thousands of rounds of ammunition went flying in all directions to the discomfort of friend and foe. Things now began to happen with bewildering speed.[23]

Tigers!

Durnford-Slater was made aware of the presence of a Tiger tank at 5:00 a.m. on 14 July, but said he could do little to counter its massive firepower with his lightly armed force:

> Pooley's men had no sooner joined us than someone shouted they could see a tank, [and] Corporal Pantall, looking through a hedge, could see a large German Tiger facing us no more than 200 yards away. Almost immediately it opened fire with its heavy machine-gun and began spraying the corner of the field 5 Troop were in. There was no cover and in open formation they dashed for a wall at the roadside. In doing so many were killed and some, like Tony Butler,[24] were killed outright. Some took cover behind a large stone pill-box but it received a direct hit and crumbled like a pack of cards causing many casualties.[25]

The Germans and Italians put down a storm of mortar, rifle and machine-gun fire on the beleaguered commandos. As the Tiger tank approached the bridge, it pounded away with its 88mm gun, causing casualties to mount among the commandos at

---

23 P. Young, *Storm from the Sea* (Nottinghamshire: Wren's Park Publishing, 2002), p. 98.
24 Lieutenant Anthony Danvers Butler, Royal Armoured Corps, attached to 3 Commando, was killed in action on 14 July 1943, aged 27. He is buried in Catania War Cemetery, Sicily.
25 *Commando Veterans* <www.commandoveterans.org> (accessed 23 December 2018).

German paratroopers use the terrain to stealthily work their way towards the Malati Bridge.
(Author's collection)

an alarming rate. It was by then obvious that the commandos were facing German paratroopers as well as Italian troops. Durnford-Slater recalled the accurate 88mm fire from the Tiger:

> I was conferring with Charlie Head in an olive grove when a large branch above me was sliced clean off by an 88 shell and fell on top of me. A minute later another shell parted my hair. All this time there had been a flow of enemy traffic from Messina. As the lorries came, we shot them up. I had stationed a troop a hundred yards up the road to deal with such matters and now the noise was heightened by the bursting ammunition in these burning lorries.[26]

Lieutenant Erskine sat with his men of 3 Troop amid a perfect storm of fire, watching as the German paratroopers skilfully manoeuvred to gain the most advantageous position for the coming counter-attack:

26   J. Durnford-Slater, *Commando: Memoirs of a Fighting Commando in World War Two* (London: William Kimber, 1953), p. 144.

A lorry came up the road from the direction of Lentini and for some reason the German paratroopers let it come on. My Bren-gunner could have destroyed it but there seemed to be no purpose in giving his position away. It trundled past me and almost got to the north end of the bridge before one of our people hit it with a Piat bomb and the whole works exploded. Live shells and burning explosives of all sorts showered the area for perhaps ten minutes. At that moment a Tiger tank arrived from up the road and started machine-gunning the general area and firing at the pill-boxes with its main gun. German soldiers could also be seen moving a few yards then going to ground, all the time steadily encircling us. I saw one little group, carrying between them a heavy machine-gun, get up from only 20 yards away on my right, dash five yards and then hide, then get up again and again go into cover. They were obviously going into a flanking attack manoeuvre but got into dead ground to give covering fire when their main body charged. Even today after 36 years I still often wake up at night seeing those machine-gunners.[27]

Durnford-Slater became very angry as he watched his men taking casualty after casualty and joined in the killing match to take his revenge on the enemy. As he approached one lorry that had been hit, a huge German came towards him. Durnford-Slater's luck held, as Lieutenant George Herbert was on hand to dispatch the German with a burst from his automatic weapon. Herbert told Durnford-Slater in no uncertain terms to move back from the main action and continue to organise the commandos.

Yet another German ammunition lorry arrived from the south and tried to cross the bridge amid the chaos and exploding ordnance. Lieutenant Cave, a recent new arrival with the commandos, was manning a PIAT anti-tank gun when the lorry moved across his front, giving him a close and clear target. He fired his PIAT at point-blank range and the vehicle disintegrated in a fireball with an enormous roar, killing all on board along with Lieutenant Cave, who was too close to escape the blast.[28] Casualties were mounting quickly as the German paratroopers became ever bolder. Major Butler had both ankles broken by an exploding grenade and was escorted from the battlefield by two men who had found a bicycle with which to carry him. Sergeant Frederick Hopkins, MM, fought on courageously until two fingers were shot off his right hand; he walked to the rear saying, "That's the lot, I'm finished with shooting." What he didn't realise was that he had two severe wounds in his chest. He died later that day.[29]

Durnford-Slater, understanding that something must be done about the Tiger tank if the position was to be maintained, called over Lieutenant John Pooley. He

---

27   *Commando Veterans* <www.commandoveterans.org> (accessed 20 December 2018).

28   Lieutenant George Charles Montague Cave, Devonshire Regiment, attached to 3 Commando, was killed in action on the Malati Bridge on 14 July 1943. He is buried in Catania War Cemetery.

29   Sergeant Frederick Walter Hopkins, MM, Bedfordshire and Hertfordshire Regiment, attached to 3 Commando, died of his wounds on 14 July 1943, aged 27. He is buried in Syracuse War Cemetery, Sicily.

Men of the 50th Northumbrian Division doggedly fight their way forward to get to the commandos at the Malati Bridge. (Courtesy of J. Verity)

pointed out a house a short distance in front of his position and told him to get his troop into it and try to shoot up the tank with his PIAT. As the two men talked, mortar bombs were falling all around. Pooley left with his men in extended line, the colonel watching them go:

> The tank opened up with its machine-gun and I was horrified to see the entire line fall together and then breathed again when they picked themselves up. A moment later they were in the house and, using it for cover, they fired at it with everything at their disposal, but unfortunately the Piat was beyond its effective range.[30]

The 50th Northumbrian Division, which was meant to have relieved the commandos at dawn on 14 July, was still battling its way forward against the determined opposition of Battle Group Schmalz and Heilmann's paratroopers. After holding the bridge for the best part of the day, and in the face of constant attacks, the commandos who survived were not enough to hold their position. They were forced to fight their way out to avoid capture or death and make for friendly lines.

---

30   J. Durnford-Slater, *Commando: Memoir of a Fighting Commando in World War Two* (London: William Kimber, 1953), p. 145.

Head for the hills

On the morning of 14 July, Lieutenant Erskine realised he was fighting a losing battle and had received no orders as to what to do next. The bridge and surrounding area were being shelled heavily, and the German paratroopers kept up a steady stream of small-arms fire upon the defenders:

> It was now daylight and the commando sat in a totally untenable position. There were now three Tiger tanks in sight and it was obvious we had to withdraw if we could. A group of mortar bombs fell on the bridge every half minute or so. The tanks kept up a constant machine-gun and heavy gun fire, the enemy was softening us up, trying to shock us so we would surrender in the attack we knew was coming. No messages reached me and we were totally exposed on the south side of the river. My senior sergeant suggested that the lack of action from our people must mean the commando was withdrawing. I told the men that we would cross the river bed, climb the far bank and then run straight up the road into the smoke of the bursting mortar bombs. As we ran a bomb picked up the sergeant and threw him forward and although slightly wounded, he got up and ran on to safety. I fell onto the road in full view of the tank which sent a burst of machine-gun fire that tore my haversack to pieces as I lay face down on the road. As soon as more mortar bombs fell and the smoke and dust rolled over me, I got up and ran on.[31]

Durnford-Slater realised that 50th Division was not going to get to the Malati Bridge in time to relieve the commandos. Consequently, he decided that the surviving troops should split up into small groups, lie up during daylight hours and make for their own lines when darkness fell. The seriously wounded who could not be moved would be hidden and made as comfortable as possible before being left. Both officers and men felt bad about leaving them, but there was no other choice. Durnford-Slater, moving off with one party, noticed to their front some olive groves that would give them total concealment until nightfall. To get to this cover, the group would have to move over an open ploughed field. As they did so, men were spotted moving about on the far side. Lieutenant Herbert said they were Germans but was overruled by Durnford-Slater, who claimed they were British. As they approached the middle of the open field, they came under heavy and accurate fire. Durnford-Slater yelled "you're right" and started running:

> The ground was dry and every bullet kicked up a little cloud of dust, but we kept on going and finally got out of the field and behind the crest of a small hill. Just then we saw more men ahead of us. George [Herbert] said 'Now we've had it, don't be a bloody fool any more John, let's pack it in.' But this time I was right,

---

31   *Commando Veterans* <www.commandoveterans.org> (accessed 20 November 2018).

they turned out to be John Pooley and a party from his troop. We all got into a very deep ditch and lay down, resigning ourselves to wait until dark.[32]

The remaining troops moved to the rear under constant fire. Captain Ruxton was wounded and sent to one of the leading sections. Captain Young led his men across the open field in extended order, and later described their steady progress under fire looking as if the men were "moving steadily as if on parade". He reached the colonel in the grove and was filled in regarding the present dire situation. Lieutenant Charles Head had been brought this far, though wounded, by Sergeant Darts, who carried him on his shoulders. Four men were detailed to carry Head on a gate, using it as a stretcher. It was very heavy, so a number of civilians were rounded up; they were reluctant to lend a hand, so Cummings gave one of them a heavy punch and fired his pistol over their heads to encourage them. A relatively new officer reprimanded him, telling him that they would get into trouble from the Germans if they helped. The only reply he got was, "That won't break my heart." The rumble of a tank could be heard in the distance, and Peter Young and his men prepared a welcoming party for it. However, the tank failed to make an appearance and the troops continued on their way. Young joined the colonel on a ridge; he was now with a group of men hiding behind rocks and facing the bridge in a line. The whole area was being shelled and mortared, and swept by machine-gun fire. It was hard to spot the mortar positions that were tormenting them, but in the bare landscape a small farmstead could be seen and it seemed possible that this was the location of the enemy mortar crew. Young put a few shots into the farmhouse and the firing stopped:

> Still this exploit didn't improve matters much. There was still an 88 firing at us and from time to time machine-gun fire swept the ridge. I had hoped that when we were reorganised, we would advance and attack the bridge from both sides, but with tanks about that would have been an invite to destruction in such open country. In the hills we would be comparatively safe from the *panzer* troops. John [Durnford-Slater] therefore decided that our best course was to split up into small bands and make our way across country to Augusta. Calling the troop commanders together he gave out his orders speaking quietly and quickly as he always did. 'It's obvious that 50 Div can't reach us so there's nothing more for us here, lie up where you can during the day and make your way back to our lines tonight.'[33]

Unknown to the retreating commandos, the hills they were to make for held another menace: the German paratroopers of the 3rd Battalion of the *Fallschirmjäger* Regiment who had landed on 13 July. The last to leave were 6 Troop, having been given orders to cover the withdrawal. Parties retreated in good order, with many within sight of

32   J. Durnford-Slater, *Commando: Memoirs of a Fighting Commando in World War Two* (London: William Kimber, 1953), p. 147.
33   P. Young, *Storm from the Sea* (Nottinghamshire: Wren's Park Publishing, 2002), p. 102.

other groups as they moved up the mountain. These men had been fighting continuously for hours, and many now felt tired and in need of rest and sustenance. In the distance, large shells could be seen exploding on a high ridge near Lentini. This was the artillery and naval barrage that accompanied the attack by troops of 69th Brigade as they fought furiously to take Mount Pancali in order to get to the Malati Bridge.

Durnford-Slater waited for nightfall before continuing on his 10-mile hike to safety. At the Agnone–Lentini road, enemy troops were encountered; as the commandos fled, bursts of machine-gun fire followed them on their way. They were lucky and took no casualties. Durnford-Slater continued:

> The rest of the way was plain walking and plenty of it. Finally, we reached an Eighth Army anti-aircraft position. The last thing I remember before falling asleep was George Herbert draping a borrowed great coat over me.[34]

'I need more men'

Peter Young looked around and wished he had a few more men with him to return to the bridge area and shoot up any soft-skinned vehicles that came along. He found another group of commandos consisting of John Budd, the signals officer who was wounded in the leg, Ned Moore, the medical officer, and Lieutenant Clive Collins with 10 other men. This group of weary and ragged men set off downhill through trees in the direction of the bridge, then moved through orange groves and along the valley of the Leonardo River. The few oranges they picked from the trees had been left by the locals and were shrivelled and in poor condition, but it was better than nothing. In the heat of the day, they pushed on to the main road. Observing it from an embankment, they saw a sight that lifted their spirits, as Young subsequently recounted:

> There were troops moving north [along the road] and armour manoeuvring along a hillside farther west. We felt pretty certain that the Eighth Army had arrived and at this moment a soldier ran up and reported that a party of the Northumberland Hussars had contacted us, [so] I went to meet them. They were very friendly and said they would provide rations. A liaison officer came up and promised to send ambulances. We spent the night in a house called Sanciolo, about a quarter of a mile from the bridge which was still intact.[35]

Lieutenant Erskine met up with others from 3 Commando, and as they headed for the safety of the British lines they had to move through enemy-held territory. At one point they captured 20 Italians and considered killing them as they could not keep prisoners in their situation. After much discussion, they simply told the prisoners

---

34 J. Durnford-Slater, *Commando: Memoirs of a Fighting Commando in World War Two* (London: William Kimber, 1953), p. 148.
35 P. Young, *Storm from the Sea* (Nottinghamshire: Wren's Park Publishing, 2002), p. 105.

to clear off and let them go. They then pressed on, hoping to find the elusive 50th Division, but as they did so were themselves taken prisoner by German paratroopers. The *Fallschirmjäger* were under orders from Hitler to execute all captured commandos on the spot, and for a while it looked as though that was their fate. However, the German paratroop officers were not at all keen to carry out such a task and told their prisoners to leave, saving their lives too. By now the Germans were under fire from the lead elements of the 50th Division as they neared the Malati Bridge. Erskine and his little group waved a white flag and were rescued by men of the 5th Battalion East Yorkshire Regiment, 69th Brigade, 50th Division.

A Forlorn Hope

Up to 30 men never received Lieutenant Colonel Durnford-Slater's orders to make for Augusta, instead heading for the place they had landed, Agnone beach, in the hope that the landing-craft were still there. Moving back the way they had come, using the railway line for direction, they picked up other men on the way until the group numbered about 40. As they neared the beach, they came under mortar and machine-gun fire from high ground to the south. The whole group split up, and in the confused fighting, Trooper Thomas Jennings, MM, headed back inland and hid under cactus bushes with a comrade that evening to evade the enemy:

> Lots of ditches and odd noises so we took it steady, [and] later we opened up our emergency rations without permission of an officer and ate well. Next morning while hiding under a bridge we heard footsteps. We looked out and saw three Germans so we got back under cover.[36]

Other men got nearer to the beach and attacked the Italian positions they encountered. Troop Sergeant Major Ernest George White, DCM, and his men captured an Italian headquarters:

> This was a very heavily defended building held by a dozen or so people. There were machine-guns everywhere and lots of grenades. Best of all there were some clean clothes, Italian KD [khaki drill] uniforms.[37]

Captain Ruxton withdrew with his group in the direction of the beach. They advanced in extended order towards a dry valley, but before they could reach it, they came under accurate enemy fire from the front and both flanks. The commandos went to ground and began to return fire. Ruxton ordered his men to give him covering fire as he leapt forward, followed by others. They were met by heavy machine-gun fire, Ruxton falling to the ground after being hit numerous times. Outgunned and outnumbered,

36   Manuscript forwarded to author, T. Jennings, 1989.
37   Correspondence with author, E. White, 1991.

the commandos had no choice but to surrender. German paratroopers moved in and disarmed their prisoners. The wounded were taken to a cave to be treated, while Ruxton was given medical help by a German doctor but later died of his wounds.[38] His men buried him there. Many men escaped their captors, some being killed as they tried to flee; Lieutenant Pienaar[39] was hit as he attempted to get away.

Eventually the Germans pulled back as the Eighth Army approached, leaving the wounded to be attended to by the British. The commandos who had escaped capture could hear the roar of vehicles close by, accompanied by the sounds of marching boots. As one group looked in the direction of all the noise coming towards them, an English voice was heard to say, "I'm fucking browned off with all this." It was only then that they knew all was well; it was some infantry of the York and Lancaster Regiment complaining as they advanced. Ambulances arrived from 151st Brigade, picking up the wounded where they found them, the other commandos guiding them to wounded comrades who were glad to see friendly faces.

The troops 3 Commando had been facing were three battalions of the Hermann Göring Division's Koerner *Panzer* Grenadier Regiment, an Italian Tactical Group under the command of Colonel Tropea and a combined force of German and Italian tanks. These units had fought bravely and with tenacity. At first sight, it might be thought that the commando operation at the bridge was a failure, especially considering the heavy casualties taken by 3 Commando: 153 killed, wounded and missing. But what they did achieve was vital, as by their skill and daring, the commandos ensured that the German and Italian forces in the area did not destroy the Malati Bridge, keeping the route open for the Eighth Army to continue its advance up the coastal road to Catania. The attack caused much confusion in the enemy rear, forcing them to divert resources of men and materiel to the coastal area. Montgomery recognised the commandos' achievement and had a stone plaque carved which renamed the bridge 'No. 3 Commando Bridge' in their honour. After the battle, he commented to Durnford-Slater, "That was a classic operation, I want you to get the best stonemason in the town and have him engrave 'No 3 Commando Bridge' on a good piece of stone. Have this stone built into the masonry of the bridge." Durnford-Slater commented, "I was only too delighted to obey Monty's order."

69th Brigade reaches the Malati Bridge

At 5:00 p.m. on 14 July, the lead elements of the 50th Northumbrian Division, the 5th Battalion East Yorkshire Regiment, reached the bridge at Malati and took it intact. In their haste to retreat, the Germans had not had time to destroy the structure.

---

38 Captain Anthony Fane Ruxton, MC, 2nd Battalion Royal Ulster Rifles, attached to 3 Commando, was hit leading an attack on an enemy position on the retreat from the Malati Bridge. He died of wounds on 14 July 1943 and is buried in Syracuse War Cemetery, Sicily.

39 Lieutenant W.F. Pienaar, General Service Corps, South African Forces, attached to 3 Commando, was killed in action during the retreat from the Malati Bridge on 14 July 1943, aged 21. He is buried in Syracuse War Cemetery, Sicily.

Private Norman Hardy, of the 5th East Yorkshires, recalled the hard march to get there and the sight that greeted their eyes:

> We were forever on the move in this horrible heat. Water was in short supply as the follow-up units got left behind in the fighting, [and] we were having a right do to make headway. We were all grousing but I suppose it had to be done, there was no option. What a state my mates looked in, covered in dust and muck with their clothes torn, [but I] suppose I looked just as bad. We met some commandos who had a hell of a time holding this bridge we were heading for, but when the forward company got there the enemy had gone. The bridge had taken a hell of a battering. Dead commandos and Germans lay about the ground in all kinds of positions. Patrols were then sent out and other companies came forward to join us.[40]

Sergeant Max Hearst, also serving with the 5th East Yorkshires, trudged on through the heat and dust with his men. Short of water, sleep and food, they concentrated on putting one foot in front of the other to get to their objective:

On their advance to the Malati Bridge, troops of 69th Brigade pass through a ruined Sicilian village. The enemy dead scattered around the street bear witness to the severity of the fighting here. (Courtesy of *The War Illustrated*, December 1943)

40   Interview with author, Norman Hardy, 1991.

We had to fight like hell to get forward to the Malati Bridge to relieve the commandos. We could hear the action being fought there during the morning but couldn't get to the poor sods. When we did get there, Fritz began to withdraw to the other side of the river as they saw our columns approaching. The surviving commandos were in a terrible state; the dead were laying all over the place and they all looked so young. We went over the bridge and prepared for the expected counter-attack which thank God never came. I was with a strong defensive platoon and we stayed here all night as vehicles and tanks poured into our bridgehead. We were all exhausted and when we were relieved, we slept like the dead.[41]

41   Interview with author, Max Hearst, 1990.

4

1st Parachute Brigade enters the fight, 13-14 July

At this point, the 151st Brigade took the place of the exhausted 69th Brigade as the troops leading the advance of the 50th Northumbrian Division. On the night of 13 July, the 1st Parachute Brigade, consisting of 145 aircraft packed with troops – 126 towing Horsa[1] and Waco gliders carrying anti-tank guns and artillery – was flying towards Primosole Bridge and the Plain of Catania. The drop was to commence at 10:00 p.m., with the gliders landing at 1:00 a.m. the following morning. As the aerial convoy moved en masse 5 miles from the coastline, they were fired on by their own ships lying off Malta and the Sicilian coast. Heavy enemy flak added to their problems and dispersed the convoy in great confusion; 11 planes were shot down and three others were lost in the sea, while 26 never dropped their loads, returning fully loaded to their North African base. Only 30 craft deposited their troops on the correct drop zone, nine dropped them just outside the target, but 48 were wide of the mark by anything up to 20 miles. Out of the 1,856 men who set out on what was christened Operation *Fustian*, only 295 landed close to or on Primosole Bridge.

As Squadron Leader Peter Davis piloted his Albemarle, towing a Horsa glider, flak burst around him. He said the battle was in full swing over the drop zone:

> I've never seen such a sight: fires, flares, flak of all sorts and searchlights. [It] only needed Mount Etna to blow off now to make the scene complete. We escaped with a lot of loud bangs and one hole under the wing. I do not like being fired at on tow.[2]

Private Thomas E. Davies of the 1st Parachute Brigade looked out of the small windows of the Dakota aircraft he was in to see heavy concentrations of flak around them:

---

1   Horsa: Airspeed AS 51 troop-carrying glider.
2   Correspondence with author, Peter Davis, 1990.

Night falls as British paratroopers drop into the battle zone. (Author's collection)

The plane bucked and rocked drunkenly and red-hot sparks flew past the portholes. Every rivet of the machine screamed in protest, then with a terrific lurch we plunged recklessly seaward. The frightening roar of the engines drowned our cries of 'Get off my bloody legs' as we were thrown on top of each other into an untidy heap at the front of the aircraft. Panic set in fast as we tried to untangle ourselves in order to make for the door, the angle of the plane making it virtually impossible. The engine noise now rose to a crescendo and we caught a quick flash of the mountainous waves of the angry sea below. Then by some Herculean effort and the grace of God, the pilot had the plane righted again and flying on an even keel. With great relief we were able to struggle back to our feet once more, adjusting our loads for action stations and taking up our positions ready for jumping. However, not much time had elapsed before word was passed around that we were on our way back to our base in North Africa and would not be dropping in Sicily after all. Frustration and a sense of helplessness hung over us like a blanket. Hardly anyone spoke. Every glance was expressive and full of significance.[3]

Private Frederick Moore of the 1st Parachute Battalion recalled flying over the Mediterranean and crossing the Sicilian coast:

3   Conversation with author, T.E. Davies, 1990.

We were fired on by our own invasion fleet and the pilot took evasive action as we neared the coast. Then to counter an attack by a German plane he again took violent evasive action, pitching us forward to the floor of the aircraft, an ominous sign. As we crossed the coast, we stood up and hooked up our static lines. I was jumping number two after the 2nd Lt and so had a perfect view through the doorway. Although it was well after 10:00 p.m. and would normally be dark, the landscape seemed ablaze with what seemed like burning undergrowth and haystacks. I could clearly hear the noise of anti-aircraft fire above the roar of the engines.[4]

Major G.H. Seal, of the 21st Independent Parachute Company, the Pathfinders who went in just ahead of the main force, reflected on his departure:

Private Thomas E. Davies of the 1st Parachute Brigade. (Courtesy of M. Denney)

The operation was suspended for some reason for 24 hours. But on a beautiful clear evening of 13th July we re-assembled. The CO 1st Parachute Battalion, Alistair Pearson, was wearing no badges of rank, a plain khaki shirt and dirty plimsolls. We then knew the job was on. At about 8:30 p.m. we took off from Tunisia and had a quiet flight, though it seemed much longer than a direct route would have taken. Light flak was fairly regular and I remember reflecting briefly that it wasn't a bad firework display. Our American pilot was flying very low, in fact standing in the doorway I was disconcerted that I was able, in the gloom, to discern quite easily the individual branches of the trees.[5]

Private W.J. Collins was in a Horsa glider being towed to Sicily when his craft came under intense and accurate fire from land and sea and was forced to crash land into the water quite a way from the shore. He recalled:

4   Correspondence with author, F. Moore, 1991.
5   S.W.C. Pack, *Operation Husky* (London: David and Charles, 1977), p. 139.

As we hit the water I was forced through the top of the glider and as I reached back inside, I caught hold of Pte Arkwright and pulled him out onto the wing, then a couple more as others were emerging. It was not long before the glider started to break up and the only thing keeping the wrecked parts from drifting away was the wire attached to them all. In the dark, searchlights from the shore were sweeping the water and when a crashed glider was spotted, we could hear the machine-gun fire on the unfortunate lads in the water. We were too far away to be spotted. I lay on the wing with the other lads and held on as best I could as I had no lifebelt, nor could I swim.[6]

Lieutenant Colonel John Frost, CO of the 2nd Battalion Parachute Regiment, had a less eventful flight to the island:

At the expected time we turned westward toward Sicily and headed to what was obviously a fully alerted defence. From the door and the windows of the aircraft we could see streams of tracer moving upwards. A number of fires were burning on the ground and smoke was rising from several other places. I could glimpse the mouth of the river and the high ground to the south of it. Our aircraft flew steadily on. The gum chewing crew chief ordered us to our various states of readiness and the aircraft throttled back to the recognised best parachute speed. Despite all the distractions from the ground we were all duly dispatched to our duties down below.[7]

Brigadier Gerald Lathbury, C/O of the 1st Parachute Brigade, was only half an hour from his departure from his RAF Albemarle. He and his men were sorting themselves out and getting hooked up ready for the off. The area around the exit door was cleared and the nervous men took up their positions. Lathbury took his place at the exit and looked down at the sea:

As I gazed down, I could see the sea in the moonlight. The red light went on with two minutes to go and still no land. Then I saw the waves breaking on the shore and a moment later caught a glimpse of the river. My eyes were rivetted on the red light. The flak had begun and the aeroplane was very unsteady. One burst lit up the inside of the fuselage and we could distinctly smell the fumes. After what seemed an eternity the light turned green and I tumbled forward through the hole.[8]

Lieutenant Colonel Pearson, commanding the 1st Battalion Parachute Regiment, flew over Mount Etna in his Dakota when he realised that he was miles from his drop zone and the pilot was heading back where they had come from. He struggled out of

---

6   Correspondence with author, W.J. Collins, 1991.
7   J. Frost, *A Drop Too Many* (London: Cassel, 1980), p. 178.
8   H. Pond, *Sicily* (London: William Kimber, 1962), p. 120.

his parachute harness so he could get to the cockpit to see what was happening. One of his paratroopers had been an RAF officer, and as he passed him Pearson said, "Can you fly one of these things?" The paratrooper replied that he could. When he got to the cabin, the co-pilot was crying with his hands over his face, saying, "We can't, we can't go in there." Pearson understood at once what was going through the minds of the crew:

> Then all of a sudden there was the clatter of machine-gun fire and I could see all these ships below belching fire at us. I could see clearly blobs of fire on the ground and thought they were burning Dakotas, [and] what was going through the crew's minds was going through mine as well. I said to the pilot 'There's nothing for it boy, we've got to do it, if your co-pilots no good I've no hesitation in shooting him.' I pulled out my revolver and the pilot continued his protests, so I said, 'I could shoot you as well.' He said, 'You can't do that, who'd fly the plane?' I said, 'Don't worry about that, I've a bloke in the back who can fly this.' 'Yeah but he won't know how to land it.' 'No one asked him how to land the bloody thing, you don't think he's going to hang about to land it do you? He'll be stepping out very sharp.' He decided very reluctantly to go in and I got back in my parachute harness.[9]

Private Joseph Smith, who served with the 21st Independent Parachute Company, watched Lieutenant Colonel Pearson go to the front of the plane but had no idea why he had done so:

> I was jumping number six or eight with a bloody great kitbag of lights and batteries and Colonel Pearson was a couple of places behind me. The comic-opera of the Yank's flight discipline doesn't now bear recall. Alastair P did unhook at one point when we were overdue, went forward, came back and hooked up again. On the next run in we did get the red and the green [lights], the latter coming miles too early. The stick had to be held back by 1 Para's IO [Intelligence Officer], who was jumping number one, until we were over the road. There was no attempt to throttle back and on exit my kitbag was literally torn from my leg.[10]

Corporal Stanley Brown, also with the 21st Independent Parachute Company, was the first ready to jump. As he stood in the doorway waiting for the order to go, he had a grandstand view of the leading aircraft formations as they crossed the Sicilian coastline:

> As we approached the island, we were met with what appeared to me to be a solid wall of anti-aircraft fire. Tracer formed the most remarkable display of fireworks

9   M. Arthur, *Forgotten Voices of the Second World War* (London: Ebury Press, 2005), pp. 230-31.
10   Correspondence with author, J. Smith, 1989.

I have ever seen. It seemed to me to be quite impossible to pass through it unscathed. The pilot must have had similar thoughts because we did a violent bank and headed towards the sea. This performance was repeated many times over the next hour. I could hear the rattling of shrapnel on the fuselage and the stick behind me were being thrown all over the place.[11]

The Commander of the 21st Independent Parachute Company, Major John Lander, was in a glider that was shot down by enemy fire, plummeting to earth and killing all on board.[12]

As the paratroopers of the 21st Independent Parachute Company fell to earth, the scene that greeted them was akin to Dante's *Inferno*. Private Robert Smith recalls how he hung in the air and viewed the terrifying scene below:

Fires were burning to the four points of the compass and I could see the bridge shining in the light of the moon. Machine-gun and small-arms fire intensified as I approached mother earth and then I was on the ground, hugging it grimly in a depression that was not nearly deep enough. As I lay on the ground a plane was hit in the under belly and I saw a pin-point of flame then almost simultaneously she exploded.[13]

Lance Corporal Albert Osborne, of the 1st Parachute Battalion, fell out of his plane into a scene of utter chaos. However, his chute opened and he headed for the drop zone:

We were all keyed up for a hot reception from enemy flak as we reached the coast of Sicily. We got one alright and more than we were expecting, there was flashes from all over the place, it was terrifying. Our aircraft was hit in the port engine, it choked up and stopped. From then on, the aircraft was bumping, swaying, diving and climbing to dodge the flak. We were tossed from one side of the plane to the other. We scrambled to the door as best we could and looked down on fires everywhere. Then came the red light [action stations] then the green light and out we went. It was just like jumping into an inferno, the countryside for miles around was ablaze and tracer bullets were coming up at us from enemy machine-guns on the ground. On landing I went to find the anti-tank weapons-container, [but] its parachute had failed to open making all the weapons in it unserviceable. We found another container that contained weapons and headed off towards our objective.[14]

11   Correspondence with author, S. Brown, 1990.
12   Major John Lander, Commander 21st Independent Company, Parachute Regiment, Army Air Corps, was killed in action on 13 July 1943, aged 47. He is buried in Catania War Cemetery.
13   Correspondence with author, Robert Smith, 1989.
14   *Pegasus Archive* <www.pegasusarchive.org> (accessed 16 September 2016).

Brigadier Lathbury recalled falling to earth from what seemed to be a very short drop:

> There was the accustomed rush of air, followed by a sharp jerk and then the impression of stillness. I hardly had time to realise what had happened when I hit a piece of soft plough [earth]. It was obvious we had been dropped much too low, in fact the pilot had turned due south from the river and dropped us on high ground overlooking the Catania Plain and some three miles from the right place. His reading of 500 feet on the altimeter represented just 200 feet above this high ground. It was only just high enough but I could not have cared less at the time.[15]

Lieutenant Peter Stainforth, with the 1st Parachute Squadron, Royal Engineers, hit the ground hard, with blazing reeds and grasses all around him:

> As I floated down the whole dropping zone seemed to be on fire, [as] tracer bullets had set the tinder dry stubble alight. There was no time to get my bearings before I landed with a heck of a thwack on my back in a deep ditch. I felt something warm trickling down my leg, [and] I thought 'Oh my God I've been hit!' I pulled my hand away and found it to be water, [as] my water bottle had burst and was crushed flat. When I got my breath back, I picked myself up and set about gathering the rest of my chaps and finding our weapon containers. Fortunately, we were all complete, but two of our weapon containers [were] missing.[16]

Sergeant H. 'Cab' Callaway, attached to the 3rd Parachute Battalion, was dropped in the wrong location some distance from Primosole Bridge and in enemy-held territory:

> Our plane was caught in searchlights and there was very heavy anti-aircraft fire. As we jumped tracer bullets came up at us from all directions. On reaching the ground it was obvious that we had been dropped on the wrong DZ [drop-zone] and were in the middle of a well defended enemy location. I made my way to where the containers should have been and I picked up my NCOs on the way. We crossed the river and on the other side I made contact with seven other paratroopers from the 3rd Battalion. There was no sign of Lt Mansfield or the section sergeant. Fires were burning all around us and machine-gun and rifle fire was coming at us from all sides.[17]

Callaway and his small group set off to find other men of their unit. Having no idea of their location, they stopped in a shell-hole to get their bearings and to take cover from the fire that was flying all around them:

---

15   H. Pond, *Sicily* (London: William Kimber, 1962), p. 120.
16   M. Arthur, *Men of the Red Beret* (London: Hutchinson, 1990), pp. 84–85.
17   Manuscript forwarded to author, Brian Cook of Carnegie Heritage Centre, Hull, 2017.

We looked up and saw a Dakota caught in heavy anti-aircraft fire which burst into flames and lost height rapidly. Two parachutes opened and seemed to come down with the plane. We continued to make our way across country when we came to another large shell-hole, we had no sooner taken cover in it when we saw a plane and glider crash in the distance. I asked for three volunteers for a patrol to get the lay of the land and also to do anything possible for the occupants of the plane and glider that crashed. The patrol consisted of L/Cpls Buttery and Watson and Pte Easton. I told them that the rest of us would remain in our present position until the moon went down. Later we heard shooting coming from the direction the patrol had taken and after waiting until the agreed time we changed our position and headed for the river.[18]

Lieutenant Anthony Mutrie Frank, MC, of the 2nd Parachute Battalion, hit the drop zone 20 minutes ahead of schedule, but could only find five of his men in the area, as he later recounted:

After waiting approximately thirty minutes by the container that held the spare arms we came under fire from a building, so I decided to move off with what men I had to try and neutralise them. We got to within thirty yards of the machine-gun position and silenced it with Bren and Sten gun fire. We were then held up by more machine-gun fire. Germans came out of the farm buildings and an exchange of grenades and automatic fire took place, at the end of which the enemy withdrew back into the farm houses. During the engagement my number two on the Bren was wounded in the leg.[19]

Lieutenant Colonel Frost, of the 2nd Parachute Battalion, landed heavily in a ditch quite close to his pre-arranged position and was in sight of the 'Johnny' features (hills). However, many officers could not be found and the whereabouts of the other companies was unknown, as he recalled:

Most of the fires we had seen from the air were stooks of corn burning and not crashed aircraft as we had feared. However, the streams of tracer were there and enemy weapons of various calibres were being fired at all approaching aircraft. Enemy artillery was firing air-bursts in our general direction. When I tried to say something important to my entourage my words were blotted out by a peremptory crack from above."[20]

Only a handful of Frost's headquarters had arrived, and it became obvious that all was not well with the battalion. Dakotas continued to fly over the area at varying heights, but none of them were in formation. Gliders came in almost silently; some

18   Ibid., 2016.
19   *Pegasus Archive* <www.pegasusarchive.org> (accessed 2 April 2020).
20   J. Frost, *A Drop Too Many* (London: Cassel, 1980), p. 178.

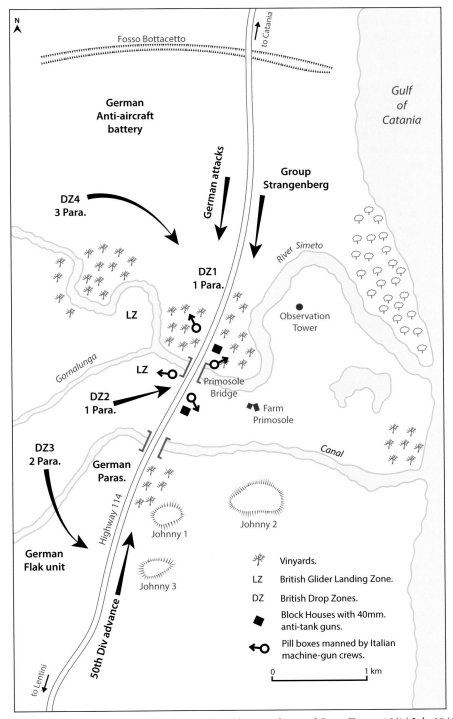

The British 1st Parachute Brigade at Primosole Bridge. Landing and Drop Zones, 13/14 July 1943.

were caught in the beams of searchlights and riddled with flak and machine-gun fire. As the numbers of aircraft coming over gradually petered out, Frost moved off with about 100 men towards his objective:

> By this time my knee was really painful, but I was able to pole myself along quite well. We passed brigade headquarters on the way. I remembered it was Brigadier Lathbury's birthday and I wished him many happy returns. On the way I met Mervyn Dennison with a small party from the 3rd Battalion, who was vigorously destroying all the telephone lines he could find near the main road.[21]

As the bell rang alerting them to be ready for their jump, Lieutenant Colonel Pearson stood up in the Dakota with his men from the 1st Parachute Battalion. As he did so, he thought the approach was being made very fast, as well as downhill:

> Out I went over the DZ and I didn't think my chute had opened, because I was down on the deck as soon as I jumped. I'd gone out number 10 and my knees hurt but I was alright. My batman at number 11 was alright but the remainder of the stick suffered serious injuries or were killed. I was very angry. We got to our RV [rendezvous] and soon discovered the burning Dakotas were no more than haystacks alight. With only about 200 men, including a couple of platoons from 3 Para, I formed a defensive position around the approaches to the bridge.[22]

Fires illuminated the area as the paratroopers tried to gather their senses and bearings. Artillery and flak fire were constant as small groups assembled and made for their respective objectives, and Primosole Bridge was duly captured in the early hours of 14 July. The Italian force defending the bridge fled in panic when a glider collided with one end of the structure. As dawn broke, other British paratroopers arrived at the bridge and engineers dismantled the explosive charges strapped to the steel girders. Alistair Pearson organised the defence of the now-secured objective with 120 men of his own 1st Battalion, two platoons of the 3rd Battalion and three anti-tank guns. The weapons left in the area by the Italians and Germans were collected and employed by the paratroopers to make up for their own losses.

Private Bob Priestley, of the 2nd Parachute Battalion, had landed some distance away from his objective, the hill named Johnny 1, and found himself in close proximity to the German defenders:

> We flew in at almost sea level until the approach then went up to about 500 feet. Equipped with all our gear we thought this is a pantomime, [and] it was. All hell broke loose, ships and artillery opened up and we all stepped out of the planes. [It was] one hell of a drop. What a job it was sorting things out, [as] we

---

21   Ibid., p. 179.
22   M. Arthur, *Forgotten Voices of the Second World War* (London: Ebury Press, 2005), p. 231.

shouted for our comrades and [were] answered in German, and this went on for some time. Eventually we got more or less organised and set off for our objective, Johnny 1, named after our colonel John Frost.[23]

Once on the ground, Brigadier Lathbury began searching for the rest of his stick, but there was no immediate sign of them. A lorry rumbled past on a road a few hundred yards away, and large fires were burning to the north. Realising it would have been fatal to linger, he took a compass bearing and set out in the direction of the fires with his batman, Private Lake. They passed through the rocky agricultural countryside, avoiding places of habitation. Lathbury then found a parachute container and armed himself with a rifle and ammunition:

> It was now about midnight and only a few stragglers amongst the aircraft were still coming in. One Horsa glider came over our heads at about 100 feet. It was clearly visible in the light of the fires and every German machine-gun and light flak gun turned on it. We could see about five streams of tracer going through the fuselage, then it disappeared into the darkness and a moment later we heard it hit the ground with a crash. We found the dropping zone and were met by Major David Hunter and it was obvious things had gone wrong. Only a very small part of Brigade Headquarters had arrived and most of the wireless sets had gone astray, one having fallen in the river. There were no communications with any of the battalions and no one knew what had happened.[24]

Not all aircraft and paratroopers were lucky enough to make the landing unscathed. Many gliders were shot down before they could land, some riddled with flak and machine-gun fire veered wildly off course and others made rough landings only to be engulfed by fire as petrol tanks on the vehicles they carried burst into flame. Several gliders were released by their towing aircraft only to be blasted out of the sky as they passed over the battlefield. The large airborne fleet had now lost the element of surprise, and indeed had stirred up a veritable hornet's nest.

German paratroopers south of the bridge were digging in as they waited for their own reinforcements to arrive near the Johnny 2 position. They set up machine guns and posted sentries. The Germans were experienced and well trained, and now prepared for the fight ahead of them. Their weapons containers and other equipment were hidden under the cover of trees.

Lieutenant Martin Poppel[25] remembered:

23   Correspondence with author, Bob Priestley, 1994.
24   H. Pond, *Sicily* (London: William Kimber, 1962), p. 121.
25   Lieutenant M. Poppel served in Poland in 1939, Holland and Narvik in 1940, Crete in 1941, Russia from 1941–43, Sicily and southern Italy in 1943, Normandy in 1944 and Holland/Lower Rhine 1944–45. He was captured by the British 6th Airborne Division on the Rhine and was a prisoner of war until late 1945 when he returned home.

Everyone was encamped under olive trees, cleaning weapons and equipment, doing a fry up or just basking in the sun. The whole farmstead was now excellently camouflaged with no indication of any military presence. Once they had got themselves into defensive positions and checked their weapons, as per the *Fallschirmjäger* rule of 'my weapon first then myself', the men began to carry out their own personal admin such as cooking, eating, washing and sleeping. As the British liked to brew up their tea, the Germans liked to brew up coffee. Due to shortages of coffee back in Germany the men were issued with ersatz coffee, known to the men as nigger sweat, which was made from acorns. Accompanying the coffee would be a slice of old man or tinned meat. The men soon settled into their routine.[26]

Lieutenant Martin Poppel, 1st *Fallschirmjäger* Regiment. (Courtesy of A. Fairfax)

The German paratroopers on the ground expected their own reinforcements to be arriving. As Lieutenant Poppel looked at the aircraft roaring overhead, he initially believed they contained his compatriots:

> At 10:00 p.m. aircraft suddenly appear overhead and our own sentries are shouting 'German paratroopers!' We know that reinforcements should be landing or making a drop sometime. But shit, shit – when the signal flares light up the eerie darkness, we can see white parachutes. In an instant we realise what's going on, British airborne troops overhead.[27]

The local Sicilian population looked on with fear as the paratroopers floated to earth and the sounds and sights of battle assaulted their senses. Stella Drezet, a 10-year-old at the time and living in the small village of Puntalazzo near Catania, recalled:

---

26   M. Poppel, *Heaven and Hell: The War Diary of a German Paratrooper* (Kent: Spellmount, 1988) p. 127.

27   M. Poppel, *Heaven and Hell: The War Diary of a German Paratrooper* (Kent: Spellmount, 1988), p. 129.

I was too young to know what was happening but I remember one day there was an explosion and shrapnel landed close to me. My mother came out of the house and shouted for me to get inside and I remember an American plane flying over us. I recall the parachutists coming down, although they were too far away for me to see where they landed. We found this very frightening as we did not know what these soldiers would be like.[28]

Private Frederick Moore was nervous as he waited for the signal to jump with other men of the 1st Parachute Battalion:

First a red light came on, then a green one and then we were clear of the aircraft. Although we seemed to be descending quite rapidly and we seemed to be drifting apart. I hit the deck in regulation fashion but quite hard and as I looked up, I could see the tell-tale trail of tracer bullets curving upwards to the remainder of the stick who were still suspended in mid-air. As I gathered my parachute, I realised that two of my rigging lines had been severed, presumably by the self-same tracer bullets. Standing up I looked for my 2nd Lt, but in vain, I never saw him again. Together with the remainder of the platoon we set a course for our objective. On the way we encountered a number of Italian troops, some with suit-cases, all eager to surrender. Leaving them protesting bitterly we proceeded on our bearing with the sounds of battle growing ever more acute as we neared our objective.[29]

Major Nino Bolla, on the staff of the Italian 213th Coastal Division, was sent a message from the headquarters of the Italian Sixth Army that German paratroopers would be making a drop on the evening of 13 July, but before he could ask for confirmation the line went dead. Consequently, he could not be sure the signal was correct. He watched the Germans dropping on their landing zone and sent out patrols to make contact, but he soon heard the sound of hundreds of aircraft approaching from the sea and realised that this could not be a German force. As he went out into the night, he looked up:

In the starry sky the enemy planes flew low over the plain; the parachutists' drop followed a few seconds later. One had the impression of watching a dance of the goblins, first suspended in the air and then descending slowly and mysteriously to earth. Some of the gliders caught fire as soon as they touched the ground and the spectacle from my vantage point was tragic and beautiful. One heard the first pistol shot, then machine-gun fire, then the crash of hand grenades. The defence of Catania had begun.[30]

---

28   *Pegasus Archive* <www.pegasusarchive.org> (accessed 20 January 2019).
29   Ibid.
30   H. Pond, *Sicily* (London: William Kimber, 1962), pp. 123–24.

The British landing caused panic among the Italian defenders, with some units deserting. However, a hard core of Italian troops, led by good officers, remained in their positions. Primosole Bridge was defended by General Carlo Gotti's 213th Coastal Division, but few of them remained to fight. The defence system just south of Catania was commanded by Brigadier General Azzo Passalacqua, and during 13 July the remaining Italian formations were withdrawn to a line north of the Simeto, where they dug-in and prepared their positions. The few German parachutists who had dropped during the night of the 13th crossed the river the following day and dug-in alongside the Italians. The remainder were cut off for two days south of the Simeto.

Take the bridge!

Brigadier Lathbury, commanding the 1st Parachute Brigade, and his brigade major, David Hunter, gathered together as many paratroopers as they could find in the initial chaos. Figures were silhouetted against the distant glow of fires, and many groups of men could be seen amid the constant chatter of machine-gun fire. Slowly, Lathbury's group of about 40 men moved up a dry dyke within 500 yards of Primosole Bridge. A small patrol sent out to reconnoitre the bridge returned to report that there were about 40 paratroopers on the south bank of the Simeto, and Lathbury had no reason to believe that the bridge had been captured. Lathbury organised his men into attack formation:

> We set off down the river bank, [and] an officer, sent forward to see if the bridge was held, signalled back with a torch that it was. As we approached, we could see a crashed glider quite near the bridge and heard the sound of English voices. Thirty yards from the bridge a figure loomed up out of the gloom: he was a parachutist from the north side who said that the 1st Battalion had just captured it from the north bank. The next ten minutes will always remain confused in my mind. Somehow, I had got ahead of the rest of the party and was quite alone, except for David Hunter's batman. We climbed up the embankment and onto the road and began to walk across the bridge. Facing me was a lorry with an 88[mm] gun in tow. I assumed it had been captured, but a few seconds later several grenades were lobbed out and landed at our feet. Matters were soon under control and, after I had been patched up and restored with a large tot of whiskey, I found I could get about, if somewhat slowly. While all this was going on there were sounds of strife from the north end of the bridge, where a lorry full of Germans had been demolished with an anti-tank grenade. Incidentally it was my birthday, but I have had many better ones. My other two battalion commanders, Alastair Pearson and Yeldham, had now arrived but they could only muster about 120 men between them. The sappers had removed the demolition charges from the bridge and the defences were organised. It was beginning to get light and I expected the enemy to react at any time.[31]

31   Ibid., p. 123.

Lance Corporal Albert Osborne, who made his way to the bridge in the darkness with others from the 1st Parachute Battalion, recounted:

> We could still hear German voices quite near and bullets were flying around all over the place. We got 200 yards from the bridge when the attack started and we let fly with everything we had. A small tank followed by an armoured car and a truck came down the road, [but] it didn't take long to put them out of action, one of the lads fired an anti-tank gun at the tank and two bombs were thrown at the other two vehicles. This just smashed them to bits and killed all the occupants. The taking of the bridge only took 30 minutes but it was stiff fighting and there were some awful sights on the bridge.[32]

Frederick Moore was in one of the groups selected to attack the bridge, and went along an embankment with his comrades:

> We proceeded in single file, [when] suddenly a speeding vehicle passed us on the road above our ditch, almost before we had realised the threat to our plan. Following a loud explosion, the vehicle burst into flames accompanied by the screams of pain as the occupants perished. A little further along a figure, standing in the middle of the road above, proved to be an Italian soldier. He had been ignored by those in front of me as they passed him but my instinctive reaction was that it would be dangerous to leave him behind us as we advanced, so I climbed the embankment and motioned him to come with me. Without warning a grenade landed between us and exploded. My facial wounds were serious and the blood pouring from them saturated my smock. I was put to one side with wounded.[33]

Lieutenant Peter Stainforth set his group of engineers to work dismantling the demolition charges that had been set under the bridge:

> The Germans had put barbed-wire road blocks at both ends of the bridge, but opened them up to allow a truck towing a field gun to pass through just as our assault party charged in. In the firefight that followed Brigadier Lathbury was on the receiving end of a grenade and got several splinters in him. So, when I came up there was the Brigadier, trousers round his ankles, bent over having shell dressings applied to his backside. As mine was the only sapper section to arrive the Brigadier told me to get the demolition charges off the bridge as quickly as possible. The charges were obvious enough, but it was difficult to distinguish detonating cable from the masses of field telephone cables that they had laid. But it didn't matter, it all went the same way. We climbed up the girders at both ends and set about the cabling with machetes and chucked

---

32   *Pegasus Archive* <www.pegasusarchive.org> (accessed 16 September 2016).
33   Ibid. (accessed 20 January 2019).

the whole lot in the river, explosives and all. Then we examined the piers and found that they, like a lot of continental bridges of the time, had been built with chambers to take sacks of powder explosives. So, all we had to do was to pull out the sacks and dump them in the river as well, [and] within half an hour the job was done.[34]

"Fight the Barbarians"

By the early hours of 14 July, the British paratroopers were in possession of Primosole Bridge and hastily prepared a defensive perimeter manned by the remnants of 1st and 3rd Battalions. At 3:00 a.m., an enemy convoy led by a German armoured car towing a 75mm artillery piece made its way to the bridge from the south, totally unaware that the British were there. The paratroopers were on the alert and made ready to receive them. Slowly, the line of vehicles approached the bridge as the paras took aim upon their unsuspecting victims. The order was given to fire and a PIAT projectile smashed into the lead vehicle, which at once burst into flames, lighting up the night and blocking the road. This was immediately followed by a storm of fire that ripped through the soft-skinned vehicles, while grenades exploded around the column and machine guns burst into life with devastating effect. The rear vehicles of the convoy managed to turn off the road and head back the way they had come. When the firing stopped, the paratroopers unhitched the 75mm gun and pushed it to the northern end of the bridge, where it would be used when the enemy reinforcements arrived. The smell of burning fuel and rubber hung in the early morning air as the vehicles blazed and the men returned to their positions, not wanting to be lit up as targets for any lurking enemy snipers in the area.

Weapons on the Italian trucks were siezed by the paras, making up for their own losses during the drop. As the Italian convoy burned in the night, it provided a beacon for men scattered over the surrounding countryside to home in on. But it also highlighted the British positions to the watchful enemy, whose observers were constantly looking on as the scene unfolded. Lieutenant Colonel Frost sent a liaison officer to the bridge on a captured Italian motorcycle to report the situation on the 'Johnny' features to Brigadier Lathbury. He informed him that Johnny 1 was held by the 2nd Parachute Battalion, whose men were dug-in on the summit. Johnny 2 had been taken and then lost because of a lack of men. Lathbury now had a good idea of the overall situation and knew that all his objectives had been taken, but his forces were badly depleted and the enemy was growing in strength. As he marshalled his men, he must have had doubts as to whether they could hold out until the 50th Northumbrian Division reached them from the south.

---

34   M. Arthur, *The Men of the Red Beret* (London: Hutchinson, 1990), p. 85.

Lieutenant Anthony Mutrie Frank watched figures moving up a farm track towards the 2nd Parachute Battalion command post. It soon became apparent that they were Germans with British prisoners in tow:

> We let them cross the bridge and then shot up the guard, killing one and severely wounding the others. Other Germans were attracted by the noise and came down the track, [but] we opened fire on them when they reached the north side of the canal bank. They made a brisk reply as they took up positions on the bank. We engaged them with grenades and automatic fire for about ten minutes.[35]

The confusion of the night evaporated with the clear Sicilian dawn on 14 July. The struggle to hold the vital bridge would now begin in earnest. In the lull before the storm, both sides had prepared themselves for the coming battle, whose outcome would determine failure or success for Montgomery's attempt to seize Catania and bring the campaign to a swift end. The morning of 14 July began with still no sign of the 50th Division, whose lead elements continued to battle their way to the Plain of Catania. The troops of the division were exhausted, many suffering from chronic diarrhoea and short of water. The men advanced in a haze of white dust for mile after mile, with strained faces sweating under their steel helmets, looking for all the world like unearthly apparitions. With the heat rising to 35 degrees centigrade in the shade, the 50th Division pushed back stubborn German and Italian forces, who made a stand at every opportunity. The road leading to Primosole Bridge was littered with the graves of the Northumbrians, whose corpses were identified by the sign of the 'double T' on their shoulders.

Sgt 'Cab' Callaway and his men had still not found any other British paratroopers. When they got to a river, they took cover in the reed beds, where they rested up and hid throughout 14 July. All around them, Axis forces were on the move:

> One of the sentries pointed out to me a German patrol with two British airborne prisoners in tow. I also saw half-tracks carrying German infantry. Jerry tanks, probably Hermann Göring [Division] Mk IVs, were advancing east along the road approximately 200 yards to our front. Later that day we tried to make our way to the bridge which was our original objective but the enemy between us and the bridge was too strong.[36]

Lieutenant Colonel Frost, by now limping badly with the injury he had incurred as he fell to earth, sheltered with a small party in a dug-out on one of the 'Johnny' positions as the battle unfolded. By 5:30 a.m. on 14 July, 140 men of the 2nd Parachute Battalion were in position on Johnny 1, with no communications and no supporting

---

35   *Pegasus Archive* <www.pegasusarchive.org> (accessed 1 March 2020).
36   Manuscript forwarded to author, Brian Cook of Carnegie Heritage Centre, Hull, 2016.

weapons. At 6:00 a.m., the Germans made the first move, and machine-gun fire could be clearly heard from Johnny 2. Frost recalled:

> By 6:30 a.m. a mortar bombardment was added to the machine-gun fire and the battalion had nothing with which to reply effectively as the enemy fire became more and more accurate. Their mortar fire was all the more deadly on the rocky ground and the number of our casualties began to grow. The long dry grass to the south of the positions caught fire, [and] the smoke from this became an effective screen behind which the Germans were able to improve their positions and the intense heat from the flames forced our own forward elements back to a small and dangerously constricted perimeter. The [enemy] machine-guns firing from Johnny 2, the mortar bombardment, the smoke and flames made life for anyone lying in the open hazardous in the extreme. There had been no time to dig-in before the attack commenced and most of the men were lying behind and among rocks and stones. There was still no support of any kind available.[37]

In the early hours of 14 July, Frost's 2nd Parachute Battalion took the full weight of the German counter-attacks. The 1st *Fallschirmjäger* Machine-gun Battalion held positions between Johnny 2 and Johnny 3, preventing any British attempt to take the bridge by way of Highway 114. The British paratroopers holding Johnny 1 were subjected to intense heavy machine-gun and mortar fire, resulting in many casualties. The British had nothing with which to counter the German heavy weapons; all they could do was cower in the holes they had scraped into the sun-baked earth and take their punishment. Lieutenant Colonel Pearson heard the sound of firing from his rear and realised Frost's men were in trouble. The British were astonished

Lieutenant Colonel John Frost, 2nd Parachute Battalion. (Courtesy of V. Hollis)

by the presence of crack German troops attacking from the west, just south of the Simeto. The 'Green Devils' (German *Fallschirmjäger*) and 'Red Devils' (British paras) fought it out around Johnny 3, which eventually fell to the attacking Germans. From this strong observational position, they rained down a withering fire on the British. The war diary of Frost's 2nd Battalion stated:

---

37 J. Frost, *A Drop Too Many* (London: Cassel, 1980), p. 181.

Fallschirmjäger mortar teams poured a deadly hail of bombs onto the positions held by the British paratroopers around Primosole Bridge. (Author's collection)

08:00 a.m.: forward troops are withdrawing inside the perimeter. At this time, it was apparent that we were under machine-gun fire from three sides and the enemy were closing in on us, not in very great strength but with heavy fire power and considerable skill. A great deal of sniping had taken place on both sides.[38]

In bitter fighting, casualties began to mount on both sides. Blazing grasses to the south forced the British into an ever-shrinking perimeter, their ammunition was running low and it became increasingly obvious that any enemy co-ordinated attack could not be held off.

Frost had a Forward Observation Officer with him, Captain Francis Vere-Hodge, who was trying all morning to contact a cruiser lying off the coast, HMS *Newfoundland*.[39] Vere-Hodge's perseverance was rewarded when his radio finally came to life at 9:00 a.m. Frost recounted what happened next:

Almost immediately the high-velocity medicine began to arrive with a suddenness and efficiency that completely turned the scales. The principles of surprise, economy of effort, concentration of force and flexibility were amply demonstrated by one officer, a signaller and a wireless set. What had seemed like imminent defeat was staved off and from then on, the danger receded. Once

38   C. Whiting, *Slaughter over Sicily* (Barnsley: Pen & Sword, 1992), p. 135.
39   Captain Francis Vere-Hodge, MC, 2nd Battalion Parachute Regiment, entered the Church after the war and died on 15 December 2013 at the age of 94.

the easement came it was possible for our posts to move forward again and Bombs P B Panter [Support weapons expert] discovered a deserted, but fully operational, Italian howitzer battery concealed in the valley next to Johnny 1. He and his 3-inch mortar crews, whose weapons had failed to arrive, soon had the Italian guns in action.[40]

The situation was saved by the 6-inch guns of HMS *Newfoundland*. Once radio contact had been made by Vere-Hodge, high-velocity shells from the cruiser began to arrive with frightening precision among the German forces, tearing great holes in their ranks as they advanced: men were blown into the air by the force of the explosions and the attack petered out. The danger thus receded, despite an attack by Messerschmitt Bf 109s, flying at tree-top level with machine guns blazing.

Counter-attack

Captain Francis Vere-Hodge, MC. MID. 2nd Battalion Parachute Regiment, forward observation officer at Primosole. (Courtesy of *The War Illustrated*, December 1943)

As this battle raged around Johnny 3, the defenders holding the bridge were left in relative peace. However, this was not to last, and during the middle of the morning a German Focke-Wulf Fw 190 fighter strafed the area around the bridge with heavy machine-gun fire. The defenders on the bridge could hear the sounds of fighting on the 'Johnny' positions and stragglers were still arriving in the perimeter, but they had seen little sight of the enemy yet. The Germans now knew the British paratroopers were holding the bridge, so began to prepare an assault force to retake it. The British looked on as truckloads of German troops approached in the distance, dismounted and closed with them on foot. The defenders on the bridge then brought the captured 75mm gun into action, putting four rounds into the trucks as the infantry were getting off them, and followed up with high-explosive mortar rounds. This well co-ordinated artillery attack drove the Germans back. Having launched two successful ambushes, the paratroopers settled down once more into

40   J. Frost, *A Drop Too Many* (London: Cassel, 1980), p. 183.

Alert British paratroopers await the enemy. (Author's collection)

their defensive positions. Next, the Germans made preparations with a mixed force of 350 men scraped together in Catania, supported by a Flak battery of the dreaded 88mm guns.

On 14 July, German aircraft activity began in earnest as a flight of Fw 190s and Bf 109s approached down a valley from the north. The aircraft hugged the ground so as to hide the noise of their engines from their prey until the last minute. They caught the defenders completely off guard because of the speed of their arrival; most men only became aware of the attack when the fighters' machine guns began to rake the bridge area. Crashed Horsa gliders made good targets. With their mission completed, the German aircraft turned and headed back to their base at Catania airfield.

By noon, the Germans had brought forward their dual-purpose anti-tank/aircraft 88mm guns, and once the gunners had got their range, proceeded to plaster the bridge with high-explosive shells and air bursts for over an hour. Amid this inferno, the defenders could only lay down and wait. The bulk of the British paratroopers were north of the river, facing Catania, and it was here that the first counter-attacks came in just after 1:00 p.m. German troops appeared out of the haze and launched a determined attack which was repulsed with heavy losses. This was followed by another attack from the right flank which forced the British to shorten their defensive perimeter and use up more of their precious ammunition. The clash was evolving into a well-organised set-piece battle, with co-ordinated infantry and air attacks and artillery barrages. The *Fallschirmjäger* rallied their men to keep up the momentum of the attack. At 2:00 p.m., German machine-gunners poured a hail of fire into the British bridgehead to keep the defenders' heads down. An hour later, the 88s resumed the barrage on the bridge, under cover of which more German troops were brought forward with further artillery pieces. Once in position, and out of range of the British, they started to plaster the pillboxes at the ends of the bridge. Before they began, however, there was a strange lull in the fighting as an elderly man riding a bicycle came down the road, watched by troops from both sides. The aged cyclist avoided the bodies on the bridge, and as he passed said good morning to Pearson, who returned the greeting. He then peddled across the bridge and out of sight.

Red Devils: Green Devils

More German 88s were brought forward, the defenders on the bridge enduring a tempest of steel exploding around them as the shelling reached a crescendo. Shrapnel screamed through the air and clattered off the iron girders of the bridge. The British were pinned down, with any movement above ground becoming impossible. Under cover of this barrage, the German paratroopers closed with the British forward positions and they clashed in hand-to-hand fighting. The *Fallschirmjäger* were soon in amongst the British positions in increasing numbers, starting to gain the upper hand as they winkled out the defenders trench by trench.

Private Herman Kuster took part in this vicious fighting and later wrote home of the savagery of the action at Primolo Bridge:

> British *Fallschirmjäger* landed and we fought a battle to hold an important bridge across the Simeto River. They fought like tigers and eventually took it with terrible losses. The fighting was horrific, with men milling around shooting and bayoneting each other as they were so close together. I have never seen men fight one another the way that both sides did in this battle.[41]

The British were being forced back to the bridge as the German *Fallschirmjäger* closed in. Brigadier Lathbury, standing near the south-eastern pillbox where his brigade headquarters was situated, contemplated how long he could hold the bridge without extra support and with dwindling supplies of men and ammunition. The determined enemy he now faced was being reinforced constantly, slowly forcing its iron-like grip on the British paratroopers holding the bridge.

Captain Desmond Robert Gammon of the 1st Parachute Brigade, who was in a pillbox at one end of the bridge, recalled the devastating effect of the fire from the 88mm guns as they fired solid armour-piercing shot:

---

41   Manuscript forwarded to author, H. Wernamann, 1989.

British paratroopers take up a position near a ruined farmhouse. (Courtesy of M. Denney)

At any moment the Eighth Army must come, but time wore on and no Eighth Army. I noticed that the pillbox on my extreme left was taking a bashing. To this day I swear as each round of solid shot struck the pillbox it keeled over and bounced up again. Perhaps it was the heat haze of dust or my fevered imagination. It was made of concrete, but I swear it did. I realised that each pillbox in turn was to take its punishment and that mine was next. Suddenly there was a crash, fumes and dust and something hit me in the chest. I could hardly see. Where's the door? Had it collapsed? A shaft of light and I groped my way out into the blinding sunshine.[42]

Private George Pratt of the 1st Battalion Parachute Regiment fired his Bren gun at the attacking German troops from the firing slit of his pillbox, but ammunition was low and he had to make every round count:

My Bren gun hardly stopped firing the whole time, then one of the lads next to me was shot in the face and his head literally exploded, showering me with bits

42   Manuscript forwarded to author, G. Worthington, 1991.

of flesh and bone. Like an automaton he staggered backwards before colliding with the wall and sliding down it, leaving a big blood smear where the back of his head had contacted the wall. Not five minutes later the young lad who'd landed with me got killed. He was flung onto his back having been shot in the chest, blood pouring out of the wound. How I didn't get killed I don't know, as enough bullets were coming through the slit to kill a dozen of us. Jerry was only 80 yards away by then. At that range it was difficult not to hit someone and I can honestly say I shot quite a few.[43]

The lack of ammunition for the defenders was becoming serious and casualties continued to mount from the heavy artillery fire. At the southern end of the bridge, a surgical unit of the 16th Parachute Field Ambulance managed to perform numerous operations in tremendously difficult circumstances. The wounded were evacuated on a mule-drawn cart, with Sergeant Stevens, RAMC, running alongside braving the flying shells and bullets. He was awarded the Military Medal for his courage, having saved many lives.

The German paratroopers now began to take their first prisoners. Major Rudolph Bohmler made the following comments on his British counterparts:

There was considerable mutual respect between the two opponents. They were splendid fellows, each single one an athletic type. Now it was clear that the British had air landed and that we were involved with colleagues, it was really a pity one had to fight against such spirited types who were so similar to our own German paratroopers. They did not seem to be annoyed that they had been captured by their German brothers-in-arms.[44]

The only radio contact that the British troops on the bridge made with the outside world was at 9:30 a.m., when they got in touch with the 4th Armoured Brigade and were informed that they were having great trouble getting through to relieve the men holding the bridge. All radio contact was lost at 10:00 a.m., never to be regained. British Army radio sets were notoriously unreliable, and all too often gave out at critical moments.

"We can't hold on!"

The battle being fought out along the Simeto and around Johnny 1 was a fierce fight for survival, with no quarter asked for or given as the British and German paratroopers continued their close-quarter fighting. The British looked in vain for the relieving force throughout the hours of daylight, and with the guns of HMS *Newfoundland* no longer able to be called into action to stem the German assaults,

---

43   Correspondence with author, G. Pratt, 1989.
44   Manuscript forwarded to author, H. Wernamann, 1989.

the senior British officers at the bridge were forced to the conclusion that they could not withstand the increasing pressure for much longer. The *Fallschirmjäger* troops crept forward under cover of the fire from their 88s, using stunted trees growing near the river as a shield and setting fire to the thick dry reed beds on the river bank, which burned furiously and gave off clouds of acrid smoke. The men on the bridge then gave covering fire as their comrades on the northern bank withdrew in the face of the intense German pressure, and by 5:30 p.m. the situation was so bad that the order to abandon the bridge was given. Those troops that were able to fell back to the 'Johnny' positions under heavy fire, leaving behind their dead and wounded comrades.

George Pratt remembered how the superior German firepower slowly ground down the British defensive positions one after the other:

The final blow was [provided by] the shoulder-fired *Panzerfaust* anti-tank rockets. The Germans began using them once they were within range, about 60 yards. I got the order I had to hold on and give the wounded men cover as they withdrew over the bridge. I was praying they would get a move on so I could get the hell out of there before the bunker got flattened. When I heard the whistle, I knew it was time to move and none too soon, [as] first they took out the bunker on the left [and] then it was my turn. The moment I skidaddled out the door there was a huge explosion and I was thrown to the ground. I got up and sprinted across the bridge."[45]

Corporal George Stanion of the 3rd Parachute Battalion was hit in the back of the neck and knocked unconscious for a time.When he came round, he saw German machine-gunners in positions where his comrades had been:

A shell burst in front of me and under cover of this I ran back to the bridge but the battalion had gone. I couldn't cross the bridge because it was under fire so I went into the reeds and ran into some Jerries and was captured. Then apparently our chaps started firing into the reeds and two Jerries got hit in the head straight away. The others went back and I crawled along through the reeds, which were smouldering in parts. I got to the point where they met the water and I slipped into it and dog-paddled over to the other side where I lay in full view of both sides. I feared that if I tried to identify myself that I would be shot. It was then about 4.30 in the afternoon and I lay there waiting for darkness to come.[46]

Private Stainforth of the 1st Parachute Battalion, firing a captured Italian Breda machine gun, soon ran out of ammunition. He felt a sudden lack of purpose when he could no longer carry on the fight:

45   Correspondence with author, G. Pratt, 1992.
46   M. Saliger, *The First Bridge Too Far* (Oxford: Casemate, 2018), p. 177.

Our ammunition was now virtually finished and our guns fell silent one by one as their limited stock ran out. Rifle ammunition had gone to feed the Brens and very few of the men had any left. Our own Vickers was down to its last belt and only occasionally rattled off a round or two. The Vickers gunner fired one last burst, then flinging the gun, tripod and all, into the bushes, he and the rest fled. Without looking back, we squirmed through the undergrowth, down the embankment and went like the wind.[47]

Primosole Bridge had been in British hands for just 16 hours. Private Bob Priestley and his comrades were caught in a hail of mortar bombs and forced to withdraw as their situation was so desperate:

A lot of men died there and almost all my friends died there. To name a few: George Weir,[48] Bob Whittle,[49] Harry Coppard[50] and lots of others. Ken Stuart and myself were blown up by a mortar bomb. We then escaped to the quarry as it was called, [and] on the way we encountered a barbed wire fence. I don't remember very much, having been wounded in the ankle, but it would appear I pushed poor Ken into the barbed wire and ran over him. All I wanted was a drink and Ken threatened an Italian prisoner he would shoot him if he did not hand over his water bottle, which he eventually did. I took a good drink and nearly choked as it was full of *vino*. I was then taken to the first aid post and after a short time I was returned to duty. Doc Gordon had little mercy, and quite right. On my return I was walking back to Johnny 1 when I saw a dog cart coming down the hill pulled by Ken. I almost threw a fit, [as] we had been together for what seemed like a lifetime, then someone gave the order that it was every man for himself.[51]

Pte Joseph Smith, one of the Pathfinders, was retreating when his friend, 'Stan', felt the call of nature and needed to stop, with Smith standing guard:

Back along the ditch we went and into an orange grove. Here Stan decided he could no longer resist the urgent call of nature. He very decently went behind a tree and lowered his trousers. At this juncture the last of the brigade came pounding through the trees saying that Jerry was hot on their heels. There was nothing for it but to join the retreat at top speed with Stan holding his carbine

---

47   C. Whiting, *Slaughter Over Sicily* (Barnsley: Pen & Sword, 1992), p. 155.
48   George Weir must have survived as he is not listed in the Commonwealth War Graves Commission archives.
49   Corporal Robert Whittle of the Parachute Regiment, Army Air Corps, was killed in action on 14 July 1943, aged 25. He is buried in Catania War Cemetery.
50   Corporal Henry William Albert Coppard of the Parachute Regiment, Army Air Corps, was killed in action on 14 July 1943, aged 32. He is buried in Catania War Cemetery.
51   Manuscript forwarded to author, J. Young, 1991.

and small pack in one hand and his disarranged trousers in the other.[52]

At 7:35 p.m., Brigadier Lathbury had finally and reluctantly made the decision to abandon the bridge and to pull back in the direction of the Johnny hills, from where what was left of the British paratroopers could keep up a suppressing fire on the Germans and prevent them laying new explosive charges under the bridge. At 9:15 p.m., Lathbury's men moved under cover of darkness to a place of relative safety.

Little did they know just how near the relieving British column was.

In the early hours of 15 July, Corporal Stanley Brown peered out into the darkness and could hear someone approaching his position. "Who goes there!" the Pathfinder challenged, to which the reply came, "Durham Light Infantry".

Brigadier G.W. Lathbury, DSO, commander of the 1st Parachute Brigade. (Author's collection)

52   R. Kent, *First In: The Airborne Pathfinders* (London: Batsford, 1979), p. 67.

5

Crossing the Simeto
The 50th Northumbrian Division and the battle for Primosole Bridge, 14-17 July

That night the Germans did not advance any further, but the British relieving force did. At 7:30 p.m., Sherman tanks of the 44th Battalion Royal Tank Regiment arrived near Johnny 3, followed by a company of the 9th Battalion Durham Light Infantry. The Germans took one look at the tanks and withdrew to the northern bank of the Simeto and prepared themselves for the expected all-out attack by the British. The troops of the 50th Northumbrian Division were worn out, as during the day they had covered some 20 miles on foot in the blazing Sicilian summer heat. Consequently, they were in no fit state to commence offensive operations immediately. Acute shortages of transport had, not for the first time, affected the outcome of a major campaign. When the men of 151st Brigade reached Primosole, they were told they would lead the assault to retake the bridge the next morning. Those who had arrived got what sleep they could, but the last troops of the brigade did not make it to the bridge area until around midnight.

Lieutenant David Fenner moved forward with the 6th Battalion Durham Light Infantry from Lentini, and as they approached the Johnny positions came upon evidence of the heavy fighting that had taken place there:

> As we progressed north, we passed lots of our parachutists who had been dropped wide and too far south. We reached a road junction called Dead Horse Corner a mile or two south of Primosole. Here we found a number of dead paras, British and German, and fighting was still going on just in front. It was an unpleasant place full of unpleasant sights and smells.[1]

When Lieutenant Fenner reached the Primosole area, he settled his men down for the night. He recalled the bitterness expressed by the British paratroopers he met after they had fought so well and then been forced to withdraw:

---

1   Manuscript forwarded to author, I.R, English, 1989.

Primosole Bridge, July 1943. The farm buildings on the far bank can be seen clearly.
(Author's collection)

During the night two tired paratroopers came up the road to the battalion. They had captured the bridge but could not hold it any longer. Most of their mates were dead or captured. So deep was their sorrow that they tried to talk the I/O and C/O into waking the lads and making an attack right away. There were tears in their eyes and anger in their voices as they talked. To the best of their knowledge they were the only ones left from the battle and it was definite that the bridge was in German hands. They swore they were coming in with us and were taking no prisoners.[2]

Other paratroopers who had remained lost in the Sicilian countryside and had not found their units survived as best they could, trying hard not to be taken prisoner. Sergeant 'Cab' Callaway and his small band of paratroopers had been hiding from the German troops since they had dropped miles from the bridge at Primosole, and for two days had been lost among strong enemy forces. They decided to split into two small groups and make their way back to friendly lines, causing whatever damage they could inflict on the way, as Callaway recalled:

Time elapsed and we were getting very tired and hungry. We came upon a farmhouse and decided to attack it as our hunger was getting the better of us. We rushed into the farmhouse but were amazed to find six Sicilians inside who welcomed us with open arms. There we ate and slept in rotation. During our time there, planes were passing overhead and bombing about 600 yards west of the farm. We learnt from the civilians it was an Italian airfield. We left that night and made for the airfield to do whatever damage we could. We set fire to two planes and then got out as quickly as possible. We met no opposition but

2   Correspondence with author, I.R. English, 1989.

it was a very short stay as we had seen German patrols in the vicinity during the day. For two days we carried on hiding and crawling and infiltrating. We came across a crashed and burnt out aircraft, [but] all the occupants were burnt beyond recognition and we couldn't get any identity discs off the bodies. What appeared to be the body of the pilot was found 20 yards from the plane. The following day we were found by a unit of the Eighth Army.[3]

A distant thunder

The night of 14/15 July was not to be restful for anyone. The sound of gunfire could be heard from the direction of the bridge as the surviving paratroopers kept up a steady fire on the Germans whenever they attempted to replace explosive charges under the bridge. At 3:00 a.m., Italian armoured cars approached the positions of the 9th Battalion Durham Light Infantry from the direction of Lentini. They had been cut off by the advancing Durhams and were now trying to rejoin their parent unit, but the Durhams heard the noise of their engines and made ready to receive them.

Captain Jim Kennedy, who was serving with the 9th Durhams, described the subsequent events:

> The battalion had gone to ground at the end of the day at either side of the road, which was beginning to descend towards Primosole. During the night seven armoured cars [later found to be Italian commandos] drove as silently as they could up the road. Everyone lay silent waiting for the officer near the anti-tank gun in defilade and he waited until all seven had passed. When the last one was along-side the anti-tank gun fired and at close range it couldn't miss. The car stopped dead in its tracks, the other cars tried to move off the road, two managed to drive uphill off the road and away [they probably knew the country] and the others were dealt with. No prisoners were taken.[4]

Private Ernest Kerens lay behind a stone wall with his 9th Durhams comrades:

> Things were more or less ready when the first enemy vehicle started to come through us. The anti-tank gun had been pulled just clear of the road and those men awakened were crouched down behind the low wall that verged it with weapons in their hands. The enemy consisted of six or seven large life-boat shaped vehicles and were packed jam full of heavily armed Italian commandos. [They looked] for all the world like so many life-boats and they could be driven [from] either end. [They were like] open boats just asking for grenades to be tossed into them. Nobby [Lieutenant Colonel Clarke] had not managed to caution men all the way through the battalion and a guard at the far end let fly at them, then

3   Manuscript forwarded to author, Brian Cook, 2016.
4   E.W. Clay, *The Path of the 50th* (Aldershot: Gale and Polden, 1950), p. 187.

all hell let loose. At the beginning the commandos were brave. Just out of Italy, they were going to make a name for themselves. They could not see who was attacking them or from where, so they put up a solid wall of fire from all sides of their armoured boats. Our lads behind the wall, without even looking, tossed grenades into the boats like so many balls in a bucket at the fairground. Those further up the hillside fired at the flashes of their guns. The Italians realised that they had run into a hornet's nest and decided to withdraw. The rear car started to beat a hasty withdrawal and as it passed the anti-tank gun the latter let fly and it burst into flames. The second managed to squeeze past but not before at least one grenade had

Private Ernest Kerens, 9th Battalion Durham Light Infantry. (Courtesy of Ralph Hymer)

exploded in it. As the third tried to get past it was hit by a shell and the road was well and truly blocked. The three remaining still poured a withering fire into our hillside but this subsided as grenade after grenade exploded in them. The air was filled with flying steel and bits of Italians, [and] those able to do so threw themselves out of their machines and took cover on the opposite side of the road. A lot of them were dead or dying and their screams and cries almost drowned out what was left of the battle.[5]

During this action, Kerens could hear his officer, Lieutenant Vischer, calling for him for a full five minutes, but could not get to him while the fight was in full swing, as machine-gun fire had his section pinned down. Kerens continued:

I eventually found him only to get the usual derogatory remarks. He ordered me to take Itie prisoners back. Just my luck, I'm going to miss my breakfast as I did my yesterday's meals. As we went back along the road the war hadn't finished and there was still the odd bullet whistling around. The prisoners were glad to come with me, [and] I don't think they liked Mr Vischer's company either.[6] By now it was quite light and we passed the first two armoured cars both still burning merrily. I had to keep my eyes on my prisoners and on the many mutilated and

5 Manuscript forwarded to author, I.R. English, 1990.
6 Lieutenant H.A.C. Vischer, 9th Battalion Durham Light Infantry, was wounded at Primosole on 17 July 1943.

dying lying all around. One of the latter might decide to take an enemy with him when he left this life. First one then another would give himself up, [and] I had eleven at the finish. As we passed the dead, dying and mutilated bodies of their comrades they wept and crossed themselves. One poor blighter had both his legs blown off and was still conscious. We propped him up against a tree and put a cigarette in his mouth, but judging by the amount of blood around him it was obvious he was doomed. There were many wounded and my charges were reluctant to leave them but there was nothing we could do for them. As we walked towards the rear a tearful and angry voice from the hillside screamed 'kill them, kill the bastards, kill the hump-backed gets, they have got Johnny Hall'.[7] It was Arthur Thompson, he was crying like a baby and through his tears I could feel his hate. A bullet had killed Johnny outright. I felt it too as he and I had been in the same training battalion in Blighty. We had fought together all the way up the desert. But after seeing what we had done to the other Ities I could feel no hate for those who were left and I told Arthur so, [but] he said, 'then turn your back for two minutes and I will'. With Arthur in his present state I thought it sensible to add a little haste as we carried on up the road. My prisoners gave me no trouble, stunned by what they had been through. Pale and dazed they walked quietly in front of me talking in whispers among themselves. I thought it's a lovely morning, the birds are singing and there are flowers in the hedgerow. Maybe that's how it was, that's how I remembered it, or was it that I was just glad to be alive?[8]

In the early hours of 15 July, the 8th Battalion Durham Light Infantry settled down for the night but were roused by the racket coming from the 9th Battalion's sector nearly 2 miles away. They listened to the violent machine-gun fire and explosions in the night, and at 4:00 a.m. they stood to their arms in readiness for an attack that never came. It was not until daylight that they were informed of the night's events. In the early hours, the 8th Battalion was ordered to breakfast before daybreak, advance and take over the positions vacated by the 9th Battalion. The 6th Battalion was ordered forward to occupy the positions vacated by the 8th Battalion on the high ground west of the road overlooking the Simeto.

Lieutenant Peter Lewis, of the 8th Battalion Durham Light Infantry, watched his weary men as they marched off the road to get what rest they could:

In our bivouac areas, with the knowledge that the morning would most certainly bring action of some sort, the exhausted infantry stretched themselves out on the hard ground to try to get a few hours' sleep before dawn. They were unlucky, [as] at 4:00 a.m. there was violent automatic fire and frequent explosions from the direction of 9th DLI's positions. The 8th Battalion immediately 'stood to'.[9]

7   Private John Robert Denton Hall, 9th Battalion Durham Light Infantry, was killed on 16 July 1943, aged 28. He is buried in Catania War Cemetery, Sicily.
8   Manuscript forwarded to author, E. Kerens, 1990.
9   P. Lewis, *The Price of Freedom* (Durham: Pentland Books, 2001), p. 24.

Lieutenant Fenner, of the 6th Durhams, greeted his brother officers of the 8th Battalion and wished them good luck:

> We settled down to make ourselves at home in our new surroundings. There was a large tent in the company area and from the evidence of uniforms and empty bottles about the place we concluded it had been a rest camp for *Luftwaffe* personnel. It was not long before certain members of the platoon had donned German greatcoats and were parading around in them and admiring the padded shoulders, [and] cries of 'aye aye spiv' rang around the place.[10]

The first phase of the battle for Primosole Bridge was over. For the British airborne forces it had been a bitter disappointment, as of the 1,856 paratroopers who had flown from North Africa, only 16 percent ever came into action on the objective, and one-third were never dropped. Many who did were captured and an unknown number were missing. With their work done, the paratroopers could now leave the battle to the men of the Durham Light Infantry, but for the *Fallschirmjäger* there was to be no relief. Indeed, during the night the German paratroopers worked hard strengthening their new positions in preparation for the ordeal to come.

An anonymous Durham officer described the scene before him:

> "From behind us the road wound down from Lentini and was joined by a subsidiary road. This junction was an appalling shambles of broken sign posts, destroyed pill-boxes and smashed telephone wires, as well as seven or eight dead mules of an Italian pack train. The smell was dreadful and soon earned the name 'Dead Horse Corner'. After coming round a bend, the road ran straight to the bridge, although there is a sort of elbow before it runs between the girders. There was a glider lying on its side not far from the bend, and that was the only visible trace of the heroism of the airborne troops. On the enemy's side of the river, thick vineyards seemed to extend right down to the banks on both sides of the bridge for four or five hundred yards, and beyond the bridge there were a couple of stone-built farms on either side of the road.[11]

The officers and men of the 9th Durhams looked down from their vantage point at the ugly iron structure of the bridge. They would soon have good reason to remember that sight. In the fading light, a group of Durham officers approached the bridge. The bitter fighting that had already taken place there was obvious to them as they looked upon this scene of desolation in silence. Dead British and German paratroopers, in their distinctive smocks, lay where they had fallen, while blackened burnt-out vehicles and reeds on the river banks were still smouldering. It was with heavy hearts that they returned to their comrades to plan the attack for the next day.

10 H. Moses, *The Faithful Sixth* (Durham: Durham County Books, 1995), p. 98.
11 H. Pond, *Sicily* (London: William Kimber, 1962), p. 134.

The 9th Durhams attack, 15th July

The plan for the morning attack was for a conventional frontal assault. Lieutenant Colonel A.B.S. Clarke did not like the hastily put together plan, but his divisional commander, General Sidney Kirkman, had Montgomery breathing down his neck to achieve even greater speed in breaking through to the Plain of Catania. Imperfect as the plan was, it would have to be put into operation. At dawn on 15 July, the area around the bridge was as quiet as the grave as the men of the 9th Battalion Durham Light Infantry moved to their starting point. At 7:30 a.m., the silence was broken as the guns of the 24th and 98th Field Regiments, Royal Artillery, opened fire on suspected enemy positions. Shells rained down on the Germans, with earth-shaking detonations. From the rear of the Johnny 2 position emerged Lieutenant Colonel Clarke's 9th Durhams, supported by the Sherman tanks of the 44th Battalion Royal Tank Regiment, who began their advance up Highway 114. The Durhams spread out in attack formation, with the tanks interspersed among their ranks. The barrage still thundered and roared before them as it pummelled the German positions. Many wondered how anyone could survive such a storm of high-explosive and flying steel. The Durhams plodded remorselessly on over open ground, fixed bayonets glinting in the sun as they approached the bridge and a smokescreen was laid down by the artillery. The German paratroopers held their fire until the Durhams were only 50 yards distant, and the leading platoons were cut down like corn before the scythe. The follow-up platoons suffered a similar fate. The tanks were forced to remain with their commanders' hatches closed down as the German machine-gunners sprayed them with fire, which meant the tankers could not identify enemy targets. As they had done on other occasions, the 151st Brigade was making an attack on a narrow front against strong positions held by first-class troops. The surviving Durhams reached the southern bank of the river and the Germans withdrew to the north bank. German troops hidden in the vineyards and the unseen sunken road now opened fired on the attackers, inflicting more casualties. Some of the Durhams attempted to swim the river, but many were shot as they did so. By 9:30 a.m., the remains of C Company had managed to get across the river, where the fighting was at close quarters. The tanks, however, were unable to cross the bridge as an 88mm gun was firing straight down the road and over the bridge.

Private Reg Pope was with C Company of the 9th Durhams and recalled the resolute defence the German paratroopers put up:

> The Germans defended the area around the bridge really well. My mate from down the road from where I live was killed in the fighting, which was very rough. There were unseen snipers everywhere picking men off from the vineyards. When we finally crossed the bridge and got into the vineyards the enemy was so close, we were engaged in hand-to-hand fighting.[12]

12   Interview with author, R. Pope, 1991.

Private Kerens returned from delivering his prisoners in time to watch the 9th Battalion's attack:

> They started to cross the river and then all hell broke loose. On the other side of the river suddenly a row of square heads with machine guns and rifles popped up. Soon the river ran red, literally, with the blood of the Durhams. Some did reach the other side, scamper up the bank and engaged the enemy in hand-to-hand fighting, but there was not enough to hang on to what they had gained. We in HQ Company went down to see what we could do to help, [but] there wasn't a lot. We stopped just short of the river and fired at anything that looked Tedescish [German]. One or two of us went into the river to rescue the wounded. It wasn't easy, [as] bullets buzzed about like angry bees. The bloke nearest to me had himself to be rescued.[13]

The 9th Battalion was forced back over the river, leaving their dead and wounded in enemy hands. They then lined the southern bank, from where the Durhams kept up a harassing fire on the Germans and successfully prevented them from placing fresh explosive charges under the bridge.

An anonymous account, written shortly after the attack by a trooper of the County of London Yeomanry observed:

> I have never seen such carnage, real Frederician soldiery of the old type.[14]

Colonel John Frost of the 2nd Parachute Battalion, who had a grandstand view of the failed Durham attack from the nearby high ground, commented: "We had never taken part in such an operation and having seen this we were determined never to do so."

Lieutenant Fenner, of the 6th Durhams, was sent forward to contact the 9th Battalion survivors who were east of the road on his right on a forward slope:

> My first contact was with two soldiers of the 9th. They were grey-faced with fatigue and stress. Their appearance was descriptive of what they had just been through: a forced night march through hostile territory, a daylight attack, driven back by a German counter-attack and finally pinned down in the open, subject to shelling by 88 airbursts. They moved like automatons and quietly told me where to find the acting company commander. From him I heard the story of the 9th DLI's fight and loss of friends. I returned to my company area where we were topped up with rations, water and ammunition, but still no blankets.[15]

---

13 Correspondence with author, E. Kerens, 1992.
14 A. Graham, *Sharpshooters at War* (London: The Sharpshooters Regimental Association, 1964), p. 122.
15 Manuscript forwarded to author, W. Ridley, 1990.

Lieutenant Peter Lewis, with the 8th Battalion Durham Light Infantry, recalled a hot meal being brought to his men in the afternoon, along with the news that a rum ration would be issued before the next attack, which would be led by the 8th Battalion:

> At dusk a troop of Sherman tanks from 44th RTR took up positions 200 yards south of the river to give covering fire to A and D Companies immediately prior to the assault. During the evening the 6th Battalion moved into the 8th Battalion's area.[16]

The German paratroopers had not only selected their defensive positions with great skill but had also been aided by the density of the vineyards on the north bank of the river. Within the vineyards were numerous olive trees, extending to a depth of 400 yards, and behind the vines ran a sunken road, later named by the Tommies 'Stink Alley' because of the stench from dead men, cattle and horses. This feature was unknown to the British, as little could be seen beyond the vineyards; between the rows of vines, visibility was limited to 10 yards. In the late morning of 15 July, General Kirkman ordered a fresh attack to take place that afternoon by the 8th Durhams, led by Lieutenant Colonel Lidwell. It was to have a much heavier artillery barrage than the earlier attack, with tanks adding their firepower to proceedings. Lidwell outlined the plan in the presence of Brigadier Lathbury, two parachute colonels and Brigadier John Currie of the 4th Armoured Brigade, even though he had grave misgivings about it. But Kirkman was insistent and had Montgomery in the background constantly demanding results. Despite his reservations, Lidwell would put the plan into operation, knowing full well that this kind of frontal attack was suicidal, as the 9th Battalion's earlier assault had shown. However, Montgomery wanted the bridge captured, no matter what the cost, as it was holding up the advance of the whole Eighth Army. Sat listening to the deliberations was Lieutenant Colonel Alastair Pearson of the 1st Parachute Battalion. He was dog tired, unshaven and covered in grime from the battle, but could contain himself no longer. In a loud voice, the dour Scot exclaimed, "Well if you want to lose another bloody battalion that's the way to do it." The officers present do not seem to have been annoyed by his remarks, but simply asked him how he would do it.

Pearson spoke of a ford about a mile downstream which he had used when withdrawing the previous night. He said the enemy was not in sufficient numbers to cover the whole of the far bank, it being most likely their forces were concentrated near the bridge itself, and the delivery of such a left hook would take them by surprise. Pearson offered to act as guide over the river for the 8th Durhams, but then told Lidwell:

> After that you're on your own, I'll cross that bridge and be up that road as hard as I can bloody well go.[17]

16   P. Lewis, *The Price of Freedom* (Durham: Pentland Books, 2002), p. 29.
17   C. Whiting, *Slaughter Over Sicily* (Barnsley: Pen & Sword, 1992), p. 150.

Lidwell reported back to his superiors, and much to his relief the operation was postponed until the following morning. In the distance, the permanent barrage rumbled and thudded ominously as A and D Companies of the 8th Battalion were led by Pearson to their crossing point downstream on the night of the 15th. The long column of men marched in silence through the darkness, and as signal flares occasionally shot up into the sky they froze until it was realised that they were not meant for them. Yet this was the lull before the storm, which the veteran soldiers of the 8th Durhams knew only too well.

Lieutenant Peter Lewis moved forward with his company of the 8th Battalion:

> It was a clear moonlit night, [and] at 10pm exactly the two assaulting companies left the assembly area and marched to their forming up place where they met Colonel Pearson and some of his paratroopers. They had gone down at dusk to tape a route from there to the river.[18]

The 8th Durhams ford the Simeto, 16 July

At 12:50 a.m., the silence was broken as the British artillery barrage opened up with a deafening roar, targeting the vineyards beyond the Simeto, while the heavy machine guns of the Cheshire Regiment raked the entire area. Sherman tanks of the 44th Royal Tank Regiment joined in with their heavy Besa machine guns. This devastating deluge of fire was kept up without pause until 2:00 a.m., when the whole weight of the barrage moved to the area north of the bridge. In this cacophony of noise, A and D Companies crossed the Simeto in single file without too much difficulty. The water was only some 4ft deep, except where a shell had fallen and then it doubled in depth. A number of men were completely submerged as they walked into these shell holes and had to be rescued.

Once across the river, the two companies formed up rapidly under cover of the far bank and headed in an easterly direction for the bridge, hampered by the closely planted vines. Their assault took the enemy completely by surprise; many of their number had been killed or wounded in the barrage, and the main body pulled back 300 yards in the face of the attack. With tracer rounds cutting through the night air over the heads of the attackers as they rushed the bridge, speed was essential. The night was filled with shouts and explosions as the Durhams quickly dispatched the few remaining defenders with bayonets, small arms and grenades. Both companies established themselves on the Catania road, using a ditch that ran alongside it for cover. Regathering their senses, the Germans laid down a heavy fire with mortars and machine guns that swept the entire area. The Durhams had only a limited view of their surroundings due to the density of the vines, trees and long grasses, and had to be constantly on the alert for any German counter-attack.

---

18   P. Lewis, *The Price of Freedom* (Durham: Pentland Press, 2002), p. 29.

A Company cut through the barbed-wire defences they found and rushed the pill-boxes at the northern end of the bridge, routing the Italian defenders with grenades, bayonets and automatic fire. Some 500 yards from the Catania road, into the vineyards where the river turned sharply to the north, was the company's objective. The road they had to cross was swept by machine-gun fire, and more belts of barbed-wire entanglements had to be cut, but the attackers made it to their objective with only light casualties. The men quickly dug-in, still under constant fire. The Germans were so close that they could hurl grenades into the Durhams' positions. Lieutenant Lewis was not happy with the position, but made the best of a bad situation:

> The company dug-in quickly with entrenching tools about a hundred yards north of the river bank. A Spandau was constantly sweeping the area and small parties of Germans harassed the company by throwing grenades at close range. The whole area was thickly covered by vines, shrubs and tall grass. There was a fair number of trees, making it difficult for us to see what was happening in front, even when standing up. It was without doubt the worst defensive position A Company had ever occupied and it required constant vigilance to keep the persistent German paratroops at bay.[19]

The first phase of the battle had been successfully carried out, and now it was up to B and C Companies of the 8th Battalion to cross the bridge. Lieutenant Colonel Lidwell had arranged for three different kinds of communication to be available when contacting the waiting companies, in the hope that at least one of them would work. The first was a mortar flare, but in the dark and confusion of the advance, mortars and flares had become separated. The second was wireless communication, but these sets had been saturated in the river crossing and were useless. The final hope lay with a universal carrier with a radio that was stationed at the southern end of the bridge. Captain G.H. Lohan, the carrier platoon commander, and Lieutenant A. Pridham of B Company took up their allotted position in the carrier, Pridham having earlier reconnoitred the bridge for mines, demolition charges and suspicious wires. As they reached their post, they came under fire and received a direct hit. Captain Lohan,[20] the driver and wireless operator were killed outright. Lieutenant Pridham was seriously wounded and had to be dragged unconscious from the wrecked carrier, but survived. He recalled:

> I landed near Avola on D-Day. I lasted only until the crossing of the Simeto and the Primosole Bridge battle and was probably the first member of the Eighth Army to cross the bridge. I was later the only one to live of four who returned to the bridge in the carrier which was knocked out on the south

---

19   P. Lewis, *The Price of Freedom* (Durham: Pentland Books, 2002), p. 31.
20   Captain Gerard Harris Lohan, South Staffordshire Regiment, attached to the 8th Battalion Durham Light Infantry, was killed in action at Primosole Bridge on 17 July 1943, aged 32. He is buried in Catania War Cemetery.

side of the bridge. I made contact with a tank lying near a wrecked glider just south of the bridge.[21]

Lidwell crossed the bridge to find a scene of carnage. It was too risky for him to walk up the road and over the bridge to where the Durhams were waiting. The only other possibility of getting a message back was to use one of the Sherman tanks on the other side of the river as a link. Lidwell approached a stationary tank that had its engine running, but with so much firing going on he could not make himself heard. He climbed onto the tank and tapped the commander on the head, but as he did so every hatch slammed shut and nothing would entice them to open up again. Lidwell walked back to the road, when out of the darkness came a figure on a bicycle, a War Office observer called Major Wigram. Luckily for him, the Durhams were not trigger happy. His arrival could not have been more opportune; he listened to the commander of the 8th Battalion, turned around his bicycle and took back orders for B and C Companies to advance at once.

This breakdown in communications had delayed things considerably, and dawn was about to break as the companies left their assembly areas. The troops marched past the smouldering universal carrier in single file and over the bridge, avoiding mines that lay on the road surface.

Lieutenant Lewis, who led B Company up the left-hand side of the road, recounted:

> Harry Walmsley was leading C Company on the right of the road, [and] the two companies passed the wrecked Bren carrier and crossed the bridge quickly, carefully avoiding the mines (some German, some British) that had been left on the surface during the fighting of the previous day. My company drew level with blazing farm buildings on the left of the road when somebody shouted, 'Push on B Company there's only a few Ities up front.'[22]

Without warning, German machine guns then opened up on the leading sections at point-blank range. These were no Italians, but well-concealed German paratroopers, and the Durhams had walked straight into them. The Durhams scrambled for cover in the ditch running along each side of the road. Lieutenant Richard Holloway led his platoon forward in an attempt to rush the German positions, but he and his men were cut down before they had got very far. In the first few seconds of firing, the forward sections of B and C Companies fell in this murderous fire. Had it not been for the protection of the ditch, B and C Companies would have been totally wiped out. The remaining Durhams were then up and advancing towards their unseen tormentors when the whole of the leading section was shot down as they pressed on into the dense vines on either side of the road. In the half-light of dawn, there began a lethal game of search and destroy as the Durhams and the German paratroopers hunted each other down. It was every man for himself in that grim killing ground, with the

21   S.W.C. Pack, *Operation Husky* (London: David and Charles, 1977), p. 138.
22   P. Lewis, *The Price of Freedom* (Durham: Pentland Books, 2002), p. 33.

Men of the 50th Northumbrian Division move to the attack. (Author's collection)

added confusion of being unable to tell friend from foe until the last moment. No quarter was asked for or given in this vicious close-quarter encounter.

Lieutenant Lewis continued:

> Three hundred yards north of the bridge the first shots were suddenly fired as a prelude to twenty minutes of the fiercest hand-to-hand fighting the 8th Battalion had ever experienced. In the darkness and in the shadows of giant poplar trees flanking the road, the men of the leading sections of both companies got to within a few yards of the German machine-guns before the enemy opened up at almost point-blank range. In the first few seconds of firing the forward sections of B and C Companies were badly mauled. The German fire was murderous and it practically wiped out the leading platoon of B Company, led by Lt Richard Holloway. If it had not been for the ditch there is no doubt that Holloway's platoon would have been shot down to a man.[23]

Fallschirmjäger troops would appear without warning and shoot their opponents from just a few yards. The Durhams stalked the Germans silently in the darkness, approaching them from behind where the machine-gunners lay and bayoneting them to death. As the Durhams returned the enemy fire, Lieutenant A.F. Jackman led his men forward, but most of them were shot down when almost on top of a German

---

23   P. Lewis, *The Price of Victory* (Durham: Pentland Books, 2002), pp. 34–35.

machine-gun post. The gallant officer was badly wounded, but his desperate charge forced the enemy to withdraw. Company Sergeant Major Matthew Brannigan led his men through the vines and accounted for several enemy paratroopers with his bayonet within the space of a few minutes. The scene was lit up by flashes from the muzzles of guns and exploding grenades in the most savage hand-to-hand fighting the men had experienced.

Peter Lewis advanced cautiously through the vines:

> It seemed as though there was a German behind every tree or vine and every bush. The whole situation was unreal, almost fantastic. Both sides fired at trees by mistake and both sides threw grenades until it was realised that the exploding bombs were just as likely to kill friend as foe. Within the space of twenty minutes the two sides had fought themselves to a standstill. Some of the company had reached the German positions in the sunken road where, after a fierce fight they were all killed or wounded. They still held the sunken road, the key to the whole of their defensive positions.[24]

The 8th Battalion was now established in a position nearly 400 yards deep to the north of the bridge, with nerves strained to the limit as the men waited for the inevitable counter-attack. The German paratroopers still held the sunken road, which was the key point in the whole defensive position. The rear section of the battalion's B Company, comprising 40 men, were under the command of Captain D.A. Neale and still situated in the roadside ditch when CSM Brannigan, one of the few survivors of the close-quarter fighting, brought him news that the rest of the company had ceased to exist as a fighting force. Neale, knowing nothing of the sunken road, decided to lead his men forward to their original objective. They left the ditch about 60 yards south of the sunken road but had moved across the fields for only some 40 yards when the concealed *Fallschirmjäger* troops opened up with grenades and accurate and heavy small-arms fire that forced the Durhams to go to ground. As daylight broke, Captain Neale finally spotted the sunken road. However, his men were unable to press on to their objective, which was beyond the sunken road, nor could they afford to stay in their exposed position. To the rear, Neale could see a high embankment near a farmhouse, and as he took his men to the relative safety of this feature, the German paratroopers emerged from their hiding places and made a bayonet charge against the Durhams' rear. They overran the rearguard commanded by Sergeant F. Mitchinson, who feigned death until the paratroopers had passed by and then opened fire on them with his Thompson machine gun. Mitchinson's act threw the Germans into confusion and allowed the majority of the Durhams to withdraw. CSM Brannigan[25] stood his ground in the face of the German counter-attack, spraying them with

---

24   P. Lewis, *The Price of Freedom* (Durham. Pentland Books 2002) p34/35.
25   Company Sergeant Major Mathew John Brannigan, MM, 8th Battalion Durham Light Infantry, was killed at Primosole on 17 July 1943, aged 28. He is buried in Catania War Cemetery.

machine-gun fire and taking a heavy toll of the attackers, but was himself killed. His selfless actions saved the lives of many of his comrades. The 30 surviving Durhams reached the embankment, where Captain Neale formed a defensive position as the Germans withdrew to the sunken road. C Company was in a similar situation, while A Company, which had so far got off lightly, would soon also have to come to grips with the *Fallschirmjäger* fighters.

Counter-attack!

The Germans launched a violent assault against the 8th Durhams on 17 July, and with the first shock overran two platoons after fierce fighting at close quarters. Lieutenant Frederick Clarke and Sergeant Crawford used their Thompson sub-machine guns to inflict heavy casualties on the paratroopers until they were both hit, Clarke fatally.[26] The fighting continued, with casualties mounting on both sides, but the Germans outnumbered the Durhams, whose two platoons were driven back to the Simeto. Some of the Durhams were also forced back across the river as the situation became even more desperate.

Private Ralph Hymer found the terrific volume of fire being directed onto his platoon of the 8th Durhams made their position untenable, and he and his comrades were driven back by the German paratroopers:

> There was a big wine place situated there and it was held by German crack troops who were well dug-in. They gave us hell and we were driven back and left with no option but to cross the river again. They shot the living daylights out of us. Our packs were so heavy that they were dragging us down into the river. The water was red with blood as we had to pull back and scrambled up the bank. Mortaring and shelling was going on all the time. But the cruel machine-gun fire was non-stop and accurate.[27]

German snipers had tied themselves high up in poplar trees, where they were out of sight and proceeded to take a heavy toll of the attackers. Lieutenant Lewis was targeted by one of them:

> Short bursts of automatic fire were coming from the tall poplar trees on the side of the road where German paratroopers had strapped themselves in the branches of the stronger trees so that they had freedom of action with their weapons and could shoot downwards. I was shot in the shoulder by one of them and lost consciousness for a while. When I came round a German paratrooper was kneeling beside me, [and] he spoke urgently and in good English 'How

---

26   Lieutenant Frederick Clarke, Ox and Bucks Light Infantry, attached to 8th Battalion Durham Light Infantry, was killed on 17 July 1943, aged 23. He is buried in Catania War Cemetery.
27   Interview with author, R Hymer, 1991.

many divisions are there?' Before he had time to repeat the question there was a burst of automatic fire and he fell forward on his face. I managed to drag myself a few yards to a shallow bomb crater where I propped myself up on the lip of the crater.[28]

Sergeant Ray Pinchin found his section of the 8th Durhams pinned down behind a low stone wall by the terrific volume of fire coming from the *Fallschirmjäger* positions:

> The battle was flaming noisy and very bloody. It caused us all a lot of grief as the fire was so intense and from very close quarters. After we had crossed the river that night, we took up a defensive position behind a low stone wall and I told the lads to dig in. Most of us kept our heads well down but a few tried to see what

Private Ralph Hymer, 8th Battalion Durham Light Infantry. (Courtesy of Ralph Hymer)

was going on and kept sticking their heads up to get a better view. I remember shouting at the top of my voice 'get your bloody heads in'.[29]

Although the British artillery barrage on the German positions was in full swing, many shells were falling short, inflicting serious casualties on the Durhams still in the bridgehead. Lance Corporal F.H. Spink volunteered to contact the gunners, even though it meant going out into the open, with shells and machine-gun fire still sweeping the surrounding area. He bravely carried out his mission, in doing so saving the lives of many of his comrades. He was later awarded the Military Medal for this courageous act.

By 6:00 a.m., the 8th Battalion was still in close contact with the enemy, with the distance between the German paratroopers and the Durhams as little as 20 yards in some parts of the bridgehead. The Primosole bridgehead was under constant and accurate small-arms fire. The beleaguered British troops, knowing how precarious their position was, looked to their rear in the hope that reinforcements would arrive soon. Men could not cross the river, but tanks could, and the welcome noise of tank engines and creaking tracks was heard as two Shermans lumbered over the bridge. As the tanks of the 44th Battalion Royal Tank Regiment moved up the road, they

28 P. Lewis, *The Price of Freedom* (Durham: Pentland Books, 2002), p. 35.
29 Correspondence with author, R. Pinchin, 1996.

German paratroopers of the Machine-gun Battalion raked the Primosole bridgehead with heavy concentrations of fire. (Author's collection)

came under fire from a German 88mm gun 800 yards north of the bridge. Both tanks rapidly withdrew and crossed the bridge back to the southern side, to the great disappointment of the infantry.

The badly wounded Peter Lewis lay motionless in his shallow crater as the battle raged around him:

> Two Germans arrived and I watched them as they set up their machine-gun and fired a burst at any sign of movement. They took no notice of me and this was not surprising. The bullet that had hit me skimmed down the right-hand side of my face, nicked my right earlobe and went clean through my shoulder without touching any bones. However, the side of my face was covered in blood and to the Germans I must have looked more dead than alive. The sweltering heat of mid-day was almost unbearable and the wounded [German and British] were in a piteous state. I shouted '*Wasser bitte*' at the top of my voice several times. It was about twenty minutes or so before two German paratroopers crawled towards me through the thick vines and tall grass. It was slow and painful progress through the vines but we made it to the sunken road without being shot at and I was carried on a stretcher to the German HQ.[30]

30   P. Lewis, *The Price of Freedom* (Durham: Pentland Books, 2002), p. 35. Lieutenant Peter Lewis was captured by German paratroopers at Primosole and taken back to Catania Hospital

The 6th and 9th Durhams ford the Simeto and enter the bridgehead, 17 July

Despite 16 July being a day of hard fighting for the men in the bridgehead, they held firm in the face of fierce *Fallschirmjäger* counter-attacks. General Kirkman, commander of the 50th Division, now decided to launch a stronger attack with the rest of the 151st Brigade on 17 July: the 6th and 9th Battalions were to ford the river, the 6th leading at 1:00 a.m. and the 9th following an hour later. A creeping barrage would be laid down before them, with 159 artillery pieces firing as the men crossed the river and moved into the bridgehead. Once established, the 6th Durhams were to advance on the left of the Catania road to their objective some 1,500 yards distant. The 9th Battalion would then advance on the right of the Catania road to their objective, also 1,500 yards distant. Sherman tanks of the County of London Yeomanry would then move over the bridge to exploit the breakthrough.

Lieutenant David Fenner prepared his men of the 6th Durhams and led them forward into a battlefield that was already full of dead, wounded and the detritus of war:

> Rum had been issued before we left and was of some comfort in this limbo period where we had little to do but occupy our thoughts with the grim and inevitable prospect ahead. We reached a dry ditch running towards the river and began moving through a battle-field where our parachutists and the Germans had fought. All around the vegetation had been burnt by phosphorous bombs and tracer bullets and evidence of the fighting was everywhere. The ditch contained many burnt bodies, one completely blackened, sat upright staring sightlessly at each member of the battalion as he struggled past in the moonlight. The only sound came from the bursts of harassing fire from the Cheshire machine-gunners and the bull frogs croaking in the reeds. We paused before the leading company entered the river, bayonets were fixed and machine-guns cocked. Ben Dickenson, the platoon runner and the oldest soldier in the platoon, argued with Connel the sergeant about the need to fix bayonets. He said he had never found it necessary to use one, [and] I cannot remember the outcome of this disagreement but I did appreciate the easing of tension it produced among us. Then we were on the move to the river.[31]

Private Harry Wilkinson of C Company was short in stature and remembered the difficulties he faced when crossing the river:

> We crossed the river first and me being small, about 5ft 4ins, it came up to my shoulders but somebody had got a rope across and I think we nearly all managed

for treatment. He was then taken to mainland Italy, where he made a daring escape and was eventually picked up by resistance fighters. With their help, he made the long journey back to England and survived the war.

31   H. Moses, *The Faithful Sixth* (Durham: County Durham Books, 1995), p. 257.

to grab hold of that. It was a heck of a shock for me going into that icy water in the dark. I believe one or two of the chaps got swept downstream.[32]

Lieutenant Fenner led his men down the river bank, and once across he immediately launched them into the attack:

We slid down the bank into chest-high water again in single file, guiding ourselves by hanging onto a wire stretched across the banks for this purpose. Below the far bank the battalion bore left and then turned to face the enemy with the three assaulting companies in line. So far all had gone well. Our objective, the sunken road, was some 500 yards away through the vineyards. It needed a few more minutes to pass before zero hour when someone said, 'what are we waiting for' [and then] another voice said 'let's get stuck in'. Then followed a general move by the leading platoons up the bank and through the vineyard towards the sunken road. My recollections of what happened after that are confused, [but] firing began at isolated Germans seen running away, then from the direction of the road came a murderous fire from the Spandaus located there. The gunners were firing past us at knee-height. The line of infantry kept on going in spite of men being hit, until we were struck by heavy concentrations of artillery. Some of this was probably enemy DF [defensive fire] but in the opinion of those who had been shelled by our own gunners on previous occasions we were in our own barrage. Ben Dickenson was clear on this point and he shouted 'when I get out of this, I'll do those bloody gunners'. He sounded a bit optimistic. Shells were now dropping all around, then it stopped and lifted and groups of men got up and moved on through the cactus hedge into the sunken road. An hour after dawn we saw some Germans coming along the sunken road, about 20, all wearing green face veils. We went for them and shot them up pretty badly – there were screams of 'Kamerad'. There was a lot of shooting, [but] suddenly it was over and we took about 8 prisoners, all but two being wounded. Mark organised what remained of the company into a defensive position astride the road. There were elements of two platoons and we started to provide some sort of protection for ourselves by scraping away at the hard ground with our pathetic entrenching tools. The older soldiers acquired the much more efficient German article and were soon digging in at great speed. The place was littered with German equipment, Spandau machine-guns, belts of ammunition and corpses. Our prisoners were all parachutists, [and] one spoke good English and told us that 3 days ago they had been in the south of France. A fierce battle was in progress to our right where the 9th Battalion were going in. Apart from the pop of small-arms fire where we were was comparatively quiet now. In the first light of the summer's day, we dug in while the stretcher bearers attended to the wounded lying thick in the vines."[33]

32   Correspondence with author, H. Wilkinson, 1991.
33   Manuscript forwarded to author, I.R. English, 1990.

German paratroopers of the Heavy Weapons Battalion man a rarely seen gun, the 7.5cm *Leichtgesschutz* LG Recoilless Rifle. It was peculiar to this airborne force. (Author's collection)

Lance Corporal George Worthington, MM, was a stretcher bearer that day with the 6th Durhams and was awarded the Military Medal for his bravery in saving many of his comrades. He remembered events with typical unassuming modesty:

> I remember before the attack they came round with the rum ration to give us a bit of Dutch courage. I'd reached the stage in my army life that I thought well let's get into it and if I come through fair enough, if I don't then so be it. That's the attitude I took on board at the time and when I came out of the battle, I was informed I'd been nominated for the Military Medal. Nobody was more surprised than myself. They tell me I got it because when we'd gained our objective we were pinned down by heavy fire. Jerry was no respecter of stretcher bearers or whatever. I was all keyed up and went out with other people and started bringing in casualties. They said I had worked with complete disregard for my own safety until everything had been dealt with. It lasted for about three hours I think and then we were pulled back. There were all these vineyards and pillboxes, [and] it was a hard battle, the ground favouring the defenders. The only thing we could see at night was the gun flashes. When hit, some casualties would take it quietly, others would let you know they were there, but that's only natural. We didn't bring in any Germans even though there was plenty laid about the place. They suffered as heavily as we did.[34]

34   Interview with the author, George Worthington, 1989.

Private Wilkinson's C Company was in the thick of the action among the mass of vines, and he had a narrow escape:

> There was quite a bit of fighting and shooting going on while we laid among the vines and I think our barrage got some of our own men. I know the earth was literally heaving, and I do mean heaving, with the explosions. Sergeant Dunn had managed to get to us. He was slightly in front of us and he shouted for us to go forward. I was getting up and my feet slipped, I fell more or less forward and I remember this little Irish laddie, he raised himself a little higher and I just heard him shout out. He'd got a bullet through the neck and it had whizzed over the back of my neck and gone clean through him. He was gurgling and spilling blood from the mouth, [and] he seemed to scramble up and turn round to go. I was pretty hot on Sergeant Dunn's heels, only about 12 yards behind him, [when] we came across the sunken road in front of us and we broke through a cactus hedge. Because of the noise of the barrage everybody was being split up and chaps were shouting as to the whereabouts of their platoons. Jerry was answering us and as soon as a chap popped up his head they were getting shot. Sergeant Dunn shouted, 'look out!' I looked to my left and there was a big German para about to break through the cactus hedge to go across the sunken road. When he fired, I fired. Later on when we were clearing up, we saw him laid down in the lane with his pack on fire."[35]

Lance Corporal George Worthington, MM.
6th Battalion Durham Light Infantry.
(Courtesy of George Worthington)

The 9th Battalion followed the men of the 6th over the river, into the vineyards beyond and to the right of the bridge. They could move only with the greatest difficulty, the thick vines causing them to lose their bearings. To avoid the severe enemy fire, the battalion veered towards the bridgehead held by the 8th Battalion. Many of the 9th Durhams' companies were understrength, their numbers having been drastically cut down after their attack on the 15th. The Germans then gathered their

---

35   Manuscript forwarded to author, H. Wilkinson, 1993.

forces for a counter-attack, which was launched at around 6:00 a.m. against the 9th Battalion.

Private Reg Pope, with the 9th Battalion Durham Light Infantry, was part of a mortar team as the attack came in. He recounted what happened:

> Primosole Bridge was a pretty grim place. We managed to get over the bridge and took up a position on the other side near a brewery or something. We put our mortars behind the brewery. And the Germans sent their Hermann Göring Division into the attack, [but] we absolutely murdered them. The numbers of dead were tremendous. We were so close when they made this counter-attack [that] we had to remove the charge from the mortar shells and fire with just the primary charge. There was no other way of getting such a short range so as to be effective. It

Private Reg Pope, 9th Battalion Durham Light Infantry. (Courtesy of Reg Pope)

was a terrible sight after we'd withdrawn. German bodies lay everywhere.[36]

Private Ernest Kerens, with HQ Company of the 9th Durhams, found himself in the thick of the action:

> The rest of us went on with Nobby [Lieutenant Colonel Clarke, DSO] down the side of a big farm building where a lot of the 8th Battalion were dug-in. We ran across the road in a mad dash, through a field and into a deep ditch that ran next to it. With a CO with you there are things done more dangerous than with a 2nd Lt. Now we were in the thick of bullets and grenades. Some of our carriers had got across the bridge and were moving up the road in the direction of Catania, [but] they didn't get very far because of the heavy opposition. About 40 yards from us, two enemy paratroopers dashed out of a farm building and put something that exploded under one carrier. Charlie Sollis and myself fired at them two or three times. I don't know if we hit them but they gave up the idea of doing it again. From the other end of our short trench a German tank fired. I dug myself into the side of the trench until it went away. In a battle like this nobody knows who's who and there were now less than a score of us left. Nobby

36   Interview with author, R Pope, 1989.

got the men on one carrier to ask for a smoke screen which was put down and we ran like the devil the way we had come.[37]

Private Kerens and the survivors of HQ Company arrived at a deep hollow or shell hole 40 yards from the bridge and settled down as best they could. The bridge was under constant shellfire, and as there had been no opportunity for burial parties to do their work, dead bodies were everywhere. He recalled that the sunken road was packed with them:

> "As usual I went in with the IO [Intelligence Officer] and the CO [Commanding Officer] at the head of HQ Coy's little column. There were explosions all around me but I went. As we crossed the ground, which was more holey than Godly, I suddenly got a painful uppercut which floored me. A nose cap from a shell hit me and almost fell into my hand. I lay stunned for a few seconds but as my senses returned, I realised that this was not the safest place to be and I dashed back to rejoin the CO and the rest who had by now returned to the other side of the road. My cut wasn't big. I wiped the blood off a couple of times but it soon stopped. The battalion now was advancing under heavy fire and it was slow going. All day we hung on to half a mile of land, every inch of it hard won."[38]

No quarter!

As the Durhams and German paratroopers fought it out, there was great slaughter in the small area around the bridgehead. The air was alive with the whine of machine-gun fire, the flash of tracer and the snap of rifle bullets. The 6th and 9th Battalions of the DLI advanced well beyond the bridge in the face of stiff enemy resistance. The Durhams winkled out the *Fallschirmäjger* troops as they went, and their 6-pdr anti-tank guns now moved over the bridge to give them some badly needed firepower. The Durhams continued to move forward but owing to the difficulties of moving through such a congested area – with vineyards making contact with troops on their flanks impossible – companies became split up. In the thick undergrowth, numerous small isolated encounters took place. Doggedly, the troops battled their way into the enemy lines towards their final objective, mopping up any opposition on the way. As the Durhams' casualties mounted, tank support was requested and the Sherman tanks of the 3rd Battalion County of London Yeomanry rumbled over the bridge and into the bridgehead. As they smashed into the vineyards, they sprayed the undergrowth with their turret machine guns, their main guns blasting anything that moved. Any dead or wounded in the way were crushed under the massive tank tracks.

---

37   Manuscript forwarded to author, I R English, 1990.
38   Correspondence with author, E. Kerens, 1991.

The German *Fallschirmjäger* Anti-tank Battalion in action at Primosole Bridge.
(Author's collection)

In the chaos, Lieutenant Fenner, with the 6th Durhams, lost contact with his battalion HQ and the companies on his flanks. The enemy was still around him, and he said they were showing no sign of a weakening of their will to resist:

> As the light improved, we started to explore our new home and discovered that large numbers of the previous occupants were still around and full of fight. These were German parachutists dressed in their camouflaged smocks with green netting face veils, [and] they were dotted among the vines shooting everything that moved. The first hour of daylight was spent trying to cope with this menace by snap shooting and ducking smartly afterwards. Then our battalion second in command appeared with two tanks, but unfortunately we could not communicate with them, [as] we had no radio and they were completely closed down having lost too many commanders shot by German snipers when they stuck their heads out of the turret. Our only way of communication was to jump on the tank and bang on the turret lid with your entrenching tool, the commander would then open it and we could have a chat. Our battalion second in command did this and was promptly shot through the hip.[39]

The tanks retired, taking some of the wounded with them, but this brief appearance of armour had disturbed the enemy, who started to withdraw in small groups.

---

39   H. Moses, *The Faithful Sixth* (Durham: County Durham Books, 1995), p. 256.

Lieutenant Fenner spotted one group coming up the road and made sure his men were ready to receive them:

> Fortunately, we saw them first and a quick ambush was prepared from which they were unable to escape and we caught them in a cross-fire.[40]

Sergeant Thomas Cairns, serving with the 6th Durhams, remembered the vicious nature of the fighting in the vineyard as the day began to break, the men having to endure merciless fire:

> The vineyard was continually swept by enemy fire, [and] red, white and green tracer ripped through the vines, scattering the leaves and tearing through the trunks and branches. Sometimes the bullets find their mark and a man drops wriggling on the soft sooty earth, but the companies keep advancing in spite of casualties and the screams and groans of wounded or dying comrades. They advance towards the sunken road and towards the formidable line of spitting machine guns. They advance so quickly and so determinedly that the forward elements are caught up in our own barrage. Several are killed, others drop with smashed legs and ugly shrapnel wounds, and all this in darkness when control is difficult and voices are scarcely audible against the bursting shells and malicious double-barrelled crack of the German machine guns.[41]

As dawn broke, the Germans were more active than ever now that they could see their attackers. Many men trying to move through the vines were killed, and those that were wounded lay helplessly near the sunken road, any movement by them attracting the lethal attention of the German machine-gunners. The positions the paratroopers occupied were so cunningly concealed that many defied detection.

Sergeant Cairns watched in horror as he witnessed the killing of stretcher bearers by the *Fallschirmjäger*:

> To move, to disturb a vine is to ask for a deadly burst of Spandau bullets. The position is intolerable and some men who cross the road are shot in the back. Others throw themselves on the ground and engage the Germans from the flank, but he has the advantage, he remains hidden and mercilessly snipes from behind the breastwork. No one, not even the red-cross men, are safe from the murderous fire. The second in command calls for tanks and as the Shermans cross the bridge two are immediately hit, [but] the other tanks destroy the 88[mm gun] that hit them and three tanks roll into the vineyard, but still the Germans hold out. Stretcher bearers moving among the wounded are callously shot. One man carrying a stretcher is shot from a distance of 100 yards, he

40   Ibid.
41   Correspondence with author, T. Cairns, 1990.

An artillery battery laying down a creeping barrage at Primosole in support of the hard-pressed infantry in the bridgehead. (Courtesy of Jack Styan)

falls and expires almost immediately, [and] another has his fingertips shot away while carrying a wounded man.[42]

In the chaos, the Durhams still fought their way forward. Captain Reginald Atkinson, with B Company of the 6th Durhams, led his men to the sunken road and was met by ferocious fire from the German paratroopers holding that position. He said the leading section was wiped out:

> As we advanced through the vineyards, we came under the most tremendous spate of Spandau fire, which was most unpleasant. It was rather like walking down a rifle range with everybody firing at you. Eventually we reached a cactus hedge along a sunken road which was our objective. The Germans had been dug-in there but must have bolted when we got through, and fortunately we found a bomb crater we were able to get into and stayed until morning. The Germans had got back behind the cactus hedge again and fired machine guns at us as they worked back down the road to the bridge. We were in a very strong position to engage them but we were running desperately short of ammunition. Our tanks managed to get across the bridge and a lot of Germans made a dash for it. We were only 100 yards away and just mowed them down, the rest surrendered and we saw white flags going up all over the place.[43]

---

42   Ibid.
43   Manuscript forwarded to author, G. Worthington, 1990.

German anti-tank gunners continued to claim more victims, and in daylight the true extent of the carnage was revealed. The field of slaughter was strewn with the broken bodies of dead and dying men from both sides. The sight was so terrible that one German commander on the 6th Durhams' front was moved to arrange for a temporary ceasefire with the aid of a captured British stretcher-bearer. Captain Eric Fassl halted the battle momentarily to enable the wounded of both sides to be evacuated. This act undoubtedly saved many lives, as to leave any injured man lying exposed in such an area meant certain death.

Captain Fassl, serving with the 1st Company of the *Fallschirmjäger* Signal Battalion, later recorded this incident:

> When our captured medical orderly understood what we wanted we both left cover with me close on his heels, [and] had we been fired upon he would have shared my fate. He held a white handkerchief aloft and waved it. The British may well have believed at first that we wanted to surrender for immediately half a dozen flat steel helmets and caps appeared over there and I had the impression that they had clearly been waiting for this moment. However, they quickly understood what our real intention was and very soon search parties reached our positions, [and] there then followed some very tense moments while the first of the seriously wounded men were recovered. Everyone realised on both sides that an unexpected move could cause catastrophe in a matter of seconds. Fortunately, no-one lost their nerve and the business of recovery went ahead. Germans and British called out to each other to show where the seriously wounded lay, everything went well and finally two long columns of wounded, some supporting others and all bound up with emergency field dressings, left the battle-field and disappeared into the dusty glowing landscape. We allowed the prisoners to go with them and I asked our British medical orderly to call a few words of thanks to the British and let him leave with the last group of wounded. The flat steel helmets disappeared and we watched the wounded file over the bridge in the midday haze.[44]

Colonel Wilhelm Schmalz, commander of Battle Group Schmalz, commented on the event initiated by Fassl:

> The battle for possession of the bridge was so severe that at one time everyone just lay down their arms to bury the dead of both sides. In the whole of the war, it was only with English troops that I observed such events"[45]

This day – 17 July – was a crucial one for the German paratroopers and a turning point for the British. In the face of such determined opposition and after suffering such tremendous casualties, other units may have broken, but the men of the Durham

44   C. D'Este, *Bitter Victory* (Glasgow: William Collins, 1988), p. 321.
45   H. Pond, *Sicily* (London: William Kimber, 1962), p. 138.

Light Infantry stood their ground and gave as good as they got. By now the Germans had lost nearly all of their anti-tank weapons, and their commanders saw the hopeless situation they were in. To continue to resist would be suicidal, so they decided the only option left was to render the bridge unusable by loading vehicles with explosives in an attempt to destroy it. However, all attempts to do so were thwarted as the tanks of the County of London Yeomanry were now overrunning German positions. Lieutenant Colonel George Willis, CO of the armoured formation, ordered his Sherman forward to make contact with the forward squadrons, but as he did so he stuck his head out of the turret because of the poor visibility and was hit in the forehead, mortally wounding him.[46]

Major Allan Grant, MC, now took over command of the County of London Yeomanry and advanced into the battle zone. He later recalled:

> We were in reserve on the high ground overlooking the river when the Brigadier ordered me forward to take command as Colonel Willis had been killed. I got in my scout car and went down to the river and he was very angry with me because I hadn't gone in a tank. However, I went back and returned in my Sherman. There was a great deal of firing going on from the enemy machine-gunners. Chris Wrey's tank had been hit by an anti-tank shell and had burst into flames, burning him badly. Suddenly John Grimwade came up on the air and he said, 'There they are the bastards, they're in the ditch' and he fired his tank gun into them, making them scatter. C Squadron then started to pursue them in a big way. I remember one incident clearly when an infantry officer dropped into the spare driver's seat of my tank. He crouched down as he was a very tall man and closed the hatch. He looked as though he was terrified and said, 'For Christ's sake what happens if we're hit now, how will we get out?' I replied, 'firstly take off your helmet, open the hatch and you will feel much happier, we do it all the time'. I recall his answer, 'I'm absolutely terrified in this horrible thing, you're a target for everything'. I said, 'well I wouldn't change places with you for anything, you have no protection at all, we at least have armour plate'. Things were now hitting us all the time. I saw a Bren carrier of the Durhams going along a road by the river when a German popped up and threw a stick bomb at them. They were not having that and spun the carrier round and ran over him. I will always remember hearing his screams."[47]

German resistance now began to crumble, and Lieutenant Fenner of the 6th Durhams began to take more prisoners:

> We took another 15 prisoners, many wounded, including two officers. It was when these men were being searched that we had confirmation that they indeed

---

46   Lieutenant Colonel George Geoffrey Lightly Willis, DSO, 3rd Battalion County of London Yeomanry, Royal Armoured Corps, was killed at Primosole on 17 July 1943, aged 35. He is buried in Catania War Cemetery.

47   Manuscript forwarded to author, A Grant, 1989.

had been in France three days before. Most of them had tickets on them from brothels in Marseilles that showed the price, the madam's name and a space where the soldier pencilled in the name of the lady of his choice. Fifi and Zouzou seemed to be popular. Our men soon realised what these tickets meant and both Germans and British started to laugh together. This did not seem at all extraordinary at the time. Order was restored when Mark appeared with his men. He had been pinned down by this group of Germans and when they pulled out, he followed, and was pleased to see that we were alert to receive them in the appropriate manner.[48]

They've had enough!

The German paratroopers who had escaped capture, wounding or death and could withdraw in safety now pulled back 4,000 yards to the cover of the *Fosso Bottaceto*, a deep ditch that marked the outer perimeter of Catania airfield, known to the Germans as *Der Panzergraben* (tank ditch). As they did so, the Durhams counted their heavy losses Although the Germans had cracked first, this was of little comfort to the victors as they surveyed the scene of carnage. The battlefield was strewn with smashed weapons, torn and bloody clothing and equipment and the dead of both sides. Vines and trees had been ripped up by the roots and blown apart, while others were crushed into the ground as the tanks smashed through the vines. Knocked-out tanks and carriers and the vegetation on both sides of the river were still smouldering, reflecting the bitter struggle that had taken place there. The history of the 50th Northumbrian Division by Ewart Clay describes the scene as a "regular hell's kitchen".

White flags began to appear all along the sector held by the German paratroopers who were not able to withdraw. The *Fallschirmjäger* came streaming in with their arms raised to be taken into captivity, encouraged to do so by the Durhams, who prodded at them with their 18-inch bayonets.

Sergeant Stan Ferguson, serving with the 9th Battalion Durham Light Infantry, witnessed the effects of the sight of tanks upon the Germans, who, left with no option but to surrender or die, sensibly chose the former:

> I and others of the 9th Battalion were crouched in a ditch on the Catania side of the bridge, where we had been pinned down. A tank came alongside but refused to go any further because of an 88mm gun round the bend, which incidentally had been knocked out. A high-ranking officer came forward and laid down the law to this tank commander in no uncertain terms. The tank moved forward level with Stink Alley, turned left and pointed its gun down the lane. First one pair then another pair of hands were raised. I jumped into my Bren-carrier and drove up to the tank and as the Germans came out they piled all kinds of weapons into my carrier, [and] I then escorted them back to HQ.[49]

48 Manuscript forwarded to author, W. Ridley, 1990.
49 H. Moses, *The Gateshead Gurkhas* (Durham: County Durham Books, 2001), p. 251.

Men of the 6th Battalion Durham Light Infantry in positions near the ruined farm buildings at the northern end of Primosole Bridge. (Courtesy of George Worthington)

Captain Jim Kennedy, of the 9th Durhams, recalled one German paratrooper who would not surrender:

> German paratroopers, they were fanatics. One German located was camouflaged up a tree and was told to come down and surrender. He had no ammunition and just spat at the two men who had crawled across to speak to him. He just spat at them so he was shot and his body left there.[50]

Lieutenant Fenner remembered the aftermath of the battle, but even then, casualties were still being taken:

> The German withdrawal continued and we spent the day clearing up the battlefield. Men who had served in the battalion since France 1940, at Gazala, Alamein and Mareth, had not seen so much slaughter and destruction in such a small place. Now little rough wooden crosses made from ration boxes began to appear as we buried our dead. For the survivors began a few hours of respite. There was one grave of 20 men in our company area and Spandau Alley was littered with German machine-guns and parachute equipment. We equipped ourselves with Lugers and German machine-pistols, most of which were handed in later to Battalion HQ as it was 'verboten' to use captured enemy weapons. Our carrier platoon was out forward in contact with the Germans, [and] unfortunately our anti-tank guns, when coming up to join us, passed through our lines and were shot up by the Germans. A few survived to get back to us but we lost the guns.[51]

50   Correspondence with author, J. Kennedy, 1996.
51   H. Moses, *The Faithful Sixth* (Durham: County Durham Books, 1995), p. 258.

Private Ernest Kerens, with the 9th Battalion Durham Light Infantry, recorded being out on the scrounge with his friend, Private Charlie Sollis, when they entered what they thought was a large farmhouse and received a shock:

> We had made some sort of a position but had neither food nor water and in no-man's land we could see a large farmhouse less than 40 yards ahead. With a Jerry can and Charlie Sollis covering me, the two of us warily made our way towards it. It was a huge barn with the floor 6 inches deep in liquid. We tasted it and found it to be *vino*. There, wrecked by the enemy, were huge vats with the bungs knocked out. They were all around the walls but had very little left in them. We only just managed to fill half a Jerry can. Suddenly there was what sounded like a loud snore, [and] we dropped our tin and pointed out weapons at a very drunk goat that was staggering around in the corner. We enjoyed a quiet laugh, refilled our can and set off for home. As we did so others were entering from the enemy side. We did not argue with them as we did not do this killing business just for the sake of doing it.[52]

Lieutenant Colonel William I. Watson, of the 6th Durhams, viewed the battlefield with horror:

> Within these comparatively few acres there was a picture of the most appalling carnage, [and] Casa di Stefano and the buildings on the other side of the road stood in gaunt ruins. Over all there was a pall of white dust and the sickly smell of death hung on the still morning air. Soon flies and the sun's heat added to the trials of the weary victors as they set about their loathsome task of clearing the battlefield. On the Catania road the telephone poles and wires were wrecked and like the olive trees had had their limbs and tops torn from the trunks. Not far away an 88mm gun had received a direct hit, but burned-out Shermans and wrecked carriers near the bridge showed that it had not fired in vain. The sunken lane that wound its way along the edge of the vineyard, and from the shelter of whose banks, protected by the dagger sharp leaves of the cactus and the needles of the prickly pear, the German paratroopers had put up such a desperate defence, was a ghastly-shambles. Cratered with shell holes it almost beggars description. Overturned ammunition boxes, smashed panniers and broken rifles [were] mingled with torn blood-stained clothing and equipment of both sides. While the dead of Britain and Germany lay sprawled throughout its length, stink alley it was indeed.[53]

Where the sunken lane (Stink Alley) meets the Catania road there now stands a memorial cairn that commemorates the struggle the men of the 151st Brigade had there.

---

52   Manuscript forwarded to author, R. Pope, 1990.
53   H. Moses, *The Faithful Sixth* (Durham: County Durham Books, 1995), p. 258.

The original memorial cairn erected in 1943 at Primosole Bridge. The battlefield graves of men who died there are scattered around it before being taken to the War Graves site at Catania. The original cairn was eventually replaced by a more formal memorial of marble, but today it stands forgotten and neglected. (Courtesy of Ian R. English)

A carrier of the Durham Light Infantry passes a smashed-up pillbox that had been held by the British paratroopers at the northern end of Primosole Bridge. (Courtesy of Ralph Hymer)

On 20 and 21 July, drafts of reinforcements came in to swell the ranks of the 151st Brigade as they sat in the bridgehead. Lieutenant Colonel Clarke[54] and Major William Robinson[55] of the 9th Durhams went to some high ground to observe the enemy movements and arrange for a relief for the 8th Battalion. However, they were spotted by the ever-vigilant Germans, who sent over a cluster of mortar bombs and both officers were killed. Private Leslie Fallows, of the 9th Battalion, recalled the tragic event:

> Later, on the other side of Primosole Bridge, [Lieutenant] Colonel Clarke and Major Robinson stopped to have a word with us as we lay in a water duct. In the distance, from the foothills of Etna, came the sound of a 210mm as they moved into no-man's land to recce. The mortar salvo that kept our heads down claimed their lives.[56]

Aftermath

Infantry and tank co-operation at Primosole Bridge had initially proved to be ineffectual and clumsy as each unit fought the battle in its own way. Small groups of men, fighting at close quarters, had decided the final outcome in a confusing encounter that tested the fighting abilities of both sides to the extreme. Even though the Germans had surrendered this important feature, the battle for Catania was far from over. After three days of savage combat, the 50th Northumbrian Division's bridgehead extended only 1,000 yards north of the disputed bridge. Although the bridge was now firmly under British control, German efforts to destroy the structure continued, their artillery registering the range and shelling it accurately. Many more men were thus injured, some as they bathed in the Simeto. The 69th Brigade then began to cross the bridge and move into the bridgehead. The carnage that met their eyes was never forgotten by them, the large numbers of dead lying about standing out in their accounts years later.

One such was Private Bill Cheale, who fought with the 6th Battalion Green Howards:

> After the Primosole Bridge battle came to a conclusion we moved forward from our area and realised that the encounter here with Jerry had been very fierce. Bodies were floating in the river and were scattered all over the surrounding area. Corpses, parachutes and weapons lay everywhere.[57]

---

54 Lieutenant Colonel Andrew Board Stephenson Clarke, DSO, King's Own Scottish Borderers, commanding 9th Battalion Durham Light Infantry, was killed on 23 July 1943, aged 37. He is buried in Catania War Cemetery.
55 Major William Robinson, MID, 9th Battalion Durham Light Infantry, was killed on 23 July 1943, aged 37. He is buried in Catania War Cemetery.
56 Correspondence with author, L. Fallows, 1991.
57 Manuscript forwarded to author, William Cheale, 1996.

CSM Laurie Whittle, of the 5th Battalion East Yorkshire Regiment, who crossed the bridge and moved into the fighting area, also remembered the scene vividly:

> I was with Battalion HQ moving up over Primosole Bridge after the rifle companies had gone through. I noticed in the river bed this German who was the tallest man I had ever seen – he must have been nearly 7ft tall – laid there dead. Over the bridge we came to what we got to know as 'stink alley'. It certainly earned its name because there were rotting bodies everywhere, not just ten or twelve but what seemed like hundreds of bodies. On the sides of the roads and in the ditches, the Durhams were dug-in after repulsing various counter-attacks.

Private Bill Cheale, 6th Battalion Green Howards. (Courtesy of William Cheale)

> They were sat there in their slit trenches, and instead of sandbags around them they had piled up German dead, two or three high. They sat there as large as life with flies buzzing around them in this horrible stench, eating their bully beef and biscuits.[58]

Gunner Harry Wood, Royal Artillery, advance with his battery through the battle zone. He had never before seen such carnage:

> We moved forward slowly through smashed-up lemon groves and picked the odd ripe fig from overhanging trees. When we finally arrived on the Plain of Catania, what a sight met our eyes: the place was mosquito-ridden, fairly flat and had been the scene of a bloody war of attrition. Three battalions of the DLI had been involved in hand-to-hand fighting at Primosole Bridge, casualties had been heavy on both sides and the dead still lay everywhere. The whole place stank of death.[59]

Private Roy Walker, of the 5th East Yorkshires, looked on aghast at the sight that met his eyes:

---

58   Interview with author, Laurie Whittle, 1992.
59   Correspondence with author, H. Wood, 1991.

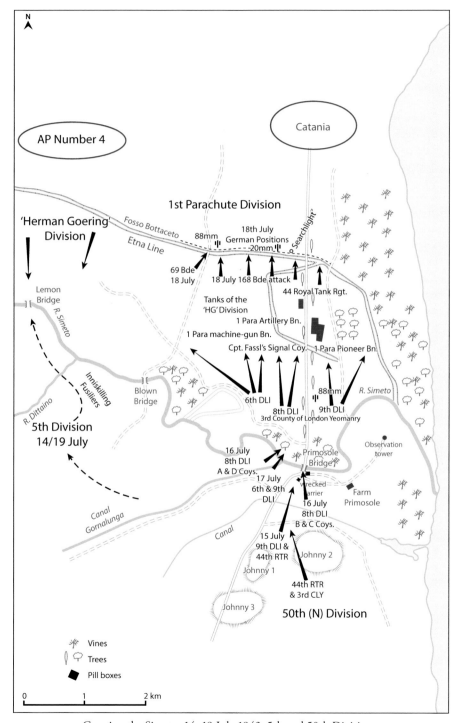

Crossing the Simeto, 14–19 July 1943, 5th and 50th Divisions.

Once we had passed over the bridge in our Bren-carriers, we had to run over the German dead to get through as there was so many of them piled up on each side. The Germans had been left where they had been bayoneted or shot. It was a terrible sight and one I will never forget."[60]

Corporal Albert Snowdon, of the 7th Green Howards, ran down the sunken lane in a carrier and was shocked by what he saw:

> There was this place called 'Stink Lane' and we had to go down it two or three times a day. We knew we were running over dead bodies in order to get through. The DLIs had been in and just left the Germans where they fell. The banks of this lane had men buried in them, [and] their heads and feet were sticking out as they'd been buried in such a hurry.[61]

The holdup at Primosole had affected Montgomery's plans, the element of luck he hoped for having never materialised. He was now forced to abandon his hopes of forcing a breakthrough at Catania. The proposed sea landings were cancelled, and the 50th Northumbrian Division was now ordered to press forward to the *Fosso Bottaceto*, which formed the most southerly defences of Catania airfield.

Private Roy Walker, 5th Battalion East Yorkshire Regiment. (Courtesy of Roy Walker)

Corporal Albert Snowdon, 7th Battalion Green Howards. (Courtesy of Albert Snowdon)

---

60   Interview with author, Roy Walker, 1991.
61   Interview with author, Albert Snowden, 1992.

6

The 5th Division at Lemon Bridge, 14-19 July

The 5th Division advanced, with 13th Brigade leading, skirting the towns of Carlentini and Lentini, following the axis of the 50th Northumbrian Division and 4th Armoured Brigade. As they reached the high ground overlooking the Plain of Catania on the morning of 14 July, they had a panoramic view quite unlike the rest of Sicily. This was a plain rich in vegetation, with cactus bushes, olive trees and almond groves. Dotted here and there were white farmhouses and other buildings. Mount Etna stood on the horizon, vapour ominously rising from its active dome. The sounds of battle to their right front came from Primosole Bridge, which 50th Division, having just relieved 1st Parachute Brigade, were trying to wrest from the enemy. The 5th Division was given orders to attack 6 miles west of Primosole over a concrete bridge (codename Lemon) spanning the Simeto and try to relieve some of the pressure on the 50th Division.

Lieutenant David Cole, who fought with 2nd Battalion Inniskilling Fusiliers, recalled the advance:

> On 11th of July 15 Brigade was fighting its way up the main road to our north against growing German resistance, [and] we spent the next two days resting in a wood. The woods were cool and there was plenty of water for washing, food was beginning to catch up with us and indeed it was good to be alive. Early on the 16th of July we were ordered to move. All that day we marched north along hilly winding roads choked with the dust of the tanks and supply convoys on the move. The sunlight glared and the heat was stupefying. Sweat and dust combined and rolled down our necks and faces like mud. Our journey took us through an ever-increasing congestion of armour, guns and lorries. Even our pipers could scarcely make themselves heard above the rumble and roar of the convoys.[1]

---

1   D. Cole, *Rough Road to Rome* (London: William Kimber, 1983), p. 43.

A sentry of the 2nd Inniskilling Fusiliers, on the northern bank of the Simeto, watches for any enemy activity at Lemon Bridge, 18 July 1943. (Courtesy of *The War Illustrated*, December 1943)

Heavily laden and parched with thirst, the men plodded along mile after dusty mile in temperatures of 35 degrees centigrade in the shade. In the afternoon, the convoy traffic began to thin out and slow, while in the distance the non-stop rumble of artillery fire, previously unnoticed, could now be heard clearly. The men of the 5th Division knew the 50th Division was now involved in fierce fighting at Primosole, and that it would soon be their turn to take part in the battle for the Plain of Catania against battle-hardened troops. On the morning of 17 July, Lieutenant Cole moved forward to the crest of a ridge overlooking the plain and never forgot the view that greeted him:

> The panorama before us was magnificent, [as] 30 miles to the north, dominating the horizon, was the misty, snow-capped conical mass, 10,000 feet high, of Mount Etna. On the plain itself we could see through our binoculars the Simeto River curling irregularly from the west down to the sea. Between us and the Simeto ran two large tributary river beds and various other water courses. These our militarised eyes immediately picked out amidst the Turneresque landscape, not for their tranquil glades but as obstacles to our tanks and transport. Between these various water-courses the land was flat and for the most part open. Beyond the Simeto the plain extended into a haze and then rose gradually

Men of the 2nd Battalion Inniskilling Fusiliers being given the rum ration before battle.
(Author's collection)

towards Etna. Along the coast, past the Simeto, the city of Catania was dimly visible shimmering in the heat. All this would have constituted a picture of great beauty and tranquillity had it not been for the thud of shells, with their tell-tale puffs of black smoke, exploding near the river. The reality was that down in front of us, concealed in slit trenches and ditches and sheltered behind buildings and whatever cover they could find, two armies were facing each other in mortal conflict. Close to where we lay was other evidence of battle, [with] on the roadside shell-shattered tanks and trucks and a burned-out armoured troop carrier with charred bodies horribly postured in a danse macabre within it. On the hillside were some dead German paratroops and several recently discarded parachutes. Down the slope just behind, our own artillery was playing a frenzied overture as they pumped out shells which droned over our heads onto the plain ahead.[2]

2   Ibid., p. 44.

As dusk fell on 17 July, the Inniskillings moved off the road to the slope of a nearby hill and found what comfort they could among the sparse scrub and rocks. The night grew colder as the tired and hungry men settled down, individuals left alone with their own grim thoughts of what the dawn would bring. The relative ease of their advance so far was about to end, and each man – ranker and officer alike – reflected on his prospects in an uncertain future. Private Albert Graves wondered, "Would I survive the coming battle? I pictured my girl at home and as I stroked my rosary prayed to God to look after me", while Lieutenant Cole reflected, "There was an emptiness in my stomach which I did not choose to identify as fear."

In the early morning of Sunday, 18 July, the men of 13th Brigade stood to their arms and made all the last-minute preparations required for the assault to come. The chill of the night air evaporated; the day was to be fiercely hot and without shade. The 2nd Inniskillings, tasked with forming a bridgehead on the far bank of the Simeto, sent forward a strong fighting patrol, commanded by Major R.C, Thomson. They came across a minor bridge over the Simeto (Lemon Bridge) and found it was still intact, though it was partly wired for demolition. Well-camouflaged German armoured vehicles were spotted in the distance. This crucial information was sent back to battalion headquarters by wireless, and the battalion commander contacted his brigade chief and issued orders for an attack to begin at 2:30 p.m. to seize the bridge before it could be demolished. In the blazing heat, plagued by flies, the company commanders stood around Brigadier Lorne Campbell, who commanded 13th Brigade, and listened in silence to their brief orders. The company commanders marked the bridge on their maps and returned to their men, who, with suitable comments, got to their feet and shouldered their equipment in the fierce heat. The companies set off down the slope, through scrub and olive trees; the anti-tank guns and other heavy equipment would have to cross a number of river beds between them and the Simeto, adding to their troubles.

By 3:00 p.m., the forward troops had spread themselves out on the plain into a practical formation for the attack. However, because of the obstacles that had to be navigated, the advance took several hours as men, sweating under their heavy loads, moved across a difficult landscape. Lieutenant Cole of the 2nd Inniskillings recalled the scene around him:

> Part of the landscape was studded, in Dali-esque fashion, with weird shapes of German aircraft, one standing absurdly on its nose, another tilted on its wing and a third burnt to a skeleton. Elsewhere the ground was carpeted, to an extent that might have bankrupted even Liberty's, with real silk, the discarded parachutes of both German and British paratroops who had, in their hundreds, successfully used the same landing area. This was a walk in the country on a blazing summer's afternoon that I, for one, shall never forget.[3]

---

3   Ibid., p. 46.

C Company, commanded by Captain Lawrence Meade, advanced to the bridge with the intention of crossing to the north bank, but came under heavy machine-gun and mortar fire. Captain Meade[4] immediately dispatched Lieutenant Harry Christie's platoon to the east of the bridge, tasked with finding a ford across the river and outflanking the German positions while the rest of the company made a frontal assault from the south. Christie's[5] platoon crossed the Simeto as planned and fought their way forward to the men holding the bridge.

By last light, the battalion was across the river and had a tenuous hold on the position. The rumble and creaking of moving tank tracks could be heard as the enemy formed up for a counter-attack. The Irishmen opened up a terrific volley, Lieutenant Christie's platoon then engaging the enemy at close quarters with bayonet and grenades, an incident remembered by David Cole:

> Then suddenly, from a few hundred yards ahead [came] a sound, quite a small sound, but one that electrified us all. It was the unmistakeable crunch of tracked vehicles [tanks] on the road. There were further noises ahead of us, [and] we could hear with frightening clarity, amidst the stillness, equipment jingling and boots rustling through the grass.

4   Major Lawrence Meade was awarded the Military Cross for acts of bravery at Lemon Bridge.
5   Lieutenant Harry Christie was awarded the Distinguished Service Order for his leadership and courage at Lemon Bridge.

Lieutenant David Cole, 2nd Battalion Inniskilling Fusiliers. (Author's collection)

Captain Lawrence Meade, MC, 2nd Battalion Inniskilling Fusiliers. (Courtesy of M Denney)

Then a German voice [was] shouting to us in strange English 'Don't fire we're the Jocks'. Sassenach that I was I knew even in Glasgow nobody spoke like that. It was clear that, out in the dark there, in addition to their tanks, German infantry were spread across our front and moving through the grass towards us. Our leading platoon shouted the challenge, [but there was] no answer, just silence. I could hear rifle bolts clicking as Harry Christie ordered his men to open fire. Then all hell broke loose, the Germans replying savagely with machine-guns to our storm of bullets. Tracer bullets streaked by like super charged flies all about us and not through the skies but just where our navels and other precious organs would have been if we had been standing up. After several tumultuous minutes the racket suddenly subsided, the tanks stopped moving and an eerie silence returned. A very precise German voice shouted somewhat theatrically 'Come on my fine fellows, we'll give you a welcome'. Then total silence again, [as] the German infantry, shaken by the ferocity of our response, had apparently, for the moment, gone to ground.[6]

This started off a series of battles that raged all night long in the small bridgehead, the determined German paratroopers trying to push the Inniskillings back as they in turn attempted to expand their position. Men made use of the slit trenches the Germans had begun to dig, while others crouched among the long grasses, busying themselves with the unreliable radios. Contact with all the companies was achieved, but the static interference caused problems and grew progressively worse. Many radio operators wondered if it was as a result of deliberate jamming. These problems became irrelevant as it soon became clear that the Germans were about to attack again. The air was full of cries as the German infantry advanced, yelling and shouting in the darkness, accompanied by the menacing rumble of tanks crunching through the undergrowth. The advanced platoons of the Inniskillings sent up flares that cast eerie shadows over the battlefield. The Germans, meanwhile, dropped to the ground to avoid being hit in the machine-gun fire that erupted from both sides. When the flares faded, the battle resumed, grenades exploding and tracer rounds cutting through the low scrub. Lieutenant Cole looked on as he saw his first man killed:

A few yards away from me along the bank I saw a man knocked back by a stream of bullets which struck him full in the chest. He crumpled to the ground and lay still. I bent over him, his shirt and equipment were soaked with blood and out of his pale face his eyes stared up at me through the dark, wide open and blind. He was absolutely dead. But there was nothing that I or anybody else could do for him and though it was Sunday God seemed to be busy somewhere else. Then, as another of our flares floated lazily to the ground, we caught glimpses of the leading German tank lumbering slowly towards us in the artificial twilight. It was an ugly squat monster, its huge gun swivelling menacingly round towards us near the bridge. From behind it came the noise of other tanks

6   D. Cole, *Rough Road to Rome* (London: William Kimber, 1983), p. 49.

revving their engines and manoeuvring off the road. A wave of horror splashed coldly over me. What for pity's sake would stop the tanks now from overrunning our forward platoons?[7]

Thoughts of doom ran through the minds of the defending companies as they listened to the terrifying roar of engines and the creaking of tank tracks. Suddenly, there was a terrific explosion and a flash of light lit up the battlefield. German soldiers were caught in the glare for a moment, frozen in a variety of poses. The tank had run over an anti-tank mine with spectacular effect as fuel and ammunition erupted in a huge fireball, incinerating the crew. The German *Fallschirmjäger* and infantry attempting to advance through the flickering light were cut down by Bren-gun and rifle fire from the British positions. The rest of the armour, not wanting to suffer the same fate as the first tank crew, came to a halt and the whole German attack lost its impetus and faded away. During the lull that followed, the officer commanding the 2nd Inniskillings, Lieutenant Colonel Joseph Patrick O'Brien-Twohig, ordered D Company, commanded by Captain Peter Slane, to cross the Simeto to the west of the bridge and outflank the Germans. They crossed without difficulty and advanced towards the bridge, but as they did so the burning tank lit up the area, exposing them to the ever-watchful Germans. D Company came under a devastating fire as they tried to force their way to the bridge. In the brutal battle that followed, another German tank was hit and exploded, adding more light to the scene, but D Company could get no further forward.

Captain Peter Marlow Slane, MC,
2nd Battalion Inniskilling Fusiliers.
(Author's collection)

The advanced troops in the bridgehead were inexperienced in battle before this day, but they withstood the attacks by the battle-hardened paratroopers and infantry of the Hermann Göring Division like seasoned veterans, keeping their nerve and holding their ground. During the night, the Germans rained down a hail of shells and mortars onto the bridgehead. The ground was torn up all around the fusiliers, steel splinters and stones hurtling through the air. Casualties began to increase, and there were cries of pain from men calling for stretcher-bearers when the barrage ceased. Moments

7   Ibid., pp. 50-51.

later, tracer bullets cut across the landscape as the German infantry recklessly
rushed forward, only to be cut down by
the determined fusiliers. The Germans
kept up their attacks throughout the
night, and the positions of the forward
platoons became very precarious.
Lieutenant Colonel O'Brien-Twohig
ordered them to withdraw and called
for a concentration of shellfire from
the divisional artillery. The 'stonk'
came down with a violent crash, shell
after shell falling on the enemy ranks,
throwing men and machines alike into
the air.

Lieutenant Cole watched in awe as
the barrage came down:

Lieutenant Colonel Joseph Patrick O'Brien-
Twohig, DSO and Bar, Commanding
Officer 2nd Battalion Inniskilling Fusiliers.
(Author's collection)

> The stonk came like a monsoon, a
> few big slow drops at first and then
> a deluge. The first shells whooshed
> lazily over our heads to crash here
> and there in front. Then their
> numbers grew and grew and grew
> until the air immediately above us vibrated with their tumultuous and crowded
> passage. All along the front the ground shuddered with the seismic upheaval of
> their explosions. Many of the shells just skimmed over the trees around us to
> burst only 40 yards away on the far side of the river, exactly where the leading
> German infantry were trying to establish themselves. When it had ended, I was
> half deaf and I was convinced that the Germans caught under it could not have
> survived.[8]

After the barrage ceased, there was no sign of any continued German resistance, and
a dozen or so dazed Germans stoop up with their hands in the air and were escorted
into captivity by a lone fusilier. Cole watched as they approached: "Amazingly a lone
limping fusilier came back with several German prisoners. He had been on the wrong
side of the river when the last barrage came down and had been joined by some
Germans who, like him, took cover under the bridge and instead of fighting it out
entrusted themselves to his care, [as] they had had enough."

The platoons at the front were very low on ammunition, but they knew it was on
its way, as other fusiliers were struggling over the landscape to bring it to them. Cole
was there when it arrived:

8   Ibid., p. 56.

Sweating gunners labouring to keep up the barrage on the German positions on the Simeto.
(Courtesy of J. Styan)

In the early hours of the morning one of our Bren carriers, loaded with ammunition, was with great difficulty brought forward to the river. The problem then
was to carry the ammunition across the Simeto and some of us, who had nothing
more urgent to do, lent a hand. I still have nightmare memories of struggling
across the river with loads of ammunition, firstly enjoying the cool touch of the
shallow water but then, as I clambered breathlessly up the far bank into what
seemed like a scene from Dante's Inferno, wondering, in a kind of academic
trance, whether any of the machine-gun bullets streaming anonymously past me
were intended for me personally. The burning tanks had set fire to the grass and
a great conflagration had spread across much of our front, [and] banks of smoke
eddied about so that when the moon was high visibility was patchy and dim.[9]

Lieutenant Robert Alexander was then ordered by O'Brien-Twohig to lead B
Company of the 2nd Inniskillings in a counter-attack across the Simeto by the side
of the bridge. As Alexander and his men filed past the rest of the battalion with
heavy hearts, their friends quietly wished them luck. Lieutenant Cole recalled: "Bob
[Alexander] passed me on the way across and I wished him luck, he paused by me for
a second and whispered to me with a smile 'It's suicide' and then went on." As soon
as they had crossed the river, the Germans opened fire with numerous machine guns,
cutting down many men before they could get very far. The survivors went to ground
and could get no further, Alexander being killed at the head of his men.[10]

9   Ibid., pp. 53-54.
10   Lieutenant Robert Alexander, 2nd Battalion Inniskilling Fusiliers, was killed in action on
      19 July 1943 at Lemon Bridge, aged 32. He is buried in Catania War Cemetery. Before the

As dawn broke on Monday, 19 July, the bridgehead held fast. D Company moved forward out of reserve with a single anti-tank gun that was pulled by a jeep driven by Fusilier Thomas James Moore,[11] who towed it into a good firing position on the north bank while under fire. The Germans kept up a sporadic fire on the Inniskillings, enabling their forward troops to withdraw. The smoke that had shrouded the area began to subside and the enemy could be seen to be pulling back. They left behind them a scene of devastation, the blackened hulks of three motionless *Panzer IVs* smouldering among the dead of both sides lying in the burnt countryside.

Lieutenant Robert Alexander, 2nd Battalion Inniskilling Fusiliers. (Author's collection)

However, even in retreat, the Germans were still dangerous foes, guarding themselves against a possible surprise attack on their rear by the British. A Bren-carrier sent over the bridge was at once hit by an 88mm shell, killing all on board, an effective reminder that although the Hermann Göring Division was withdrawing, its members were still close enough to be lethally effective.

The Inniskillings then withdrew from the bridgehead and were relieved by the Cameronians. With glazed eyes, they plodded back several hundred yards and took up a position in a dried-up tributary of the Simeto. Sentries were posted and the men dozed in the hot sun. Nevertheless, David Cole found it impossible to sleep:

> In the early hours of the morning I had taken a Benzedrine pill which the doc had given me to keep me fully awake, [and] it certainly did that. But unfortunately, it also left my mind in a whirl for some time afterwards. My ears kept ringing with the tumult of battle, my brain

Fusilier Thomas James Moore, MM, 2nd Battalion Inniskilling Fusiliers. (Courtesy of N. Hardy)

war, he was a member of the Royal Ulster Constabulary, and was an international rugby and cricket player.

11   Fusilier Thomas James Moore was awarded the Military Medal for his courageous actions at Lemon Bridge.

was full of questions without answers and, when I closed my eyes, I kept seeing the reproachful look on the face of a dead German whom I had tripped over in the dark down beside the river. Beyond that I had no real feelings. We had captured and held the bridge but I felt no elation. Our casualties had been heavy, [and] I had lost several friends and some of my own men. But I felt no ache, I was just totally numb.[12]

On the night of 19 July, the 15th Brigade put in a hastily planned attack in an attempt to enlarge the bridgehead that had been forced by 13th Brigade. However, only a basic reconnaissance of the attack area was carried out when something more in-depth was required for such an operation. Darkness was approaching when the units involved were informed of events, and poor information and the nature of the difficult terrain ensured that the attack would fail. The brigade advanced with the 1st Battalion Green Howards on the right of the line and the 1st Battalion York and Lancaster Regiment on the left. The 1st Battalion King's Own Yorkshire Light Infantry followed up in reserve. Major J.R, Elwood commanded D Company of the 7th Battalion Cheshire Regiment, which would provide machine-gun support for the attack. Artillery from XIII Corps laid down a creeping barrage that the attacking infantry followed as they moved forward at 2:45 a.m. on the 20th. The troops found their forward movement was slowed down by having to cross unknown deep ditches before they reached the railway line. The barrage they were supposed to follow thus ran away in front of them and the infantry lost their sense of direction. The German machine-gunners waited for the barrage to pass over them, then emerged from their dugouts and proceeded to pour mortar and machine-gun fire into the ranks of the attackers. B Company of the Green Howards overtook A Company in the darkness and met the full volume of the enemy's fire, being forced to retire into the ditches for some cover. The dead and wounded had to be left in enemy hands: Captain Hedley Verity,[13] Captain Lawrence Hesmondhalgh[14] and Lieutenant Arthur Johnson[15] were all mortally wounded and died in captivity.

Lieutenant Cole and the 2nd Inniskillings were in reserve after their exertions when forcing the original bridgehead at Lemon Bridge, when he received some news that greatly upset him:

> On the night of the 19th, soon after we had been relieved, 15 Brigade was ordered to go through and enlarge the bridgehead. They had a grim 24 hours beyond the Simeto during which, raked by a murderous fire, they suffered

12   D. Cole, *Rough Road to Rome* (London: William Kimber, 1983), p. 57.
13   Captain Hedley Verity, 1st Battalion Green Howards, was mortally wounded in Sicily on 20 July 1943 and died of his wounds in Italy on 31 July, aged 38. He is buried in Caserta War Cemetery. Hedley was a well-known Yorkshire and England cricket star.
14   Captain Lawrence John Hesmondhalgh, 1st Battalion Green Howards, died of his wounds on 20 July 1943, aged 28. He is buried in Catania War Cemetery.
15   Lieutenant Arthur Reeson Johnson, 1st Battalion Green Howards, died of his wounds on 21 July 1943, aged 34. He is buried in Catania War Cemetery.

heavy casualties and then had to be extricated under cover of our artillery the following night. I can still remember the speed and shock with which the news came back from the Simeto that Verity, the great English test bowler and one of my boyhood heroes, was wounded and missing. He was the second international sporting figure to be mortally hit near a bridge called Lemon.[16]

After a fierce battle, the 1st Battalion Green Howards found itself pinned down in the open and overlooked by the nearby enemy. Mortar and machine-gun fire made any movement in daylight impossible, but during the night of 20/21 July, the brigade withdrew and moved to the rear.

Captain Hedley Verity, 1st Battalion Green Howards. (Courtesy of *The War Illustrated*, December 1943)

16   D. Cole, *Rough Road to Rome* (London: William Kimber, 1983), p. 59.

7

The Etna Line
69th and 168th Brigades
enter the battle for Catania

On the night of 16/17 July, the German forces in front of Catania were reinforced by Lieutenant Colonel Erich Walther's 4th Parachute Regiment, giving a seriously needed boost to the badly mauled *Fallschirmjäger* troops that had fought the Durhams and Inniskillings. The men of the 4th Parachute Regiment took up positions along the *Fosso Bottaceto* (in an anti-tank ditch, or *Panzer Graben*), and to their west were joined by elements of Battle Group Schmalz. This area was to become the eastern anchor of the Etna Line. The Germans now found themselves in vastly superior positions to those they occupied at Primosole Bridge. With their fresh troops, plus new weapons taken from British gliders and weapons canisters, the area around Highway 114 was turned into a death trap for any British units attempting to break through to Catania.

The last phase of the battle for the bridgehead at Primosole had ended, but although the bridge was now firmly under British control, it had been captured far too late. Montgomery's hoped-for luck had never materialised, and he would have to abandon his plan of forcing a breakthrough to Catania. On 17 July, XIII Corps commander Dempsey paid a visit to Kirkman of 50th Northumbrian Division to inform him the outflanking coastal landings that had been planned would not now be taking place. The 50th Division's task was now to advance for another 2,500 yards to the *Fosso Bottaceto*. In the severe fighting at Primosole over the last few days, the 151st Brigade had shot its bolt, losing 500 killed, missing and wounded.[1] It was decided that for the next operations, it would be replaced by the 69th and 168th Brigades, who would launch another protracted and bloody attack towards Catania into the teeth of the German defences. These positions had previously been meticulously prepared by Italian engineers and were now manned by reinforced and well-armed German paratroopers.

---

1   D. Rissik, *The DLI at War* (Durham: Brancepeth Castle, 1953), p. 130.

Attack on the Fosso Bottaceto, 18 July

On the night of the 17/18 July, 168th Brigade passed through the Durhams' positions, with their central axis on Highway 114. The plan was for the 69th Brigade to then pass through in a westward movement, seize the railway line and in so doing screen the left flank of 168th Brigade.

Lieutenant David Fenner, of the 6th Battalion Durham Light Infantry, watched as the fresh and untried troops of 168th Brigade passed through the bridgehead:

> That night 168th Brigade companies deployed through the DLI Brigade bridgehead [London Scots, London Irish and Royal Berkshires], [and] were to attack towards Catania. They were very smart, [with] officers wearing the correct pattern webbing equipment, binocular cases, compass case, map-case and pistol. Our company officers favoured other-rank equipment as the pouches could be used for grenades, biscuits, tea or a compass, [and] we all carried rifles. My platoon was draped about with German parachute silk over their torn KD [battle-dress] and we looked rather scruffy compared with these new arrivals. It was 168th Brigade's first battle and we wished them well. For some reason just before the attack began a Borfors light anti-aircraft gun fired a burst of tracer to mark the axis of the infantry attack. This had often been used in the desert but seemed unnecessary under the present circumstances. I am sure the Germans were expecting an attack and this may have confirmed their suspicions.[2]

The assembly area for 168th Brigade was in vineyards that gave only low cover. It had already been the scene of bitter fighting, and the dead and wreckage of the past few days were still scattered about. The supply units bringing up the ammunition had great difficulty getting forward, having to move back and forth along a very narrow track. A reconnaissance was ordered to discover the strength and approximate location of the enemy, with carriers from the 168th Brigade and tanks of the 4th Armoured Brigade to take part. The area where the main road crossed the *Fosso Bottaceto* was thought to be the location of an 88mm gun acting in an anti-tank role, so artillery firing high-explosive and smoke shells saturated the area during the reconnaissance. Reports came in from the 4th Armoured Brigade that there was thought to be no enemy to the south of the *Fosso Bottaceto*, with those that were there only in small numbers. Very little Spandau fire came from the German line, and because of the lack of any reaction to the reconnaissance force by the Germans, it was believed that there were very few enemy troops in the area.

These reports would prove to be extremely optimistic and even misleading for the attacking brigade. In the enemy line, the newly arrived German paratroopers had prepared their positions to meet the expected attack and did not want to give away their new locations. The 168th Brigade would attack without a barrage in the hope of gaining the advantage of surprise. However, a barrage was to be

---

2   Manuscript forwarded to author, Reg Pope, 1992.

focussed on the final objective, the southern boundary of Catania airfield, from 10:45–11:00 p.m.. At 10:00 p.m., the leading troops were to leave the start line. But things began to go wrong from the outset, as the London Scottish on the right flank were not informed of the new plan until they had left the start line. The order for the Bofors gunners to fire tracer every three minutes to mark the flanks of the attack was not cancelled, and this fire was started as the attack went in, giving away any element of surprise.

The lead troops of the 168th Brigade settled down for the night in vineyards and orchards as they waited for their first great test as a fighting unit. An anonymous account left by a soldier of the London Irish paints a vivid picture of the mind-set of these young men as they spent a quiet night alone with their thoughts:

> The darkness of the night had fallen over us with all the suddenness of the eastern hemisphere. The stars glittered and shone like diamonds in a dark blue sky. The soft breeze drifted off the Mediterranean and stole sighing gently through the trees. In the orchard there was the scent of luscious fruit and our world seemed enclosed by a myriad of whispering thoughts. Only a few hours before we had landed on this island and in the dark depths of the orchard we slept fitfully or talked quietly of things which come into the minds only of soldiers waiting for their first battle. Occasionally whispers came through the darkness to the spot where I lay, queer fragments of conversations which, pieced together, showed that the men's thoughts were far from the field of battle, they were away in better days and peaceful times, in the homes they had left far behind in England.[3]

As the time for the attack approached, concern was being voiced at Divisional Headquarters as information came in reporting that *Fallschirmjäger* had been seen dropping in or close to the divisional area. The attack went in with the 1st Battalion London Scottish on the right flank and the 1st Battalion London Irish on the left. They halted as planned 400 yards short of their objectives, with the enemy taking no action. The standing barrage rumbled and flamed before them, the troops moving as close as they dared to it. As it moved on, the troops launched their assault. An anonymous soldier of the London Irish left his account of events:

> Our tongues were still but our minds were strangely active as we filed nearer, ever nearer to no-man's land. We were on the alert and the going was rough as we passed through vineyards that seemed endless. The attack was to start at once and we had hardly absorbed this news when the silent almost beautiful night was made hideous by the crash of the guns. Flares, very lights and tracer made the night as day. Ahead of us I could see a long double row of barbed-wire glittering maliciously in the light. The guns stopped and we went in, [and] I clutched my rifle like a drowning man holds on to a straw. We ran ahead

3   *London Irish Rifles*).

dodging and ducking, slipping and cursing, over hazards which we could see only when we reached them.[4]

Lieutenant Martin Poppel, serving with the Machine-gun Battalion of the German 1st Parachute Division, had just returned to duty after being wounded. He recalled the experience of the heavy, but ineffectual, barrage:

Our conversation is suddenly interrupted by an abrupt resumption of artillery fire in the sector defended by my own company. The strikes are too numerous to count, there are at least four per second, how have the British managed to move in such a massive quantity of artillery? The earth trembles and shakes so much that it seems like the end of the world. What's more it carries on for a bloody long time. Telephone connections were cut some time ago and the wind carries the clouds of powder over us. *Hauptmann* Laun reports that the artillery fire has been withstood without any casualties.[5]

Farm buildings and other strongpoints in front of the outer defensive perimeter of Catania aerodrome had not been touched by the barrage. The attacking troops pressed on into a storm of fire from the German paratroopers, and in some parts of the attack the fighting was at very close quarters. An anonymous account by a soldier of the London Irish Rifles observed:

The enemy was now wide awake and his Spandaus swept the ground over which we passed. His mortars whizzed and banged and sand, dust and earth crashed heavily around us. The man ahead of me coughed, sighed and rolled over slowly, [and] I raced past him hoping the stretcher-bearers would not be far behind as he was my friend. A carrier swept by me spitting out death. I reached the wire, fell flat and hacked away like hell and a gap was made. We crawled through and as we did so a murderous pill-box in front went up with a roar and a great flame. Well done the mortars I thought. Bayonets moved forward in relentless line, [but there was] a burst of fire and again men fell flat, some never to get up again. The section on the left was catching it hot because they were exposed to deadly fire, [and] they held on in dwindling numbers.[6]

Communication with the attacking troops was poor as some companies had advanced too quickly and were out of touch with their commanders. Not realising that some troops had actually reached their objectives, a barrage was called down on the enemy positions, only to fall on their own men and cause even more casualties. Stragglers came back with tales of massive casualties, others giving the commander of 168th

4   Ibid. (accessed 9 September 2018).
5   M. Poppel, *Heaven and Hell: The War Diary of a German Paratrooper* (Kent: Spellmount, 1988), pp. 127-28.
6   *London Irish Rifles* <www.londonirishrifles.com> (accessed 9 September 2018).

Brigade, Brigadier K.C. Davidson, a false view of what was going on, stating things had not gone exactly to plan but a lot of ground had been seized. Davidson made contact with his divisional commander, reporting to Major General Kirkman that only in a few places were the objectives achieved and that his men were now pinned down by Spandau fire 200 yards short of the enemy lines. As this was open country, it was not considered desirable to remain in such a position and the brigade was ordered to retire to the line of a ditch 1,000 yards short of the original objectives. A soldier fighting with the 1st London Irish described the scene:

> Pressing myself to the earth I choked and spluttered in the smoke from the flares and fires all around me. We had reached our first objective and the thought came to me 'would we press on or stay where we were until daylight'. The shelling died down and with it the flares, but to the left there was still the venomous spatter of the Spandaus. Darkness returned and the firing slackened, [and] the order was passed forward that we must fall back in good order. In the pale shafts of dawn, we checked up on who had come through our first ordeal and who had not.[7]

Searchlights from Catania airfield swept the area, exposing the attackers to the gaze of the German machine-gun and mortar crews. The artillery barrage made little impression on the German line, and when the infantry had attacked, they were cut down. German accounts talk of the horrific scene before them as they rained down machine-gun, small-arms and mortar fire upon the attackers. Lines of wounded and dead lay before the German positions. Some of the Germans were so moved by the plight of their enemies that early next morning they went out into no-man's land and rescued those close at hand. After yet another costly frontal attack, the 50th Division had been halted again several hundred yards short of the *Fosso Bottaceto*.

One of the *Fallschirmjäger*, Sergeant Georg Schmitz, looked at the scene before his position and was shocked by the sight of so many dead and wounded:

> "Heavy machine-gun and small arms fire greeted these brave attackers who again suffered high losses. The dead and wounded lay in rows before our positions and the cries of the wounded were heard for the rest of the night. Early the next morning we rescued some of the wounded that were near to us."[8]

As the attack by the 168th Brigade went in, 69th Brigade also moved forward on the left flank at 2:00 a.m. They were informed of the failure of the 168th Brigade too late, and some troops had already fought their way forward and onto their objectives.

Private Harry Forth, serving with the 5th Battalion East Yorkshire Regiment, volunteered to be first in to knock out a machine-gun post in an effort to lessen casualties in the first wave:

7   Ibid. (accessed 9 September 2018).
8   C. D'Este, *Bitter Victory* (Glasgow: William Collins, 1988), p. 395.

We heard there was to be a big frontal attack. I volunteered with four other lads to knock out this machine-gun post one night. We blackened our faces before we left, all equipment that rattled was taken off or secured, and personal possessions were left behind. The enemy post was well concealed – it was a deep wooden emplacement. We had to sneak up to it and when we were close enough, we lobbed in grenades. One went right into the machine-gun aperture and that silenced it altogether. As we were coming back a Jerry observation post for their

Exhausted troops of 168th Brigade go to ground to escape the deadly machine-gun fire sweeping the area. (Author's collection)

mortars must have spotted us, [as] he dropped one right in the middle of us and caught me in the leg. The lads behind me caught the lot, [and] killed all four of them. The road was higher than the ground I was laid on and a machine gun was firing over me. I could see the tracer bullets striking the road. I thought if they come much lower, I could catch it, so I dragged myself to the shelter of the road side and laid low until the early hours of the morning. Then our main attack went in to clear Jerry out of the wood, [and] the infantry passed over me as shells and mortar bombs flew overhead. As the lads passed me, I could hear them shouting. I looked down and thought I'd lost my leg as the lower part below the knee was doubled back against the upper part. The next I knew a stretcher-bearer found me and I prayed to the Lord to save my leg. I didn't want to lose it in the field. I was numb and the lower part of my body was dead.[9]

9   Interview with author, Harry Forth, 1990.

Private Forth was taken to the rear, where his condition was thought so serious that a nun was brought, clasping her rosary beads to give him the last rites. However, Forth's life was spared and his prayers answered. His leg was saved, but gave him many years of complications. He was Mentioned in Dispatches for his bravery in the face of the enemy in this attack.

In the early hours of 18 July, three squadrons of the 44th Battalion Royal Tank Regiment rumbled over Primosole Bridge and deployed in support of the 69th and 168th Brigades. On the west side of Highway 114, B Squadron took up a position among the ranks of the 6th and 7th Battalions of the Green Howards. A Squadron moved to the east of the highway and linked up with the London Scottish and London Irish. The 168th Brigade was by now under heavy fire. Harry Gratland was a tank driver in A Squadron that day, and when asked what he recalled most clearly, he replied: "I remember the terrible heat and the stench of death."

Arthur Soper drove his A Squadron tank forward to assist the badly mauled infantry:

> We in A Squadron advanced to help the London Scottish, who were under heavy fire and pinned down in the open. Charlie Hardy, my troop sergeant [and] acting troop officer, moved out to the right flank when his tank ran over a mine which blew off the track. As was usually the case the crew luckily escaped. My tank commander, L/Sgt Wally Warley, told me to change direction right and to head over to where Charlie's tank lay, the idea being to rescue the crew who were sheltering behind the knocked-out tank. While executing this manoeuvre we were fired on from a wood beyond Charlie's tank. Luckily for us the rounds went over the turret. I think the position of the angry man did not allow him to depress his gun enough to register hits, much to our relief. We reversed out of harm's way and had another go, [and] our second attempt at retrieving Charlie and his boys was successful and we withdrew as a squadron south of the bridge.[10]

An anonymous officer of the 7th Battalion Green Howards described his experience of the night attack by 69th Brigade:

> It was what might be described as the queerest night attack of all time. The orders were to move in several bounds by means of compass bearing for so many paces, but on arrival at the start line all was chaos and nearly 40% had failed to arrive, having become mixed up with the London Scottish. The barrage unfortunately went wrong and two companies had a number of casualties from it before it could be stopped over the wireless. This caused a further splitting up of companies and odd men were wandering about all over the place completely lost. Our company commander, Captain Ian Hay, crept forward unseen to deal with the first MG post when some fool of an NCO opened up with a

10   Correspondence with author, A. Soper, 1989.

German *Fallschirmjäger* stand to their arms as they brace themselves for the next British attack.
(Courtesy of H. Wernamann)

machine-gun and gave away the show. Hay collapsed riddled with Spandau bullets[11] and it was only with great difficulty the company was able to extricate itself. New orders were received and we were able to withdraw, admittedly in some confusion as it was dark and everyone had lost their bearings. The night's escapes included the crew of a carrier which received a direct hit from an 88 solid shot which went right through the vehicle and left the men untouched. One of the most trying facts about this operation was the great use made by the Boche of the searchlights on the airfield, which continually swept the ground over which we moved.[12]

The captured diary of a German soldier reveals the toll being taken on the ordinary front-line men in these constant and bloody actions:

Still near Catania, heard the German news, the stuff they are putting over is beyond description. The enemy has about half the island and they talk about engaging enemy convoys off the coast (Poor Germany). We are almost

11   Captain Ian Thomas Russel Hay, 7th Battalion Green Howards, was killed on 18 July 1943, aged 22. He is buried in Catania War Cemetery.
12   E.W. Clay, *The Path of the 50th* (Aldershot: Gale & Polden, 1950), p. 199.

surrounded again, [so] we must withdraw. Hope I get out of it. The food is bad especially the bread. They say we've got to move forward tonight, [but] yet again it is a pretty hopeless business. In the front line we settle down on a hill, it is to be held to the last round. Anyone who retreats will be shot. We hold the height with a handful of men. The enemy has tried with all weapons to take it but we hold out.[13]

A "very bloody killing match"

The situation early on 18 July was not good for the British, and both attacking brigades were ordered to withdraw to a line well short of the *Fosso Bottaceto*. The baptism of fire for the inexperienced troops of 168th Brigade and the poor intelligence they had received from the start had ensured that the first attempt to seize this important feature ended in failure.

At first light on 19 July, the bridgehead was reinforced by the 102nd Anti-tank Regiment, the machine guns of the 2nd Battalion Cheshire Regiment and two battalions of the 4th Armoured Brigade. With a few minor exceptions, the Eighth Army got no closer in July to the city of Catania, which was a mere 3 miles distant. It was not until 5 August that the city fell, 22 days after the 1st Airborne Division took the bridge over the Simeto. The struggle for access to the open ground of the Plain of Catania was to stick in the memory of the attacking forces as one of the bitterest of the entire war. Many thought it put Alamein in the shade, the stench of rotting flesh on the banks of the Simeto still clearly remembered by veterans many years later. Montgomery himself referred to it as a "very bloody killing match". His dream of a quick victory in Sicily had been halted and his hope of a swift advance on Catania came to naught.

At Primosole Bridge, a small outgunned force of *Fallschirmjäger*, with very little air cover and no naval support, had held up the entire Eighth Army and prevented the rolling-up of the German left flank. The 50th Northumbrian Division may not have broken through to the Plain of Catania, but their attacks at Primosole Bridge did succeed in drawing all enemy forces away from Catania, leaving the city undefended for five days. Had Montgomery stuck to his original plan of an amphibious landing at Catania, he would doubtless, at one fell swoop, have reclaimed the initiative and gained control of the coastal route to Messina. The Etna Line would have had one of its vital links broken, thereby bringing the campaign to a speedy and favourable conclusion for the British.

The most crucial battle of the Sicilian campaign had been fought with the use of only a fraction of the assets available to the Eighth Army. The crushing naval firepower and the ample numbers of aircraft at Montgomery's disposal were never fully utilised, ensuring that no breakthrough occurred. The official history of the war puts

13 AFHQ Papers, Public Records Office, WO 204/983.

the blame for this failure squarely on the shoulders of the 5th and 50th Divisions.[14] Although the majority of the troops of the Eighth Army at that time were seasoned veterans, they were very tired and at times browned-off. Nevertheless, the performance of the lead units of both divisions on the Simeto was awesome to behold as they doggedly fought their way forward against battle-hardened elite parachute forces in prepared positions. The lack of transport laid on by the planners and logisticians was a major factor for the inability of the ground troops to make deep and swift penetrations with their forward units. Because of the rocky and mountainous Sicilian landscape, movement was limited to the few roads already in existence. The enemy knew every turn the British took and made maximum use of their detailed knowledge of the interior to harry the invaders at every opportunity. The British forces thus pressed on down these narrow arteries, unable to outflank the enemy.

It had been a mistake by Montgomery not to use the full resources at his disposal to launch a thrust to the Plain of Catania. He had not adhered to his own rule that when trying to break a strong enemy position, concentration in strength was the order of the day. The usual criticism levelled at Montgomery is that he was too cautious, but in this instance the opposite was the case. His main fault here was not to employ the massive firepower at his command to overcome the weak coastal sector, where any breakthrough could have penetrated clear through to Messina.

A change of plan

Montgomery wrote in his diary of 21 July:

> My troops are getting tired as the heat on the plain of Catania is great. He [the enemy] is going to hold the Catania flank against me to the last. The proper answer to the problem is now to reorganise, to hold on my right while keeping up a good pressure to continue the left hook with XXX Corps using the Canadian Division. I will give 78th Division to XXX Corps and go hard for Adriano and then northwards round the west side of Mount Etna.[15]

He was now to undertake a secondary drive using XXX Corps' 51st Highland and 1st Canadian Divisions, but neither supporting the other. The Canadians, responsible for delivering the left hook from Etna to Leonforte and on to the River Adrano, were lacking in transport and were new to combat. The mountainous terrain also favoured the defenders. The offensive began unfavourably, with the Germans putting up savage resistance whenever attempts were made to breach their defences along the northern perimeter of the Plain of Catania. The badly mauled 50th Northumbrian Division was still holding the Primosole bridgehead, and a series of attacks by the

14   C.J.C. Maloney, F.C. Flynn, H.L. Davies and T.P. Gleave, *The Mediterranean and the Middle East: Sicily 1943* (London: HMSO, 1954), p. 354.
15   B. Montgomery, *El Alamein to the River Sangro* (London: Hutchinson, 1948), p. 198.

5th Division that were delivered north of the Simeto, with the intention of seizing Misterbianco, met with failure. As at Primosole, all that was achieved was a tenuous hold on the northern bank of the Simeto, the troops of the 5th Division taking heavy casualties as they tried to widen the bridgehead.

The Canadians were supposed to have taken Leonforte by the night of 19 July, but because of the skilful delaying actions being fought by the German forces they did not achieve their objective until 22 July. At the same time, a number of bloody actions were being fought by the 51st Highland Division, which secured a crossing over the River Dittaino and captured the village of Gerbini and nearby area. The Scots encountered fierce German resistance and were checked at Sferro, unable to cross the Simeto some 2,000 yards south of Gerbini airfield. Operations ceased and the Scots took up a defensive position, awaiting the next move. Three days later, Patton's American Seventh Army advanced and took Palermo on Sicily's northern coast but was too late to intercept the eastward withdrawal of the Axis mobile forces. Patton's troops had been originally used as a flank guard to the Eighth Army's advance on Messina, but the change of plan meant they could take on an offensive role. The Axis forces now fell back in good order, delaying the British and American forces for as long as possible at every opportunity. The ground favoured the defenders, and each step back shortened their front and lines of communication, meaning that fewer troops would be needed to man the defences. Montgomery and Patton made amphibious landings in attempts to cut off the retreating Axis forces, but each time the enemy slipped away.

The 5th Division and 50th Northumbrian Division were both to find the latter part of the Sicilian campaign a hard slog as they sustained more casualties following up the retreating enemy. Captain D.L.C. Price, who fought with the Royal Artillery in the 5th Division, remembered the hazardous journey as they pressed forward towards a still very active enemy:

> The time came to press across the plain of Catania and those were a few bad hours. More than a few soldiers turned and ran. We had the luggage carrier on our vehicle carried away by an anti-tank shell while we were in it. I did a foot reconnaissance and we holed up behind a haystack until dawn. We pressed across the plain but the Quartermaster's Department of the infantry hadn't caught up and by the evening the PBI [Poor Bloody Infantry] had had no food. A German machine-gun crew fired into the positions that had been selected for a night's rest and sustenance. I remember the extensive use of mines during this phase of the affair and sitting on the bonnet of our tracked carrier looking for a disturbed surface on the paths we followed, touching the driver's shoulder to stop when suspicion arose. There was no time for sweeping ahead, [as] we had to get on. One less lucky carrier had been blown up into a tree and was lodged forlornly in a leafy grave.[16]

---

16   S.W.C. Pack, *Operation Husky* (London: David & Charles, 1977), pp. 142–43.

The fall of Catania, 5 August – 50th Northumbrian Division

The 50th Division was slow to follow up the retreating enemy, their advance heralded by an enormous barrage that was wasted on empty Axis positions. Catania was devoid of Germans, and the few citizens who had stayed were in fact organising a celebration. The Northumrbians reached the outskirts of Catania on the morning of 5 August. Lieutenant Roy Griffiths, with the 9th Battalion Durham Light Infantry, received orders to take a reconnaissance patrol into the city:

> I was summoned to Battalion HQ and there was ordered to take a large patrol, together with an official photographer, to gain entry into Catania. We went down a comparatively good road into the city and we attained the outskirts without contact with the enemy. The area was considerably damaged and the official photographer enjoyed his travels with us. I got to a point in Catania where I decided to stop and report my location. The battalion then entered the town and Captain Brian Gardner was officially handed the keys.[17]

Lieutenant David Fenner, part of the 6th Durhams, left a good account of the 50th Division's move forward:

> Several very big explosions took place behind the German lines. The bomb dumps on Catania airfield were being destroyed, giving a clear indication that the Germans would be pulling back. On 4th August we followed 8th DLI in pursuit of the departing Germans. We were harassed by enemy 88 gunfire and *Nebelwerfers*. One of the brigade support company 3-tonners received a direct hit and the ammunition exploded, destroying the vehicle and killing the crew. We passed the dead anti-tank gunners killed on 16th July when they had driven through the forward companies into the German lines in error. None of our dead at this time had been buried by the Germans, [whereas] we in 50th Division were most careful to bury all our own and the German dead. Either the Germans were too idle or perhaps it was deliberate policy to leave our dead unburied so as to depress our forward troops as they advanced. As we entered Catania, the locals were busy looting the stores and shops and paid little attention to us."[18]

Corporal Robert Cork, who fought with the 9th Durhams, remembered the good reception he received in Catania:

> On the 5th August we moved across the plain and through Catania. A great deal of looting by civilians was going on. I was given a packet that turned out

---

17   Manuscript forwarded to author, W. Ridley, 1990. A film of Lieutenant Griffiths' entry into Catania was displayed by Gaumont British News Review for 1943 and featured in the celebrated television documentary series *The World at War* (1973).

18   Ibid.

Troops of the Durham Light Infantry, 151st Brigade, 50th Northumbrian Division, enter the ruins of Catania. (Courtesy of H. Forth)

to be six boxes of three-hole razor blades. I shared them with the lads and the wine flowed.[19]

Lieutenant Colonel William Watson recalled the devastation he found in Catania and the reception his 6th Durhams received from the civilian population:

> [There were] shell holes, craters, bomb craters and smashed buildings all over the place, but somehow as if by magic the poor people came out of their holes and hovels and gave us a royal welcome. Flowers etc and nuts are thrown to us. I stop in the centre [of the town] and up come war correspondents and reporters who start writing their experiences on the steps of the tribunal. Then came the film people. We disarmed the carabinieri to the intense delight of the crowd who seized their rifles and smashed them on the pavement.[20]

Private Jim Radcliffe advanced through Catania with the 9th Durhams and caught a last view of the enemy as they withdrew:

> Jerry had just pulled out and we must have been a bit close on his heels because an armoured car suddenly appeared at the end of the street. I don't know who

19   Correspondence with author, R. Cork, 1991.
20   H. Moses, *The Faithful Sixth* (Durham: County Durham Books, 1995), p. 264.

was more surprised them or us. I know at the time I was busy smashing up some Italian rifles when there was a shout for all Bren-guns to the end of the road. There was a wall at the end and across the open hillside we could see a few troops running about, so we rested our guns on the wall and had a high old time having a go at them. Bob [Lord] was by my side jumping up and down with excitement saying, 'let me have a go' which I did.[21]

The advance beyond Catania

The advance beyond Catania was to be most unpleasant, and as the 50th Division approached Acireale, enemy resistance stiffened. Sherman tanks advanced to support the infantry, while the big guns of the Royal Navy shelled the enemy north of the town. The Germans utilised fully this difficult country, blowing numerous vital bridges to impede the British, and mines were liberally laid on the roads and tracks and in the cultivated areas adjacent to the roads. Major delays were caused to the infantry and transports, and the dangerous work of the sappers increased; they were always in demand and suffered very heavy casualties. The Germans held a series of positions, and though few in number they used the terrain to their advantage, with artillery and mortars frequently called upon to harass the advancing British troops. The Germans held a position until they were pressed, and then withdrew to the next line of defence.

Lieutenant Martin Poppel, serving with the *Fallschirmjäger* Machine-gun Battalion, was part of one section that was ordered to fight a delaying action when the British arrived:

> We can hear the sound of hand grenades and machine-gun fire from the unit on our left, they were firing on a recce patrol consisting of four Tommies, [and] one had been left wounded. Reports came in of increased enemy activity when a messenger came running in to report that Tommies were on their left only seventy metres away, [and] things could well get lively. Everyone grabs their guns and heads for the anti-tank position at breakneck speed. We jump down a wall towards them and we are there, falling on them like the devil. There was some fierce close combat before we drove them off. But they almost caught us in our combat post in this broken countryside, damn it. The boys were all superb, all joining in, [and] none hesitated or stayed out of the way. A lot of Tommies managed to get away but we brought back six prisoners and found several corpses, [and] trails of blood were spotted leading back towards the enemy lines. We had no casualties, proving that when you go in hard and courageously you get the best results. Everyone is inspired by this success and nobody pays any more thought to the fact that the Tommies had come very close to wiping us all out.[22]

---

21 Ibid., p. 98.
22 M. Poppel, *Heaven and Hell: The War Diary of a German Paratrooper* (Kent: Spellmount, 1988), p. 135.

A young infantry officer with British 69th Brigade left an anonymous account of the opposition regularly being offered by such dedicated paratroopers as Poppel:

> It was our ninth consecutive day in the front line and was also one of the worst days I have ever experienced. We soon found ourselves advancing along a dusty road past evacuated pill-boxes, [and] on our left were troops of the 5th Division. We came to a level crossing and a blow in the road held up our carriers for a time. With my leading section were sappers with mine-detectors and progress was slow. As we threaded our way up a narrow lane Spandaus rattled at us from our right front and a fusillade of air-burst shells came uncomfortably close. We grounded and the company commander came up and tried a series of plans which were bound to fail because the country was so close that we never really pin-pointed the enemy. The enemy's clever mutually supporting positions made it impossible for us to attack one post without running into heavy fire from the others. The enemy was still mortaring [us] and air-burst shells were still coming over.[23]

A new plan of attack was implemented by his platoon, but it was not long before they were pinned down by heavy enemy fire. The young officer tried to move things on and took a risk:

> I ran directly up the hill in full view of the Spandaus, [and] they soon saw me and began firing, the bullets spitting all around my heels. As I neared the top of the hill frantic voices shouted, 'hurry up sir' and I tumbled into a ditch occupied by our own troops just as a fierce burst of Spandau fire skimmed the top. When I had got my breath back, I learnt that the troops were Green Howards who had been ordered to advance up the same valley as myself but who had been held up. 'He's got the place taped' they said. When I got back to my own company HQ, I found that yet another attempt to dislodge the enemy had been made but was still unsuccessful. More serious casualties had occurred within the company. By this time, it was dusk and it was decided that we should rest and lick our wounds.[24]

Colonel Wilhelm Schmalz, commander of Battle Group Schmalz, inspected the German front lines every day without fail, as his command was widespread, holding positions from the coast to halfway across the Plain of Catania. His daily routine would start at the crack of dawn to the thunder of shellfire echoing across the flat ground being contested by the two armies and the ridges surrounding it, as he later recalled:

> The sun shone down unmercifully and everywhere was dust, [so] in the battle zone journey by car would become impossible. Moving on foot I found a good

---

23   E.W. Clay, *The Path of the 50th* (Aldershot: Gale & Polden, 1950), p. 207.
24   Ibid., p. 209.

survey point, taking cover every now and again. I met battalion reserve where everything was well prepared, [and] the soldiers had withdrawn from battle during the previous night and were waiting for the enemy in their new positions. Young faces, unwashed for days, [were] dusty and sweaty but still cheerful. Out of the horror of battle came the will to live [as] I spoke to many of them, [but] many had little to say and many [were] incoherent. We went on and came round a rocky corner as iron and steel was flying around our heads. The battle thundered and roared, raged and screamed. At first, we were flat on the ground and then up and running. This particular assault lasted for about five minutes and then gave way to silence, apart from intermittent shooting.[25]

On the afternoon of 11 August, units of the 50th Northumbrian Division occupied Giarre and Riposto. The Germans had good observation here and directed shellfire at any sign of movement, making it difficult for the advanced troops of the 151st Brigade to the north of both towns. Meanwhile, 168th Brigade moved forward and established troops on the Mascarello Ridge and in Macchia. On the morning of the 12th, the Germans were still holding their positions and 151st Brigade was relieved by the 69th Brigade. The rattle of machine-gun fire and the thud of mortar bombs from both sides echoed around the hills as they kept up the constant pressure on their opponents. The 231st (Malta) Brigade was placed briefly under the command of the 50th Division at this time, and the division itself was under the command of XXX Corps. The 168th Brigade was then taken from the 50th Division and returned to the 56th (London) Division, from where it came.

The enemy withdrew in the night, and this kind of delaying action was repeated again and again. Losses mounted, with officer casualties particularly severe as the 5th and 50th Divisions pressed on against a well-organised and ruthless foe. Right up to the end of the campaign, the forward troops were constantly being harassed by German artillery and machine-gunners. Lieutenant Fenner was ordered to take a platoon patrol of the 6th Durhams into the town of Riposto to see if it was still occupied. They found a few Italian soldiers, but the Germans had withdrawn:

We returned to our company area and settled down for the night. During the evening German artillery and machine guns opened up along the battalion front. I think it was their way of letting us know they were pulling out. The next day 69 Brigade advanced through us and moved on to Messina, which they reached on 17th August. It was over.[26]

On 30 August, the commander of the Eighth Army, Montgomery, visited the battered and depleted units of the 50th Northumbrian Division, an event recalled clearly by Lieutenant Fenner:

25   H. Pond, *Sicily* (London: William Kimber, 1962), pp. 147–48.
26   Manuscript forwarded to author, William Ridley, 1996.

Monty addressed us in a dried up river bed. He congratulated us and said we had fought long and hard under his command since Alamein. We could now have a rest, but the army was going over to Italy soon. If he ran into trouble there, he would send for us because as he said, 'I like to have the 50th Division with me wherever I go'. A great groan rose from the soldiery at this remark. He then said 'why, I might be going home', [and] false laughter followed with cries of 'ha bloody ha' from the troops. Monty departed smiling among a mixture of boos and cheers. He must have been wise enough, old soldier that he was, to know what to expect. Among the ranks of the 50th Division were some hard-bitten, cynical and lively survivors. The sort of generals' chat that may have gone down well with fresh infantrymen or those of a less dangerous branch of the army, would have been disastrous. All Monty had to offer was more of what had gone before. He handled it all very well and we respected him for it.[27]

The units of the 50th Northumbrian Division embarked from Sicily on 20 October, and the convoy they were in set sail on the 23rd. Passing Avola, where they had landed, the ships set out to sea, eventually dropping anchor off Algiers. No shore leave was granted. The voyage home was without incident, and as they passed to the north of Ireland, the ships split up, heading for the ports of Glasgow, Liverpool and Bristol, where they arrived on 5 November.

David Fenner remembered when they were duly informed of their future role in the invasion of Normandy:

Towards the end of January 1944 our commanding officer called us all together in our Nissen hutted officer's mess and said 'As you know Monty is back running things and was not happy about some of the divisions earmarked for the assault [on Normandy]. He wants one of his veteran formations to lead. We are to be an assault division to land on D-Day.' If Monty was aware of it, he had the last laugh.[28]

A *Times* correspondent who had been following the progress of the 50th Northumbrian Division wrote an article that appeared on 25 August 1943:

I always had the feeling that the sheet anchor of the Eighth Army was the 50th Division. They had the hard dirty work at Lentini and Primosole Bridge and the long slog up the coast from Catania, past Etna, through cruel country. They got less public mention than some of the other divisions because theirs was the unspectacular flank of the front. They plugged on learning the new warfare the hard way, taking their punishment and coming on for more. Tyne and Wear may well be proud of them for they are a grand division.[29]

---

27 Ibid.
28 Ibid.
29 Newspaper cutting forwarded to author, Mr Kilgallon, 1990.

8

The 5th Division, 31 July-10 August Sferro: A suburb of hell

On 31 July, the 51st Highland Division, on the left of the 5th Division, attacked the Sferro Hills. The 5th Division was ordered to move up to the Sferro railway station sector and secure the Highland Division's right flank. German forces held the high ground overlooking the valley of the Dittaino River. Lieutenant David Cole, of the 2nd Battalion Inniskilling Fusiliers, recalled this as "A colourful suburb of Hell called Sferro Station." As the lorries loaded with men of 5th Division approached their destination in darkness, the area was lit up by flames from a burning oil truck. The shattered buildings of the station were illuminated and outlined by the blaze. Wrecked lorries that had been hit by shellfire were strewn about the place, on their sides and upside down, as the men approached with heavy hearts. A Lieutenant Maybury said dryly, "First station I've seen with a decent fire in the waiting room."

Lieutenant Cole thought the whole scene unreal, like entering a set for a Hollywood war film, but all the 'props' were real:

> Chunks of masonry fell from the signal box as a shell struck it. Flames spat into the sky and heavy black smoke from blazing oil billowed over our heads. The crack of mortar bombs ripped the air. Everywhere the acrid fumes of explosives mingled with the odour of death. All this and the rattle of machine-guns, with their tracers streaking into the sky, strengthened my feeling that our change of residence was not for the better. The neighbours were far too rowdy. Crouching low we dashed over a level-crossing pitted with shell craters, then along the railway track under the shelter of the crumbling platform, climbing over heaps of debris and squeezing past overturned wagons. The visibility was, in its ghoulish way, all too good and the Germans must have enjoyed what they could see. Faces glowing red in the dancing light of the flames peered like rabbits from their dug-outs and shouted to one another above the din.[1]

1   D. Cole, *Rough Road to Rome* (London: William Kimber, 1983), pp. 62–63.

From the nearby foothills, where the 51st Highland Division was attacking, the ominous sound of explosions shook the air, and the tempo of artillery fire from both sides increased. Cole recalled the violence of the moment:

> Dead on time the whole countryside behind us erupted in a blaze of flickering light as, with a thunderous roar, the massed artillery of the Highland Division opened up, sending a torrent of shells whooshing and whining over our heads. It was as if some great monster behind us had suddenly come to life, spitting fire. A moment later our Borfors guns joined the chorus, chugging out streams of tracer shells which chased each other merrily across the sky. Finally, when we were stupefied and deaf, the Germans, their suspicions aroused, did what was expected of them and brought all their defensive fire down on Sferro. We dashed for our dug-outs as German shells began to crash down along the railway. Once again, we seemed to be living in the midst of an inferno. The ground shook under us as, with a rending crash, a shell struck the roof of the command post. Bits of steel, sandbag and railway sleeper flew everywhere and dust showered down around us. We feared catastrophe, but a moment later a dazed adjutant peeped out through the crumbling entrance and said, 'I thought I heard something on the roof'.[2]

The commander of Battle Group Schmalz had expected the attack and martialled his troops as the barrage came down. Colonel Schmalz had ordered his men to get under cover, leaving just a small number of sentries and lookouts in the line, as he recorded:

> The enemy [the British] put everything they had into it. Their artillery fire rose to a pitch, [and] we tried to estimate the density of the shells and if I am not mistaken it was around 30,000 shots in one and a half hours on one kilometre of front line. In my sector at Gerbini we managed to break through the enemy attack, but at Sferro the enemy got their own back on us for it.[3]

On the morning of 1 August, the 5th Division sent out patrols to make contact with the enemy and find out if they were still alive and kicking. One patrol led by Lieutenant Colin Grant was badly mauled by the German infantry, with Grant being mortally wounded. He and Lieutenant Cole had been friends for a long while. Cole commented on the death of his friend: "When I passed his body lying shrouded in a blanket on a stretcher I felt my spirit drain away. I remembered the good times and the talks we had about after the war, [but] now for him there would be no 'after the war'." When the commanding officer heard the news of Grant's death, he was furious

2   Ibid., p. 66.
3   H. Pond, *Sicily* (London: William Kimber, 1962), p. 164.

A German paratrooper (centre) with two *panzergrenadiers* of Battle Group Schmalz.
(Author's collection)

Troops of the 5th Division pass the outskirts of Catania on their way to Misterbianco.
(Author's collection)

and at once ordered a 'murder'[4] to be put down on every registered German position. The guns duly roared out a final salute to Lieutenant Grant.[5]

Centuripe fell to the 78th Division, and the 51st Highland Division was held up but successfully secured the high ground at Sferro, repelling German counter-attacks on the morning of 1 August. By now, it was obvious that the German forces could no longer hold the approaches to Mount Etna.

On 5 and 6 August, the 5th Division pressed forward along the left flank of the 50th Northumbrian Division, with the 17th Brigade on the right and 15th Brigade on the left. As they progressed, they had to deal with a few minor enemy posts that had been left behind. Mines and booby traps were also a constant danger, slowing the advance considerably taking a steady toll of the unwary. Misterbianco was entered late on 6 August to an overwhelming reception. Lieutenant Cole recalled a pleasurable interlude in the town:

> It turned out to be a pleasant place, [with] farm buildings, water, trees and shade. We were in the front line but nobody seemed to know quite where it was and there did not appear to be many Germans about. I chiefly remember lying on my back in the grass counting the hundreds of American bombers flying overhead with the intention presumably of flattening somewhere or other. No doubt German soldiers were lying on their backs a few fields away doing exactly the same. It was too good to last and a couple of days later we moved again to a sector a few miles to our north-west.[6]

Captain H.L. Wilson, serving with the 1st Battalion Green Howards in 15th Brigade, commanded the leading platoon of D Company and found the going hard:

> All seemed peaceful enough until just as we rounded the bend a Boche machine-gun opened up. We flung ourselves down and I wriggled forward round the bend. I could not see where it was but got a Bren-gun up and opened fire on a house, just for effect. Leaving the Bren there I got back and took my platoon off the road to the right. I got two more Bren-guns over into the vineyard and spread the sections. Then, firing from the hip, we went forward. Norman Yardley, meanwhile, had got his platoon down on the left and put a couple of well-aimed mortar bombs on the spot. The Boche then fled, leaving his guns and one man dead. We continued the advance, picking bunches of grapes off the vines as we went along, climbing up into the village [Motta] without any further opposition.[7]

4   A 'murder' was a type of engagement invented by the commander of the 2nd New Zealand Division in 1942. It entailed a concentration of a division's artillery (72 guns) onto a single point for two or three minutes. It was originally called 'Method A'.
5   Lieutenant Colin Grant, 2nd Battalion Inniskilling Fusiliers, died of his wounds on 1 August 1943, aged 22. He is buried in Catania War Cemetery.
6   D. Cole, *Rough Road to Rome* (London: William Kimber, 1983), p. 61.
7   W.A.T. Synge, *The Story of the Green Howards* (Richmond, Yorkshire: The Green Howards, 1952), p. 224.

Troops of 17th Brigade, 5th Division, enter Misterbianco on 5 August to a rapturous reception.
(Author's collection)

Stella Drezet was a young girl living in the village of Puntalazzo in the foothills of Mount Etna when the infantry of the 5th Division arrived:

> A Scottish regiment came to our village. This was the feast day of our patron saint Maria Assunta in Cielo. I was a little girl looking in awe at these people. The soldiers had rosaries dangling from their wrists and they respected our day. I stood on a bollard so I could see more but I tripped and fell off and hurt my knee. I was bleeding and one of the soldiers took off his belt, spat on it and cleaned the wound on my knee. The soldiers used to give us gelleta biscuits.[8]

On 7 August, the 5th Division was on the move again, attacking the enemy's right flank in order to threaten his position. Two mobile columns, consisting of the 5th Reconnaissance Regiment and tanks of the County of London Yeomanry, advanced swiftly and Mascalucia was cleared of the defenders. They were then joined by elements of the 50th Northumbrian Division to the south of the town, forcing the Germans to retreat. The 15th Brigade held the deserted town of Belpasso, and the nature of the hilly landscape became more and more difficult, making the movement of supporting guns a problem. Beyond Nicolosi, Axis tanks were spotted. The 13th and 15th Brigades approached Nicolosi, which was heavily mined and booby-trapped; some booby traps were even placed underneath German corpses. As the 5th Division

8   Manuscript forwarded to author, H. Wernamann, 1989.

passed through Nicolosi, the signs of recent fighting were everywhere: houses and vehicles were on fire, while dead soldiers were sprawled in the streets. British tanks, guns and lorries choked the road leading to the town as accurate German shellfire fell ahead; they were all waiting for the poor bloody infantry to clear the way.

Tremonti, 8-9 August

The 2nd Inniskillings and 2nd Cameronians debussed and occupied positions north and north-east of Nicolosi. To the north of the town, the 1st York and Lancs moved some way up the slopes of Etna, enabling their artillery observers to find many good targets for the gunners. The next task for the 5th Division was to capture the feature called Tremonti, which consisted of three conical hills clustered together beside a track leading from Padara up the slopes of Mount Etna. These strategically important hills were held by a battalion of *panzergrenadiers* of the 15th *Panzer* Division, and tanks were reported to be in Padara.

The guns of the 91st Field Regiment, Royal Artillery, and of the Sherman tanks of the 1st Canadian Division, laid down a creeping barrage that the infantry followed closely behind, passing Padara. The 2nd Inniskillings moved forward as enemy shells thudded around and among them and tracer rounds buzzed angrily over their heads. As this attack went in, the 2nd Cameronians attacked two other prominent hills – Monte Arso and Monte Gervasi – and in doing so surprised and eliminated a group of Germans who were firing on Tremonti.

The leading Inniskillings found the going hard because of the distance they had to cover and the hilly terrain as they disappeared into the smoke and confusion all around. An optimistic report was received at a sceptical Battalion Headquarters that Tremonti had been taken, but this proved not to be the case.

On the night of 7 August, Lieutenant Cole and his 2nd Inniskillings settled down in the main square of Padara:

> In the darkness the town looked sinister and hostile, [and] each shade and shape had its own menace, with spectral enemy machine-guns protruding from every door and window. The main streets swerved drunkenly this way and that and off them ran a web of murky lanes ideal for German gun-emplacements and patrols. Nor were we encouraged by renewed reports of a Tiger tank lurking round a nearby corner. This and other hair-raising information was offered to us by various Sicilians who kept slinking out of the darkness to help us. In these eerie and threatening surroundings, we barricaded ourselves in, with riflemen at every approach and Willy's Anti-tank guns poised for action. It was not to be a quiet night and as the church clock struck nine a dozen shells came whistling down to crash amongst the adjoining houses. Parts of the square crumbled around us showering us with debris and wounding two of our fellows. This ceremony was to recur at intervals throughout the night.[9]

9   D. Cole, *Rough Road to Rome* (London: William Kimber, 1983), p. 73.

In the early hours of 8 August, the 5th Division sent out patrols towards the lower slopes of Tremonti, where they were challenged in German and heavily machine-gunned, showing the enemy to be there in force. The 13th Brigade emerged from Padara and began their forward march to Tremonti in the morning mist. Immediately ahead, the three hills of Tremonti came into view; they were steeply terraced and the lower slopes were planted thickly with vines. Through these vines a maze of lanes threaded their way, each flanked by high stone walls, while the crests were strewn with patches of undergrowth and small trees. This scene of rustic peace had not yet been visited by the horrors of war, but this was soon to change. Bren-carriers and Canadian Sherman tanks rumbled past the infantry, belching out exhaust fumes and throwing stones in all directions. It was not long before the enemy machine-gun posts opened up on the advancing column, and a cluster of mortar bombs thudded into the dry earth, sending the soldiers sprawling over the ground. Lieutenant Cole recalled:

> One of our Bren carriers nosed its way up the lane and almost at once ran into a hail of bullets from invisible German machine-gunners hidden close by. A savage exchange of fire ensued and the Germans withdrew down a ditch. The leading platoon came under a blizzard of machine-gun fire and had to disperse into the vineyards. We at company HQ watched the men of our forward sections as, hiding, dodging, ducking, crawling, sprinting and sometimes dying amongst the lush vines, they worked their way steadily closer to the German positions.[10]

Two companies pressed on and eventually the lead sections reached the foot of Tremonti, where they were shielded from the withering German fire by the terracing above them. The supporting heavy weapons had by this time been brought forward and mortars put down a murderous barrage on the slopes of Tremonti. Then the Canadian tanks joined in with devastating impact as they pumped shells into the German positions at short range, and finally the Vickers machine guns of the Cheshire Regiment raked the defenders' lines with stream after stream of bullets. The roaring of the barrage thundered above the heads of the attacking troops, who were showered with debris as vines and trees that had hidden the Germans were blown to shreds. Germans were occasionally caught sight of, scurrying about the hillside as the barrage ceased. Lieutenant Roy Hingston, commanding the leading platoon, led his men up the slope, scrambling from one terrace to another, one section killing a machine-gun crew as they did so, reaching the top of the hill with fewer casualties than expected. Without pause, the Germans massed for a counter-attack. The companies on the lower slopes watched aghast as the Germans swarmed back up the hill to attack Lieutenant Hingston's platoon, whose members were busy trying to establish themselves in their new position. Firing automatic weapons and hurling grenades before them, the Germans came on until they were in the British positions, and with the two sides so closely intermingled there was bloody hand-to hand combat.

---

10   Ibid., p. 75.

Men at the foot of the hill looked on as the battle was fought for the peak, which lasted for several minutes. Hingston realised he had not enough men left to hold on, and fearing being overrun he began to extricate the survivors. The doughty lieutenant was the last to leave, keeping the Germans at bay by hurling grenades into their ranks with lethal effect. He covered his men as they retreated from shrub to shrub and terrace to terrace. When they finally arrived at the foot of the hill, Hingston had with him only nine of the men he had started out with. Other platoons also suffered heavily. It was by now obvious that it would take more than two companies to take the heights of Tremonti, and a full battalion attack by the 2nd Inniskillings was organised for the morning of 9 August.

Montgomery visited 13th Brigade's Headquarters later on 8 August and threatened to pull out the whole brigade and replace it with one that could do the job required of them. This was taken as a great insult, and the 13th Brigade was thereafter even more determined that Tremonti would be taken on 9 August, no matter what the cost.

During the early hours of the following morning, fighting patrols were sent up the forward slopes of Tremonti in darkness. Although these were ferociously engaged by German machine-gunners, they managed to return to their own lines with a prisoner. Before first light, the troops prepared themselves for the trials ahead, the Inniskillings moving forward and beginning their ascent at dawn. The momentum of their determined attack swept the German defenders off both hills in the face of some heavy machine-gun fire. Lieutenant Cole commented:

> The rest of the battalion then swept forward, the last of the Germans jumping out of their trenches after a final burst or two from their machine-guns, scurrying headlong away. The hills were found to be littered with German dead as well as a sad number of our own. The Germans had obviously had a bad time and, judging by the profusion of equipment that they had uncharacteristically abandoned, their decision to withdraw had been a precipitate one. Indeed, one of the prisoners told Willy that his battalion had been given orders to hold on to the last. It was quite clear that the Germans had been fighting here with several hundred first-class troops for every hour of delay they could gain to keep open the escape route to Messina.[11]

The war diary of the 5th Division for 9 August recorded:

> "For the past five days the division has been pushing forward against an enemy intent on withdrawal. The enemy's intention to abandon Sicily is apparent. The nature of the country, which is steep hills interspersed with lava fields, render it impossible in many places to leave the roads. The many bridges and the precipitous nature of the country render it easy for the enemy to impose delay out of all proportion to his fighting strength.[12]

11   Ibid., p. 77.
12   Public Records Office (TNA), WO 169/8711.

Once the dead were buried and the wounded evacuated, the 5th Division quickly reorganised and continued the advance, taking up positions on the road to Messina just north of the town of Trecastagni. The lead troops entered the town in a dishevelled state after their exertions of the last few days, but the whole population turned out onto the streets to welcome their liberators. Laughing and cheering, the people threw flowers at the troops and thrust bunches of grapes into their already red grape-stained hands. Lieutenant Cole wondered cynically to himself, "Had they bestowed the same treatment on the German reinforcements rushing south a few weeks earlier?" The 5th Division pressed on, with the 50th Northumbrian Division on their right. On 10 August, the 1st Battalion Green Howards reached Masacalucia and were ordered to attack the mountain village of Milo. At 5:30 a.m. on 11 August, the men of the Green Howards entered the town as the enemy were leaving on the far side. The German gunners began to shell the area: the first missile to arrive knocked down the church spire, and A Company, who were near the church, began to take casualties. During the day, the Green Howards prepared for a counter-attack that never materialised, but on the evening of the 12th, the enemy put down a heavy stonk with all the weapons at their disposal, a sure sign they were preparing to withdraw. The 5th Division was now drawn into reserve, earmarked to take part in the forthcoming invasion of the Italian mainland.

Lieutenant Cole recollected his experiences in Sicily:

> We had been in some bloody fighting and lost many men. But the nastiness had been overlaid, even at the time, by an exhilarating aura of adventure. I did not of course then realise that that sense of adventure, with its supercharged impulses of curiosity and excitement, was one of the few advantages that the infantryman new to battle enjoyed over the veteran, and that it would alas gradually fade away. Thereafter we would become much better soldiers, hardened and more expert, but we would also, to that end, have to draw more and more deeply on our innermost resources of discipline, comradeship, endurance and fortitude.[13]

13   D. Cole, *Rough Road to Rome* (London: William Kimber, 1983), p. 82.

9

Bitter victory
The end in Sicily

The battle for the Plain of Catania is remembered as one of the bitterest fought by troops of the British XIII Corps throughout the whole of the war. Montgomery's dream of a rapid advance followed by a swift and decisive victory in Sicily had turned to ashes. At Primosole Bridge, a relatively small and outgunned force of German para-troopers, devoid of naval or air cover, prevented the Eighth Army from rolling up the Axis left flank and advancing straight to Messina. The futile British airborne opera-tion to seize Primosole was an important part of the failure, but not the real reason for the total collapse of the operation. The actual cause was the cancellation by Dempsey and Montgomery of the planned amphibious landing at Catania. Although the 50th Northumbrian Division never broke the German defences on the Simeto, it did draw all available German reserves away from Catania. Had Montgomery kept to his orig-inal plan of an amphibious landing at Catania, he would have regained the initiative at a stroke and taken control of the coastal route to Messina. The Etna Line, the most vital link in the German defences, would have been overcome and the outcome of the whole campaign set in train. For five days, Catania was left undefended against an attack from the sea while Battle Group Schmalz and the *Fallschirmjäger* fought savagely to prevent XIII Corps from making any headway north of the Simeto.

Another reason for XIII Corps' poor performance was the lack of use of the naval and air resources available. The exception was the employment of naval gunfire by the 1st Airborne at Primosole, though the poor quality of the radios in use at the time prevented this happening at vital moments in the battle. Montgomery's attempt to force a lightning breakthrough to the Plain of Catania was conducted in a one-dimensional environment throughout the campaign. Although 200 requests were made for naval support and were met by the Royal Navy, they could have provided much more support if they had been called upon to do so.

As XIII Corps battled forward to Lentini and Primosole, there is no evidence that the forces on the ground made good use of close air support. A crucial campaign was being fought by only a fraction of the assets available to the commanders on the ground. The official history blames the failure of XIII Corps to advance on the 5th and 50th Divisions, stating that both these were not seasoned formations,[1] a claim that is not borne out by events. The only unseasoned troops in XIII Corps were those of the 168th Brigade, who were needlessly sacrificed by being thrown into the battle when it had already been lost. The performance of the 5th and 50th Divisions during the whole campaign was exemplary; they did all, and more, that was demanded of them, even when they knew senseless loss of life was inevitable.

One major factor in the inability of XIII Corps to make deeper and more rapid penetrations was the failure of the British logisticians and planners to provide adequate transport. Movement through Sicily's interior was severely limited to the few existing roads, which were well defended by an enemy who knew how to utilise the mountainous terrain to maximum advantage. Animal transport was needed to outflank the enemy; to do it without this was virtually impossible. Consequently, units were tactically slow; Carlo D'Este likened it to "cramming a number of corks into a bottle".[2] The area of advance for the British XXX Corps and XIII Corps was a nightmare for mechanized forces but ideal for pack animals. Indeed, companies of pack mules were originally included in the Eighth Army's original order of battle,[3] but they were cancelled by a staff officer, thereby terminating any possibility of organised pack support. After 10 days of covering enormous distances and fighting numerous actions in burning heat and humidity, many troops were left exhausted by their efforts. In hindsight, the overall lack of transport in the follow-up convoys seems to have been as great a mistake as the decision not to employ pack transport.

Not launching an attack towards the Plain of Catania with all the resources available to both XXX Corps and XIII Corps was a serious misjudgement on Montgomery's part. His attempts to break through at Catania on a one-brigade front proved futile, but he persisted with the strategy, one he had castigated others for pursuing in the past.[4] The British failure at Catania was not a consequence of Montgomery's lengthy and determined concentration of force at a decisive point, but a result of dispersing his assaults over too large an area and lacking a powerful reserve to exploit any breakthrough. Nigel Hamilton has commented: "For once Monty had let down his army by being overambitious and his lack of ruthless adherence to his own rule of concentration in strength."[5]

In Sicily, the Eighth Army had at its disposal a total of 39 battalions of infantry and nine tank regiments, plus supporting units of artillery regiments, reconnaissance units, engineers and machine-gun battalions. However, Montgomery's attempts to break through the Catania defences relied solely on one brigade at a time, and occasionally on a single battalion. As XIII Corps ran out of steam before Catania, Montgomery placed his hopes on a left hook by XXX Corps around Mount Etna. The

1   C.J.C. Moloney, *The Mediterranean and the Middle East, Vol. V* (London: HMSO, 1973), p. 114.
2   C. D'Este, *Bitter Victory, the Battle for Sicily* (London: Collins, 1988), p. 398.
3   N. Hamilton, *Monty: Master of the Battlefield* (London: Hodder & Stoughton, 1983) p. 317.
4   Ibid., p. 318.
5   Ibid., p. 181.

1st Canadian Division would attack Enna and the 51st Highland Division advance towards Paterno. By 18 July, Montgomery had already written-off a breakthrough at Catania, but the 5th Division was still ordered to move around the left flank of the exhausted 50th Northumbrian Division and attack Misterbianco, with disastrous results. Montgomery's grip on the situation was slackening, but he expressed his hopes to his chief, General Harold Alexander, that by 21 July his troops would have taken Misterbianco and Paterno and be well positioned to continue the battle around either side of Mount Etna. His optimistic predictions turned out to be illusory; in his diary he wrote optimistically:

> The attacks put in last night by the 5th and 50th Divisions did not make any great progress. Very determined resistance was met. We have definitely won the battle for the plain of Catania and we are in possession of the whole plain. Our advanced troops have got a footing on the foothills of Etna. But the enemy is securely positioned in Catania itself, which is a strong bastion. My troops are getting tired as the heat in the plain of Catania is great. He [the enemy] is also going to hold the Catania flank against me to the last.[6]

Montgomery's hopes now lay with his left hook by XXX Corps, while all along the Etna Line the Germans strengthened their defences. By dividing his forces and gambling on the left hook, Montgomery had stretched the Eighth Army dangerously thin. XXX Corps would be fighting on rough terrain over an area that was far too extensive for effective offensive operations against a determined and ruthless defender. The operations by XXX Corps turned out to be a series of actions fought by the Canadians and Highlanders, neither supporting the other. Montgomery persisted in employing his four-divisional thrust. The German forces met all attempts to break their defences with determined savagery, and all four offensives met with unfavourable results. The Canadian left hook was blocked by the tough grenadiers of General Rodt's 104th *Panzergrenadier* Regiment and the 15th *Panzergrenadier* Division,[7] keeping the Canadians at bay until 22 July. After a brave outflanking manoeuvre by the Canadians, Assoro was taken. The loss of this town shook the German forces manning the southern edge of the defences, which in turn led to the capture of Leonforte on 22 July, forcing the Germans to retire. As the struggle continued in the east and west, another series of bloody battles were underway in the sector held by the 51st Highland Division, which became held up at Sferro.

Operation *Lehrgang*

German attention now began to be focussed on the lifeline between Italy and Sicily: the Strait of Messina. Admiral Doenitz of the *Kriegsmarine* and Field Marshal

---

6   B.L. Montgomery, *Memoirs* (London: Collins, 1958), p. 342.
7   Major General Eberhard Rodt, Commander 15th *Panzergrenadier* Division.

Kesselring were holding talks that eventually resulted in the formation of an all-German transport service for the Strait under the control of the navy. Baron von Liebenstein, a naval reserve officer,[8] had been given the job of Sea Transport Leader and at once set about creating a more effective and disciplined operation from the chaotic one currently in use. Von Liebenstein took command on 28 May, and quickly set to work. He made two essential changes; the first was to organise his scattered flotillas into an efficient ferry service that was to vastly improve its daily capacity from 100 tons of supplies, vehicles and men per day to 1,000 tons. In June and July, when the Hermann Göring Division was arriving in Sicily, over 600 vehicles, nearly 800 tons of supplies and 4,000 men crossed the Strait in a single day. Heavy bombing raids by the Allies in July had no effect on the ferry service, which continued to operate unhindered. Every vessel in use had some form of anti-aircraft protection, which proved to be surprisingly effective.

Whilst Liebenstein was working his own brand of magic on the sea, Kesselring appointed an army officer, Colonel Ernst-Guenther Baade,[9] to the post of Fortress Commander of the Messina Strait. He was tasked with organising the anti-aircraft defences of the Strait, which was badly run and fragmented at the time. He was also charged with providing the German forces with the means of evacuating the island of Sicily, which he did with tireless vitality and stunning efficiency during the short time he had to prepare. He seems to have overlooked nothing. Eventually, the German and Italian flak forces totally dominated the skies above the Strait. The German evacuation of Sicily was accomplished in separate phases, the first beginning as the Allies landed in Sicily on 10 July when all non-essential German and Italian units were sent across to the Italian mainland. The result of the initial poor organisation meant enormous traffic jams as these units moved towards Messina. However, the Allied air forces did not detect them and missed a golden opportunity to inflict massive damage on the Axis forces when they were at their most vulnerable. The second phase was equally chaotic when western Sicily was evacuated as Patton's Palermo offensive began. This stage consisted mainly of the removal of massive amounts of stores and equipment. Patton's swift advance prevented the Germans from saving other valuable assets in the form of petrol dumps and weapons.

The first official indication that an evacuation was being considered came on 27 July after the fall of Mussolini. Kesselring called all of his senior operations officers to a secret meeting in Rome, and by the end of the month details of the evacuation (Operation *Lehrgang*) were finalised. By August 4, the increasing pressure from

8   Baron Gustav von Liebenstein, Naval Reserve, was the son of an army major general. He served in the First World War and left the navy afterwards, joining up again in 1940. In 1943, he was posted to Sicily as the commander of the 2nd Landing-boat Flotilla based at Marsala. He was awarded the Knight's Cross of the Iron Cross. He was born in Rastat on 25 April 1891 and died in Munich on 17 January 1967.

9   Colonel Ernst-Guenther Baade was born in Falkenhagen on 20 August 1897. He served in the First and Second World Wars and was awarded the Knight's Cross of the Iron Cross with Oak Leaves and Swords. On 5 April 1945, he was mortally wounded in an air-strike on Horsten and died in hospital at Bad Segeberg on 8 May. He is buried in the Parc of Neverstaven.

Bradley's II Corps and Leese's XXX Corps was so great that any units that could be spared were ordered to evacuate as soon as possible. Hitler never informed his troops of what was happening in Sicily, but senior commanders on the ground made sure their men knew they were to be saved and not abandoned. German morale was raised once the men realised they would not be sacrificed needlessly in Sicily. Many officers were still pessimistic about the outcome of the campaign, one anonymous German colonel writing, "In view of the Allied materiel superiority we are all fully convinced that only a few of us would get away from the island safe and sound."

This gloomy assessment was not held by all, especially those within the German navy. Indeed, the Germans made a fighting withdrawal towards the triangle that made up north-eastern Sicily, finally converging on Messina. As each line of resistance was given up, 8,000–10,000 troops would be released to make their way to the ferry sites. In the area around Messina and the town itself, each division was given a clearly defined concentration area and evacuation point. The routes they were to take to these points was now organised with thoroughness, discipline and efficiency as the men trudged through the hot and dusty landscape. The period leading up to the evacuation was a time of worry and tension; it was not known what the Allies would do to prevent it, but an Allied offensive on the Strait was expected. Operation *Lehrgang* commenced on 10 August, the first quota of troops marching to their concentration points, where they would board the Messina ferries for their journey across the Strait the following day. In early August, 13,000 German troops with all their vehicles, three tanks, ammunition, fuel and equipment crossed the Strait on von Liebenstein's ferries. All the while, the RAF kept up bombing runs on the Messina Strait targets, but they had no effect on the efficiency of the operation and the preliminary evacuation was carried out with minimal loss to the Germans. As Troina and Adrano fell to the Allies, the final German withdrawal began. Adrano was the linchpin of the eastern sector of the Etna Line, and the British XXX Corps exerted such pressure on the Germans that the Hermann Göring Division was finally forced to abandon the town to the 78th Division on 7 August. XIII Corps now began its long-awaited advance up the eastern coast road north of Catania, where it continued to meet determined opposition.

Under increasing pressure from British and American forces, the Germans were slowly pushed back towards Messina. It was amid the ruins of Randazzo, which had been pummelled to rubble by Allied bombers, that the British and American forces finally linked up on 13 August. As the evacuation continued, von Liebenstein came to the conclusion that daylight evacuation was preferable to the less-productive night operation, noting that heavy Allied bombing attacks were carried out between 9:00p.m. and dawn, when German losses and interruptions were more likely. By comparison, few heavy raids took place during the day, and these could be fended off with heavy and concentrated anti-aircraft fire. Night and day operations continued, but it soon became obvious that the greatest achievements were performed in daylight hours. The only restriction they faced was the limited number of ferries available.

General Rodt wrote in one report:

Set habits on land were reflected in the air. The most likely raid free times, apart from the nights, were what the troops called 'the enemy tea breaks', 1600 to 1800 hours daily, which were usually followed by raids until dusk. Another quiet period was during the early misty hours, during which we used to complete our transport movements. The old African campaigners were well acquainted with this behaviour on the part of the British and adjusted their actions accordingly.[10]

On 14 August there was a curious absence of air attacks, and with bright moonlight to assist them, the German ferries worked tirelessly and without pause to evacuate men and materiel. They were so efficient that the ferries had to wait the following day as there were no troops or vehicles arriving at Messina for evacuation.

What had originally been thought of as an undertaking that was likely to end in disaster became a resounding success for the Germans. The army never over-taxed Liebenstein's ferry service and all requests for ferry space were met. Allied aircraft failed to make a determined effort to impede the evacuation until the last three days of the operation: night and day raids by bombers and fighters on 16 and 17 August dropped nearly 300 tons of bombs without sinking a single Axis vessel. This half-hearted attempt to disrupt the evacuation came too late, as by then the Germans had completed the seemingly impossible. The much-maligned Italian forces also played their part in Operation *Lehrgang*, and by 16 August they had evacuated an estimated 62,000 soldiers and sailors, 227 vehicles and 41 artillery pieces. By the end of the operation, the Italians were able to boast that they never lost a man during the evacuation. The last Axis troops to leave Sicily were eight Italian soldiers who had stayed behind at Faro; they were picked up by a German assault boat at 8:30 a.m. on 17 August.

It was not until 15 August that Montgomery decided to launch an amphibious assault to speed up the Allied entry into Messina. A task force consisting of tanks of the 4th Armoured Brigade, artillery, engineers and 2 Commando landed near Scaletta some 10 miles below Messina early on 16 August. But it was far too late to hinder the German evacuation. The Hermann Göring Division had effectively blocked Highway 114, and it took a full week for the 50th Northumbrian Division to advance 16 miles from Catania to Riposto. The thrust along Highway 114 by the 50th Division continued to be painfully slow, and by the time its advanced units had got as far as Taormina they found that enormous demolitions had been carried out to impede any further advance. The first Allied troops (Americans) to enter Messina found it in ruins and abandoned: the Germans had already left. The Axis withdrawal was conducted with cool efficiency, and during the course of six days and seven nights, 100,000 troops were safely evacuated, together with nearly 50 tanks, numerous guns and 17,000 tons of supplies and equipment. The German evacuation of Sicily was executed with pin-point precision, which would have far-reaching consequences for the British when they landed in Italy. The enemy divisions that returned to mainland Italy were made up of fully armed veterans with plenty of fight left in them, as the

Allied forces were soon to find out at Salerno, Cassino and Anzio. The Allied air forces had not been able to agree on a plan to halt the enemy withdrawal from Sicily, which resulted in the entire German forces that had been employed in the defence of the island being able to escape to the mainland.

The Allied campaign in Sicily came to a dismal conclusion, having been beset from the beginning by controversy and indecision. It was fought over a harsh terrain that would prove the equal of that awaiting them in Italy. The Germans defied them every step of the way, adding the final insult by achieving one of the most dazzling strategic withdrawals in the annals of military history, leaving behind only prisoners and the dead. The Germans, defiant to the end, came away from Sicily with their pride intact, having given as good as they got. After fighting against overwhelmingly superior forces, one officer of the Hermann Göring Division wrote in his diary:

> The campaign in Sicily is over. We were far from fond of the country in which we had been fighting, but for all that we felt strange when the ferry pulled away from Messina and we had to leave the island to an enemy who was superior to us only in the material sense.[11]

The key to a swift, bold and total Allied victory in Sicily was always to prevent the Axis forces using the Strait of Messina. Had the Allies launched an operation to seize the southern tip of Calabria in mainland Italy, all enemy forces would have been trapped on Sicily. Kesselring acknowledged the fact that this action would have resulted in a "devastating Allied victory". Of all the senior Allied commanders, it was only Eisenhower who was willing to admit that the Allies had blundered and that their approach to the whole campaign had been overly cautious. The senior German and Italian commanders were universally critical of the conservative Allied tactics, stating that too much time was allowed to elapse between the fall of Tunisia and the July landings. General Heinrich von Vietinghoff, commander of the German Tenth Army in Italy from August 1943, remarked:

> From the German standpoint it is incomprehensible that the Allies did not seize the Straits of Messina, either at the same time as the invasion landing or in the course of the initial actions, just as soon as the Germans were contained. On both sides of the Straits, not only in the northeast corner of the island but in southern Calabria as well, this would have been possible without any special difficulty."[12]

The greatest failure of the whole Sicilian campaign was the utter ineffectiveness of the Allied air forces and navies in preventing Axis forces from crossing to the Italian mainland. The Allies could claim complete domination of the air, and their naval

---

11   C.J.C. Malony, *The Mediterranean and the Middle East, Vol. V* (London: HMSO, 1973), p. 182.

12   C. D'Este, *Bitter Victory: The Battle for Sicily* (London: Collins, 1988), p. 526.

forces had never been seriously harassed by enemy shipping. Meanwhile, the Allied armies outnumbered Axis forces 10-fold by the end of the campaign. Nevertheless, the Axis forces were still allowed to slip away with the bulk of their equipment. Historian Hugh Pond claimed that a major factor holding up the naval planners was their memories of the disaster at Gallipoli in 1915/1916. Many of the senior officers who had served there looked with horror at the possibility of taking their warships into the narrows and being shelled by shore batteries. US maritime historian Admiral Samuel Eliot Morison commented, "The navy was frightened, [as] the Straits smelled too much of the Dardanelles." As a consequence of this, the naval planners relinquished a golden opportunity of victory; instead, their ships lay largely idle in open waters. The air forces did not fare much better, holding back because of the large numbers of flak batteries lining both shores of the Strait.

The major tactical error of the whole campaign was that the Allied troops had landed at the southern tip of Sicily and had to fight their way up the whole length of the island. Pond states that even Eisenhower, when he saw the slowness of the advance, blamed himself for not landing at Messina from the start.[13] The campaign could then have been shortened from 38 days to as little as five days. The lack of initiative by Eighth Army commanders, the poor cooperation between the army and the air force and the navy's refusal to close with the enemy during the evacuation were the main reasons the enemy had time to get their troops off the island. The Germans justifiably termed the evacuation of Sicily "a glorious retreat", but for the Allies the struggle for the island had been a long and bitter victory that would return to haunt them.

The close of the Sicilian campaign concluded yet another bloody chapter in the history of the Second World War. German losses in Sicily are believed to have totalled 29,000 killed, wounded and taken prisoner, while the Allies lost some 12,000 British and 9,000 Americans. And now the Italian campaign – which proved an even more brutal affair – was about to begin.

---

13   H. Pond, *Sicily* (London: William Kimber, 1962), p. 212.

Appendix I

50th Northumbrian Division, Sicily, July 1943

Order of Battle

Divisional Headquarters
GOC, Major General S.C. Kirkman, CBE, MC
GSO 1, Lieutenant Colonel R.G.B Innes
AA and CMG, Lieutenant Colonel R.H. Batten
CRASC, Lieutenant Colonel G.W. Fenton, MBE
ADMS, Colonel J. Melvin, OBE, MC
ADOS, Lieutenant Colonel R.C. Gibb
CRÈME, Lieutenant Colonel G.D. Pollock, MBE

Royal Artillery

CRA, Brigadier C.H. Norton, DSO, OBE
74th Field Regiment, Lieutenant Colonel G. Marnham
90th Field Regiment, Lieutenant Colonel I.G.G.S. Hardie
124th Field Regiment, Lieutenant Colonel C.F. Todd
102nd Anti-tank Regiment, Northumberland Hussars, Lieutenant Colonel A.K. Mathews
25th Light Anti-aircraft Regiment, Lieutenant Colonel G.G.O Lyons, MBE

Royal Engineers

CRE, Lieutenant Colonel E.N. Bickford

Divisional Signals

OC, Lieutenant Colonel G.B. Stevenson

69th Infantry Brigade
Brigadier E.C. Cooke-Collis, DSO

5th Battalion East Yorkshire Regiment
Lieutenant Colonel R.B. James, DSO (KIA 1944)

6th Battalion Green Howards
Lieutenant Colonel D.J.M. Smith (wounded 13 July 1943)

7th Battalion Green Howards
Lieutenant Colonel D.G. Jebb, DSO

151st Infantry Brigade
Brigadier R.H. Senior, DSO, TD

6th Battalion Durham Light Infantry
Lieutenant Colonel W.I. Watson

8th Battalion Durham Light Infantry
Lieutenant Colonel R.B. Lidwell, DSO

9th Battalion Durham Light Infantry
Lieutenant Colonel A.B.S. Clarke, DSO (KIA 23 July 1943)

168th Infantry Brigade
Brigadier K.C. Davidson, MC

10th Battalion Royal Berkshire Regiment
Lieutenant Colonel I.R. Baird, MC

1st Battalion London Scottish
Lieutenant Colonel H.J. Wilson, OBE

1st Battalion London Irish Rifles
Lieutenant Colonel I.H. Good

2nd (machine-gun) Battalion Cheshire Regiment
Lieutenant Colonel S.V. Keeling, DSO

Temporarily attached to 50th Northumbrian Division

44th Battalion Royal Tank Regiment
Lieutenant Colonel E.D. Rash

A Squadron the Royals
Major J. Hamilton-Russel

98th Army Field Regiment Royal Artillery
Lieutenant Colonel Hon. C.G. Cubitt, DSO

No. 34 Brick
Colonel J.T. Gibson

Appendix II

50th Northumbrian Division Honours and Awards: 10-18 July 1943

Abbreviations employed in text:
VC: Victoria Cross
DSO: Distinguished Service Order
MC: Military Cross
DCM: Distinguished Conduct Medal
MM: Military Medal
BEM: British Empire Medal
MID: Mentioned in Dispatches
Bar: If a bar was awarded, it means an individual has been awarded the same gallantry medal for the second time. This bar is worn on the ribbon of the original award.

The following list has been taken from the original recommendations that were written many years ago. The author apologises for any omissions or mistakes.

Each entry features name, initials, rank and any awards already given prior to the Sicily campaign. This is followed by the award, the date it was given for, the date it appeared in the *London Gazette* and the battalion and regiment the man served in.

151st Brigade

Atkinson, R.G., Major, MC, 16-17 July, Gazetted 23 December 1943, 6th Bn DLI
Beattie, C.L., Captain, MC, 16-17 July, Gazetted 21 October 1943, 8th Bn DLI
Bleakley, H., Lance Corporal, MM, July-August, Gazetted 23 March 1944, 50th Div Signals: attached to 151st and 168th Brigades
Boyd, T.P., Signalman, MM, 16-17 July, Gazetted 21 October 1943, 50th Div Signals: attached to 151st Brigade

Cockett, A., Lance Corporal, MM, 16 July, Gazetted 21 October 1943, 50th Div Signals: attached to 151st Brigade

Connel, J., Lance Sergeant, DCM, 13 July, Gazetted 18 November 1943, 6th Bn DLI

Critchley, C.R., Lance Sergeant, MM, 16 July, Gazetted 21 October 1943, 6th Bn DLI

Daley, P., Lance Sergeant, MM, 15 July, Gazetted 21 October 1943, 9th Bn DLI.

Duckworth, MM, 13-17 July, Gazetted 18 November 1943, 6th Bn DLI

French-Kehoe, D.A., Lieutenant, MC, 17 July, Gazetted 18 November 1943, Northamptonshire Rgt: attached to 6th Bn DLI

Galloway, R., Captain, MC, 10 July, Gazetted 23 December 1943, 6th Bn DLI

Goodwin, G.T., Private, MM, 16 July, Gazetted 21 October 1943, 8th Bn DLI

Hampson, P.G., Lieutenant, MC, 16-17 July, Gazetted 21 October 1943, 8th Bn DLI

Hannah, J.R., CSM, MM, 15-16 July, Gazetted 21 October 1943, 8th Bn DLI

Horton, P.J., Signalman, MM, 15-16 July, Gazetted 21 October 1943, 50th Div Signals: attached to 8th Bn DLI

Lee, J.J., Sergeant, MM, no date given, Gazetted 23 March 1944, Army Catering Corps: attached to 8th Bn DLI

Leybourne, J.A., Captain, MC, 16-17 July, Gazetted 21 October 1943, 8th Bn DLI

Lidwell, R.P., Lieutenant Colonel, DSO, 15-16 July, Gazetted 21 October 1943, King's Liverpool Rgt: attached to 8th Bn DLI

Loveridge, D.A., Lieutenant, MC, 17 July, Gazetted 21 October 1943, Suffolk Regiment: attached to 6th Bn DLI

Mackmin, C.J.W., Sergeant, MM, 16-17 July, Gazetted 21 October 1943, 8th Bn DLI

Mitchinson, F., Sergeant, MM, 15-16 July, Gazetted 21 October 1943, 8th Bn DLI

Muir, W.J.H., Lieutenant, MC, Bar to MC, 17 July, Gazetted 21 October 1943, 9th Bn DLI

Neale, D.A., Captain, MC, 15-16 July, Gazetted 21 October 1943, 8th Bn DLI

Richards D.J., Lance Sergeant, MM, 16-17 July, Gazetted 21 October 1943, 8th Bn DLI

Robinson, R., Private, MM, 16-17 July, Gazetted 21 October 1943, 6th Bn DLI

Rose, S.S., Lance Corporal, MM, 14-15 July, Gazetted 21 October 1943, 9th Bn DLI

Saban, D.H., Private, MM, 17 July, Gazetted 21 October 1943, 6th Bn DLI

Scriven, W.D., Corporal, MM, 15-16 July, Gazetted 21 October 1943, 6th Bn DLI

Searle, S., Driver, MM, 16-17 July, Gazetted 21 October 1943, 50th Div Signals: attached to 151st Brigade

Shepherd, G.E., Lance Corporal, MM, 15-16 July, Gazetted 21 October 1943, 8th Bn DLI

Simpson, C.B., Lance Corporal, MM, 17 July, Gazetted 23 December 1943, 9th Bn DLI

Spink, F., Corporal, MM, 16-17 July, Gazetted 21 October 1943, 8th Bn DLI

Thompson, F., Sergeant, DCM, 17-19 July, Gazetted 21 October 1943, 9th Bn DLI

Wardle, F., CSM, MM, 15-16 July, Gazetted 21 October 1943, 8th Bn DLI

Whitaker, K.H., Captain, MC, 15-16 July, Gazetted 18 November 1943, Troop Commander, Somerset Light Infantry anti-tank guns: attached to 151st Brigade

Worthington, G., Lance Corporal, MM, 16-17 July, Gazetted 21 October 1943, 6th Bn DLI

69th Brigade

Bailey, J., Private, MM, 15 July, Gazetted 21 October 1943, 5th Bn East Yorkshire Rgt

Forth, H., Private, MID, 17 July, Gazetted 21 October 1943, 5th Bn East Yorkshire Rgt

Herbert, L., Captain, MC, 17-18 July, Gazetted 21 October 1943, 6th Bn Green Howards

Hood, E.A., Lance Sergeant, MM, 18 July, Gazetted 21 October 1943, 7th Bn Green Howards

James, R.B., Lieutenant Colonel, DSO and Bar, 2nd Bar to DSO, 12 July, Gazetted 21 October 1943, Commanding Officer 5th Bn East Yorkshire Rgt (killed in action August 1944)

Jebb, D.G., Lieutenant Colonel, DSO, 17-18 July, Gazetted 23 October 1943, 7th Bn Green Howards

Smith, C.G., Lieutenant, MC, 14 July, Gazetted 23 December 1943, 7th Bn Green Howards

168th Brigade

Adamson, P., Private, MM, July-August, Gazetted 21 October 1943, 10th Bn Royal Berkshire Rgt

Atwool H.R.R., Captain, MC, 16-17 July, Gazetted 21 October 1943, 1st London Scottish

Blair, C., Corporal, MM, 17 July, Gazetted 18 November 1943, 1st London Irish

Brightman, T.J., Piper, MM, 17-18 July, Gazetted 21 October 1943, 1st London Irish

Brooks, W.E., Captain, MC, 17-18 July, Gazetted 21 October 1943, 1st London Irish

Crampton, A.E., Lieutenant, MM, 17 July, Gazetted 23 December 1943, 1st London Irish

Gillan, J.H., Lieutenant, MC, 15-16 July, Gazetted 21 October 1943, 1st London Scottish

Hunnex, W., CQMS, BEM, 17-18 July, Gazetted 21 October 1943, 1st London Irish

Madigan, J.T., Sergeant, MM, 17-18 July, Gazetted 21 October 1943, 1st London Irish

Royal Artillery

Armiger, E.W., Lance Bombardier, MM, 14 July, Gazetted 21 October 1943, 124th Fld Rgt, RA

Aston, H.H., Sergeant, MM, 14 July, Gazetted 21 October 1943, 124th Fld Rgt, RA

Cubitt, G.C., Lieutenant Colonel, DSO, 10-15 July, Gazetted 21 October 1943, Commanding Officer 98th Fld Regiment, Surrey and Sussex Yeomanry, RA

Hopkins, F.W., Sergeant, MM, 16-19 July, Gazetted 23 December 1943, 124th Fld Rgt, RA

Peile, G.H., Captain, MC, 16-17 July, Gazetted 21 October 1943, 98th Fld Rgt, Surrey and Sussex Yeomanry, RA

Philips, H.J., Gunner, MM, 14 July, Gazetted 21 October 1943, 124th Fld Rgt, RA

Pike, L.L., Lieutenant, MC, 14-18 July, Gazetted 21 October 1943, 98th Fld Rgt, Surrey and Sussex Yeomanry, RA

Sharp, A.J., RSM, MM, 14 July 1943, Gazetted 21 October 1943, 124th Fld Rgt, RA

Snelling, R., Gunner, MM, 18 July, Gazetted 23 December 1943, 90th Fld Rgt, RA

Wells, G.C., Major, MC, 17 July, Gazetted 23 December 1943, 90th Fld Rgt, RA

Royal Engineers

Compton, C.A.O., Major, MC, 15-16 July, Gazetted 21 October 1943, 505 Fld Coy, RE

Hamblett, F., Private, MM, 10 July, Gazetted 23 December 1943, 1st Welsh Rgt: attached to 34 Beach Brick

Hard, L.F., Captain, MC, 10 July, Gazetted 23 December 1943, 1st Welsh Rgt: attached to 34 Beach Brick

Russel, G.Y., Corporal, MM, Bar to MM, 16 July, Gazetted 21 October 1943, 505 Fld Coy, RE

Royal Army Medical Corps

Hall, J.G., Private, MM, July-August, Gazetted 23 March 1944, 149 Field Ambulance, Royal Army Medical Corps

Appendix III

British units at Primosole Bridge, July 1943

1st Parachute Brigade, Brigadier Gerald Lathbury

1st Parachute Battalion, Lieutenant Colonel Alastair Pearson

2nd Parachute Battalion, Lieutenant Colonel John Frost

3rd Parachute Battalion, Lieutenant Colonel E.C. Yeldham

1st Air Landing Anti-tank Battery, Royal Artillery, Major W.F. Arnold

21st Independent Coy Parachute Regiment, Pathfinders, Major J. Lander (killed in Sicily on 13 July 1943, aged 47, and buried in Catania War Cemetery, Sicily)

44th Battalion Royal Tank Regiment, Lieutenant Colonel Eric D. Rash (in Patrick Delaforce's *Monty's Marauders*, Rash is reported to have been killed in Sicily, but in Ewart Clay's *The Path of the 50th* he is reported as missing in Sicily; in fact he survived the war and died at the age of 70 in February 2009)

3rd Battalion County of London Yeomanry, Lieutenant Colonel George Geoffrey Lightly Willis, DSO (killed in Sicily on 17 July 1943 at the age of 35, and buried in Catania War Cemetery, Sicily)

A squadron the Royal Dragoons, Major J. Hamilton-Russel

151st Brigade, Brigadier R.H. Senior, DSO

6th Battalion Durham Light Infantry, Lieutenant Colonel W.I. Watson

8th Battalion Durham Light Infantry, Lieutenant Colonel R.B. Lidwell, DSO

9th Battalion Durham Light Infantry, Lieutenant Colonel Andrew Board Stephenson Clarke, DSO, King's Own Scottish Borderers (killed commanding the Durhams on 23 July 1943, aged 37, and buried in Catania War Cemetery, Sicily)

98th Field Regiment, Royal Artillery, Lieutenant Colonel C.G. Cubitt, DSO

Appendix IV

Fallschirmjäger at Primosole Bridge, July 1943

1st *Fallschirmjäger* Division, Lieutenant General Richard Heidrich. In July 1943 they were stationed in France. Not all units from this division were in action at Primosole Bridge, but various elements landed and took part in the fighting there. Those that did are as follows:

3rd *Fallschirmjäger* Regiment, Lieutenant Colonel Heilman. This unit air-dropped into Sicily on the evening of 12 July and fought with Battle Group Schmalz around Lentini and Carlentini to hold up the advance of the 50th and 5th Divisions until they were cut off by the British advance. Heilman led his men out of this trap and did not join the action again until the night of 17-18 July.

4th *Fallschirmjäger* Regiment, Lieutenant Colonel Walther. This unit air-dropped into Sicily on the evening of 17 July and went straight into action.

1st *Fallschirmjäger* Pioneer (engineer) Battalion, Captain Paul Adolph (acting commander, as the regular commanding officer was on a course in Paris). This unit air-dropped into Sicily on the evening of 14 July and took up positions around Highway 114 at the northern end of Primosole Bridge. Captain Adolph was killed in action at Primosole Bridge and was posthumously promoted to major and awarded the coveted *Ritterkreuz* for his bravery.

1st *Fallschirmjäger* Machine-gun Battalion, Major Schmidt. This unit air-dropped into Sicily on the morning of 13 July and took up positions around the 'Johnny' hills, where they met British paratroopers for the first time. They fought throughout the battle for Primosole Bridge.

1st *Fallschirmjäger* Signals Company, Captain Eric Fassl. This unit air-dropped into Sicily and counter-attacked at Primosole Bridge on 14 July, retaking the bridge from the British paratroopers who held it. This counter-attack was organised by Captain Franz Strangenberg, who, seeing the dire situation at Primosole, recruited clerks, drivers, HQ staff, cooks and mechanics (200 in all) from Catania and transported them all, along with Fassl's signals company, to the battle area. The machine-gun and pioneer battalions relieved their victorious comrades on the night of 14 July, and Strangenberg and Fassl took their troops back to Catania. Fassl's Signals Company returned to the battle on 15 July.

Appendix V

4th Armoured Brigade Order of Battle OC Brigadier J.C. Currie

44th Battalion Royal Tank Regiment
A Squadron Royal Dragoons
3rd Battalion County of London Yeomanry
No 5 Coy, Royal Army Service Corps
14th Light Field Ambulance
318th Armoured Brigade Workshop, Royal Electrical and Mechanical Engineers
4th Armoured Brigade Signals Section

Appendix VI

5th British Division Order of Battle

GOC Major General H. Berney-Ficklin

13th Brigade

2nd Battalion the Cameronians (Scottish Rifles)
2nd Battalion Inniskilling Fusiliers
2nd Battalion the Wiltshire Regiment
13th Brigade Support Coy

15th Brigade

1st Battalion Green Howards
1st Battalion King's Own Yorkshire Light Infantry
1st Battalion York and Lancaster Regiment
15th Brigade Support Coy

17th Brigade

2nd Battalion Royal Scots Fusiliers
2nd Battalion Northamptonshire Regiment
6th Battalion Seaforth Highlanders
17th Brigade Support Coy

Divisional Troops

5th Battalion the Reconnaissance Regiment
7th (Machine-gun) Battalion the Cheshire Regiment
52nd Anti-tank Regiment, Royal Artillery
38th, 245th and 252nd Field Coys, Royal Engineers
91st, 92nd and 156th Field Regiments, Royal Artillery
18th Light Anti-aircraft Regiment, Royal Artillery
254th Field Park Coy, Royal Engineers

Appendix VII

XIV *Panzer* Corps Order of Battle

Officer Commanding, General H.V. Hube
15th *Panzer* Division, Hermann Göring Division,
1st *Fallschirmjäger* Division, 15th *Panzergrenadier* Division
15th *Panzergrenadier* Regiment (three battalions)
71st *Panzergrenadier* Regiment (three battalions)
129th Armoured Reconnaissance Battalion
One Coy 129th Tank Battalion (assault guns)
29th Artillery Regiment (three battalions)
One Coy 29th Engineer Battalion
313th Anti-aircraft Battalion (three batteries)
29th Signal Battalion
3rd *Fallschirmjäger* Regiment
4th *Fallschirmjäger* Regiment
1st *Fallschirmjäger* Machine-gun Battalion
1st *Fallschirmjäger* Engineer Battalion
1st Battalion 1st *Fallschirmjäger* Field Artillery Regiment
Elements of 1st *Fallschirmjäger* Anti-tank Battalion
1st *Fallschirmjäger* Signals Company

Appendix VIII

Battle Group Schmalz, Sicily, 1943 Order of Battle

Officer Commanding Colonel Wilhelm Schmalz
115th *Panzergrenadier* Regiment of 15th *Panzer* Division
Fortress Battalion 904
Fortress Battalion Reggio
3rd *Fallschirmjäger* Regiment of the 1st *Fallschirmjäger* Division
4th *Fallschirmjäger* Regiment of the 1st *Fallschirmjäger* Division
Remnants of the *Fallschirmjäger* Engineer Battalion and *Fallschirmjäger* Machine-gun Battalion, both of 1st *Fallschirmjäger* Division.

Appendix IX

1st *Fallschirmjäger-Panzer* Division Hermann Göring, Sicily, 1943 Order of Battle

Headquarters
1st Hermann Göring *Panzergrenadier* Regiment
2nd Hermann Göring *Panzergrenadier* Regiment
1st Hermann Göring Artillery Regiment
1st Herman Göring Anti-aircraft Regiment
1st Hermann Göring *Panzer* Reconnaissance Regiment
1st Hermann Göring Tank Destroyer Battalion
1st Hermann Göring *Panzer* Engineer Battalion
1st Hermann Göring *Panzer* Signals Battalion
1st Hermann Göring Divisional Support Group

Select Bibliography

Anon., *Globe Trotters: The Story of the 2nd Battalion Royal Inniskilling Fusiliers in the Second World War* (Northern Ireland: An Inniskilling Museum Publication, 2018).

Aris, G., *The Fifth British Division 1939 to 1945* (London: The Fifth Division Benevolent Fund, 1959).

Arthur, M., *The Men of the Red Beret* (London: Hutchinson, 1990).

Atkinson, R., *The Day of Battle. The War in Sicily and Italy 1943-44* (New York: Henry Holt and Co., 2007).

Barnes, B.S., *The Sign of the Double T* (York: Sentinel Press, 1999).

Barker, A.H.R. & Rust, B., *A Short History of the 50th Northumbrian Division* (London: 1966).

Beevor, A., *The Second World War* (London: Weidenfeld & Nicolson, 2012).

Blumenson, Martin, *Sicily: Whose Victory?* (London: Ballantine, 1969).

Breuer, W.B., *Drop Zone Sicily* (California: Presido Press, 1983).

Bull, S., *Commando Tactics* (Barnsley: Pen & Sword, 2010)

Clay, E.W., *The Path of the 50th* (Aldershot: Gale & Polden, 1950).

Cyril, N., *The London Scottish* (London: Clones, 1952).

Crookenden, A., *The History of the Cheshire Regiment* (London: Evans, 1949).

Delaforce, P., *Monty's Northern Legions* (Gloucestershire: Sutton Publishing, 2004).

D'Este, C., *Bitter Victory: The Battle for Sicily* (London: Collins, 1988).

Durnford-Slater, J., *Commando: Memoirs of a Fighting Commando in World War Two* (London: Kimber, 1953).

Follain, J., *Mussolini's Island* (London: Hodder & Stoughton, 2005).

Frost, Major General J., CB, DSO, MC, *A Drop Too Many* (London: Cassel, 1980).

Gilchrist, R.T., *Malta Strikes Back: The Story of 231 Brigade* (London: Gale & Polden 1945).

Graham, A., *Sharpshooters at War* (London: Sharpshooters Regimental Association, 1964).

Hamilton, N., *Monty: the Battles of Field Marshal Bernard Law Montgomery* (London: Hodder & Stoughton, 1981).

Jolsen, H.F., *Orders of Battle 1939-1945* (London: HMSO, 1960).

Kent, R., *First In: the Airborne Pathfinders: A History of the 21st Independent Parachute Company 1942-1946* (London: Batsford Ltd, 1979).

Kurowski, F., *Jump into Hell: German Paratroopers in World War Two* (Mechanicsburg, Pennsylvania: Stackpole Books, 2010).

Lewis, P., *The Price of Freedom* (Durham: Pentland Books, 2001).

Lewis, P.J. & English, I.R., *The 8th Battalion Durham Light Infantry, 1939-1945* (Newcastle: J. & P. Bealls, 1949).

Malony, C.J.C., *The Mediterranean and Middle East, Vol. V* (London: HMSO, 1973).

Messenger, C., *Commandos: The Definitive History of Commando Operations in the Second World War* (London: William Kimber, 1985).

Miller, V., *Nothing is Impossible* (Kent: Spellmount, 1994).

Ministry of Information, *By Air to Battle* (London: HMSO, 1945).

Mitcham, S.W., *Hitler's Legions* (London: Leo Cooper, 1985).

Montagu, E., *The Man Who Never Was* (Philadelphia, Pennsylvania: Lippincott, 1954).

Moses, H., *The Faithful Sixth* (Durham: County Durham Books, 1995).

Moses, H., *The Gateshead Gurkhas* (Durham: County Durham Books, 2001).

Nightingale, P.R., *The East Yorkshire Regiment in the War: 1939-45* (Howden: Mr Pye Books, 1952).

Pack, S.W.C., *Operation Husky* (London: David & Charles, 1977).

Peters, M., *Glider Pilots in Sicily* (Barnsley: Pen & Sword, 2012).

Pond, H., *Sicily* (London: Kimber, 1962).

Poppel, M., *Heaven and Hell: the War Diary of a German Paratrooper* (Kent: Spellmount, 1988).

Rissik, D., *The DLI at War* (Durham: Brancepeth Castle, 1953).

Saliger, M., *The First Bridge too Far* (Oxford: Casemate, 2018).

Saunders, H. St G., *The Green Beret* (London: Michael Joseph, 1949).

Saunders, H. St G., *The Red Beret* (London: Michael Joseph, 1950).

Synge, W.A.T., *The Story of the Green Howards* (Richmond: The Green Howards, 1952).

Waldron, A., *Operation Ladbroke: From Dream to Disaster* (Sussex: Woodfield Publishing, 2003).

Whiting, C., *Slaughter over Sicily* (Barnsley: Pen & Sword, 2006).

Young, P., *Storm from the Sea* (Staffordshire: Wren's Park Publishing, 2002).

Zaloga, S., *Sicily 1943* (Oxford: Osprey, 2013).

Index

Index of People

Index of Places

Index of Allied Units & Formations

Index of Axis Units/Formations